JLMW

THE EQUITABLE GUIDE TO
WORKING A

THE EQUITABLE GUIDE TO
WORKING ABROAD

——

William Essex

BLOOMSBURY

About The Equitable Life Assurance Society

The Equitable Life Assurance Society was founded in 1762, making
it the oldest mutual life assurance society in the world, and the first
to develop the sound actuarial principles on which all modern
life companies are based. Throughout its long history The Equitable
has steadfastly refused to pay commission to third parties for
the introduction of new business; a policy that has helped to
achieve the society's consistently low level of expenses.

The Equitable today is an international company dealing with
clients globally from its offshore base in Guernsey.

The information in this book was correct to the best of the author's and publisher's
belief at the time of going to press. While no responsibility can be accepted for
errors and omissions, the author and publisher would welcome corrections and
suggestions for material to include in subsequent editions of this book.

This edition first published in 1996 by
Bloomsbury Publishing plc
2 Soho Square
London, W1V 6HB

Copyright © by William Essex 1996

The moral right of the author has been asserted

A copy of the CIP entry for this book is available from the British Library
ISBN 0 7475 2552 8

10 9 8 7 6 5 4 3 2 1

Designed by AB3
Typeset by Hewer Text Composition Services, Edinburgh
Printed and bound in Great Britain by Clays Ltd, St Ives plc

CONTENTS

Acknowledgements   vii

Introduction   ix

Chapter One: Before You Go   1

Chapter Two: The First Year Abroad   47

Chapter Three: Financial Planning   90

Chapter Four: Planning to Return to the UK   185

Chapter Five: Useful Information   193

Index   237

ACKNOWLEDGEMENTS

I would like to thank some people for their help with this book.

Heidi Beyer at Employment Conditions Abroad, Liz Bowen-Jones at Going Places and Stephen Sweby at the Centre for International Briefing were informative on cultural questions, living-cost comparisons and preparations in general.

Donald Elkin at Wilfred T. Fry, Peter Goodman at Wilkins Kennedy and Roger Ambrose at Ambrose Associates provided useful and sometimes surprising insights into the workings of the Inland Revenue and the British tax system.

Adam Courtenay at The Money Laundering Bulletin and Yuri Bender at Offshore Financial Review gave advice, as did Dawn Smith, Henry Russell, Andrew Webb, Madeleine Wickham and Paul Ham. I'd like to thank Catherine Bremer for research beyond the call of duty on the table of worldwide emergency numbers.

Roger Collis in Antibes, Rupert Glasgow in Berlin and Kathryn Davis in Poland were among a number of expatriate friends and colleagues who answered questions. Others must remain nameless, for a reason best summed up in a footnote to some information that was sent to me. Perhaps it's instructive.

'Please remember that [they] are very sensitive about how their country is reported – so don't identify your sources. You probably know this but it's worth my work permit to emphasise. For this reason, I'm having this posted in Britain rather than faxed from here.'

Finally, and above all, I would like to thank my wife Penny for her patience and support while I was preoccupied with writing this book.

INTRODUCTION

Taking a job abroad means moving your entire life to another country. If you're married, or in a stable relationship, it also means persuading your partner to come with you. Partners, or 'trailing spouses' as the international recruitment industry calls them, have the most to lose from moving abroad. Not only do they have to say good-bye to family and friends, as you do, but they also have to put their own careers on hold for as long as your overseas employment will last. Trailing spouses don't often find jobs abroad to match what they had back home, and some countries won't allow them to work at all.

So this has to be a book for both of you. It starts, therefore, by talking through the 'soft' issues that you need to discuss – the effect on your relationship; whether life overseas will be good for you – and then suggests ways to work out whether the salary package is good enough to make the move worthwhile. Even working out what you're being offered is difficult, if the salary is quoted in another currency and calculated by reference to another country's cost of living.

You need to know three things. First, that the offer's competitive with what you could expect for the same job back home; secondly, that your spending power as a couple will not be less than at home; and thirdly, if this is a short-term assignment for a long-term employer, what will happen to your home salary when you return from being paid at overseas rates.

There is also the question of whether working abroad will be good for your career in the long term. You may be going overseas as a promotion, but once you're there, you might be out of touch with changing realities back home. The international recruitment industry has a term for this too: 'repatriation failure'. You come home and your job's changed, or it isn't there any more, or you find that you've changed. Working abroad does different things to different people, and many expatriates find that once they've tried it, life overseas is far more challenging and worthwhile and generally fun than life back home. So you need to develop contingency plans for what happens at the end of your present contract.

Of course, you may not be able to turn the job down. If you're building a career with an international company, or in a profession where the opportunities are world-wide, you might have more to think about than just the salary. If you're serious about your career, you'll have to work abroad sooner or later. This is an age of executive mobility, and being posted overseas is becoming a routine part of the job for potential high-fliers. So there are more and more candidates for senior positions who can show proven international experience. They will have the edge on any future shortlist.

Thinking about the future means facing the possibility that this will not only be good for you, but it'll transform your prospects beyond anything that can be fulfilled by your present employer. The potential benefits of succeeding abroad are enormous. You'll have a much stronger CV, and you'll have proved yourself in the eyes of your present, and any potential future, employer. You'll be in a much stronger bargaining position in your company. And if you move on – the whole world is your employment market.

The downside is, it's much easier to fail overseas than at home. You may be able to handle the job perfectly well, but you'll be subjected to all the additional stresses of working in an unfamiliar culture, among people who do things very differently from the way you've always done them. In their country, they're right. You're the one who has to adapt, if you want to make things happen.

Your home life, too, will undergo stress. Even if your partner hasn't given up a perfectly good job to come with you (and then perhaps can't find a replacement in the new country), you'll find that you have to rely on each other much more than you did in the UK. While you're getting to know people at the office, remember that setting up all the domestic networks in unfamiliar surroundings is more difficult and thankless than getting stuck into a new job. The 'trailing spouse' doesn't get a perforance bonus.

Expatriate communities tend to be close and supportive, but if you're used to a wide range of interests, activities and friends, your new life might take a lot of getting used to. Work will be closer to home, and your social life will often involve colleagues who want to talk shop. You might one day sit back and realise that your dinner party has split between 'halves' talking about the office, and 'other halves' talking about a social world of clubs, tennis matches, etc., about which you know nothing. Don't let that happen. The downside of close communities is that it can be difficult to set a distance from everybody, to claim personal space for you individually and for you as a couple. Your 'quality time' will not be easily spent alone together.

So talk it all through and do the homework before you go. But don't expect to have the time to do it properly. The expatriate world is full of stories of people who had a month, a week, or in one case just forty-eight hours to prepare for a working life in another country. You may be going on ahead, staying in a hotel room while your family follows at 'leisure', but you need to settle the preparations for all of you before you go. The short-notice stories tend to be the exceptions, but 'the thing about preparing to go,' as one past expatriate put it at a briefing seminar, 'is that it tends to fill up the time available, and then some.'

The most important thing is to do it together, and not to get stressed if you run out of time. Prepare for the job as completely as you can, and prepare for the life outside the job. Prepare for the second disruption of returning to the UK (or not, as the case may be). Keep everything as simple as possible at this stage. Take advice, and take the time to do all the things you won't be able to do once you've gone. Go out to the theatre; go out to dinner. See your friends and family.

And remember this.

It's great fun, working abroad. It's full of opportunities, and it's full of challenges. Like all the best things in life, it isn't easy. But that doesn't mean you shouldn't have a good time while you're doing it.

So whatever happens, enjoy yourself.

How to use this book

Working abroad successfully depends on planning ahead. Don't leave planning your return to the UK, for example, until it's about to happen. If you're going to take holidays in the UK, maybe it would be easier to pack addresses now for hotels, etc., rather than to try to find them once you're overseas.

At every level of seriousness, it is much better to be too early with your preparations than too late. It is also very easy to be wrong about how early you need to be. Your first priority, therefore, should be to brief yourself fully on all the preparations you will need to make, both now and later. You should, in managagement-speak, prioritize.

But the run-up to departure is fraught with preparation, excitement and anxiety, and you'll find that you don't have enough time to sort everything out as efficiently as you would like. The most important part of this book to read before you go is Chapter One. Also important (though these are summarized in Chapter One) are the tax sections (pages 92 to 130) of Chapter Three plus the section on finding advice on page 147.

Addresses are generally given for companies and other organizations where they are first mentioned in the text. All addresses are repeated (or in some cases given for the first time) in Chapter Six. Some additional names and addresses also appear in Chapter Six.

Immediate do's and don'ts

This isn't everything; this is just what you should do, think about and be aware of straight away. A checklist of slightly less immediate preparations appears on page 23, and there are last-minute checklists beginning on page 42. The page references below are to where in this book each item is discussed in more detail.

- Do work out immediately what you're going to do with your house. If you're going to sell it, you need to get it on the market quickly. If you might rent it, you need to get an agent appointed to look for tenants. If you're going to leave it empty, you need insurance. Page 28.
- Do discuss your children's education (page 80) and inform their schools that you will be going overseas. You may have to give notice that you will be withdrawing your children; at the very least, with

children at a boarding-school, you will have to arrange guardianship and appoint someone to act *in loco parentis*.

- Do tell your bank (page 26) and your tax inspector (page 26) that you will be going overseas.
- Do start to bring your UK address book up to date.
- Do open accounts with suppliers of books, etc. Books Etc., Hatchard's, The Book Bag. Investigate mail-order shopping (page 200).
- Do get the names of professional advisers (page 214). In particular, you should contact an accountant with expertise in expatriate tax matters as soon as possible (so that there is time to arrange your affairs for departure), and you should at least obtain the names and addresses of lawyers in your destination country before you go.
- Don't sell any investments at a profit before you go overseas (page 27) unless you have overriding reasons to do so. You are advised later (page 27) on setting up a bank account in your destination country, and recommended to have a substantial balance in this account when you arrive. Raising the money for this account is more tax-effectively achieved by making a loss, as in the next item.
- Do consider selling any investment on which you can realize a capital loss before you go overseas. You will be able to offset this loss against any Capital Gains Tax incurred after your return (page 112).
- Do not enter into any long-term financial commitments without considering first timing (ie, do you do this most tax-effectively before or after you go?) and secondly, whether there are offshore alternatives. The whole of Chapter Three is a reference for this item; it stresses taking advice on financial matters (on page 90).
- Do, if you are going overseas for your present employer, talk to somebody at the office about your future (page 27). Formally and/or informally, you need somebody looking after your interests and keeping you informed.
- Do discuss with your employer what briefing you will receive, and ask, in the strongest possible terms, that it be offered to your partner as well (page 30).
- Do start noting down questions that occur to you. See Chapter Five.
- Do give your family and friends plenty of notice of your departure. If you have elderly relatives, think about their wellbeing while you are away (page 18).
- Don't get so preoccupied with preparing to go that you forget to go out and enjoy yourself. Do British things that you won't be able to do overseas.
- Do put in your packing a copy of the phone directory for your home town; also the Business and Services directory for Central London. Surprising numbers of enquiries from expatriates are simply for UK-based (usually London) companies' phone numbers. Order forms for all UK phone directories at £6.50 each (and some overseas directories) may be found in the back of every phone directory.

While you're in the bookshop

There is a further reading list on page 229. Here are some immediate suggestions.

- Buy a map of the town and the country you are going to. Do buy the Michelin guide and the Rough Guide. Different books have different strengths; buy more than one. Budget travel guides tend to be good on public transport and basic etiquette. Lonely Planet city guides are widely recommended; costing under £10 these are available from bookshops and Lonely Planet Publications, 10 Barley Mow Passage, Chiswick, London W4 4PH, telephone 0181 742 3161, fax 0181 742 2772.

- Buy at least one phrasebook each. Buy a business phrasebook. Buy dictionaries.

- Buy a Good UK Pub Guide and a Hotel & Restaurant Guide such as Egon Ronay's. You will need these for forward-planning of visits to the UK. Buy a restaurant/theatre/what's on guide to your home town, for the same reason. Check your local paper or another source (look in your newsagent) or the phonebook for booking-office numbers for local theatres. You may stop over in London; pack a copy of Time Out or a similar entertainment guide for the numbers and addresses it contains.

CHAPTER ONE

BEFORE YOU GO

'What I didn't know, but had worked out for myself, was the importance of getting the details of the employment contract sorted out before I came out. I went through an agency and was offered a retailing job . . . it took a couple of weeks for us to sort out the details and get the assurances I wanted . . . but it was worth the delay and they seemed to respect my requests for clarification about pay and conditions, especially as related to my family. That said, the job description has turned out to be very wide of the mark.'

Manager recently arrived in the Middle East.

First, ask yourself the right questions

Before you start thinking about the job and the salary package and the contract, think about yourself and your partner. Ask yourself the following questions. What matters, as any successful expatriate will tell you, is not so much that you answer them, but that you think them through first.

Should you accept the job at all?

The first and most important thing about expatriate life is that it depends on stability at home. This is recognized by employers: the majority of personnel moved abroad are married. The thinking is that in unfamiliar surroundings, facing unfamiliar challenges, you'll perform better if you can share the stress.

But the corollary of that is that by going to work abroad, you place an additional strain on your relationship. You and your partner are going to depend on each other much more than you do now.

Among the unwelcome statistics: the divorce rate is higher among expatriates than it is among stay-at-homes. But equally, you'll find a lot of expatriates who'll tell you that life overseas has brought them closer together. Do you want to put your relationship to the test?

How do you break the news to your partner that you've been offered the job?

It's difficult to keep a sense of the domestic perspective on a career-making opportunity in another country.

You're coming home to somebody who's going to have to face up to far bigger changes than you are – without even a pay rise to soften the blow. You're going to an office, to do roughly what you do now, for a better package at perhaps a more senior level. Offices look the same all over the world.

Your partner is going to have to give up a career, organize most of the move (whatever your intentions, you'll be getting stuck into the job while the carpets are laid, the utilities are connected and the furniture is retrieved from the dockyard) and then cope with no friends nearby, no family, and probably no job even just to fill the time.

So, when the prospect of a job overseas turns into something that really might happen, think about what it would mean to the people around you. In particular, think about the impact on your partner.

Who might not agree to come with you, anyway. Would you refuse the job, if your partner asked you to?

Here are three suggestions.

1. Share the decision on whether to take the job, and
2. Don't just brush aside the negatives, and
3. Forget that you thought you'd agreed all this already.

The first is obvious. If you seem already to have made the decision, you're sending the wrong signals about how much you value your partner's contribution. Given the additional strain mentioned already, you'll be far better off in the long run if you can start with a shared decision.

Perhaps the second is obvious too. There are negatives. Of course there are. You'll have to face them sooner or later. Discuss any misgivings now; don't take them abroad with you.

The third suggestion? Up to now, working abroad was just an idea, something easy to imagine. Maybe you talked about a big, airy apartment in a fashionable quarter; maybe you liked the idea of meeting for lunch in the piazza on weekdays. You had fun talking about how it might be. But now it's real, and now you're going to have to say goodbye to family and friends. That's different. Start afresh.

And ask yourself:

Have you got what it takes to succeed as an expatriate?

Whatever the money, a job's only as good as where it will take you next. If you succeed as an expatriate, your CV will be stronger. If you think you might fail, you should think seriously before accepting the job.

Employers and recruitment agencies see expatriates as expensive and high risk. Expensive, because of the cost of relocation and settlement as well as what they're actually paid; high risk, because significant numbers of them fail to complete their contracts.

The reasons for failure fall into three broad categories:

- Work problems. Sometimes, the job isn't what was expected, but more often the new arrival fails to adapt to the local culture, and specifically to local business practices; this can lead to an irretrievable breakdown in relations with colleagues.
- Problems at home. Perhaps the partner has similar problems with adaptation to the local culture; more often, the failure to settle can be traced to the clash of incompatible expectations, and insufficiently expressed reservations about the move overseas.
- Dislocation. For both partners, moving overseas means leaving behind a whole support network of friends, relations and colleagues. Sometimes, one or both partners fail to establish a replacement network overseas.

You will notice that none of the above has anything to do with whether you can handle the job itself. Even where an expatriate manager fails to manage effectively, the problem is more likely to be a 'culture clash' than a failure of managerial ability. The problems to worry about are those that might arise out of a failed adaptation to unfamiliar surroundings.

Briefing courses to prepare you and your partner for being overseas are covered on page 30 (language courses on page 70). Of course, no responsible employer of expatriates will send you abroad without any preparation, and you should expect to find a budget already allocated to your briefing.

You may not. It isn't unknown for key positions to need filling in too much of a hurry for pre-departure briefing, and in a competitive world, sometimes the preparation for the move has to be done retrospectively. There are also employers who regard briefing courses as expensive, which they are, and whose recruitment techniques allow them to believe that they're taking on people who don't need briefing. If you've done a lot of box-ticking in the selection process, you may come up against this.

Psychometric and other personality tests are popular with employers of expatriates, who see a need to pick an expatriate 'type'. They work, up to a point, in that they tell your employer that you're more likely to succeed than the other candidate. But professional recruiters express concern that they're sometimes taken as guarantees.

If you're in a position to do so, you should insist on being trained. More on that on page 30. But whatever happens, you should give yourself time to think about your own strengths and weaknesses. All the non-job problems are magnified in an unfamiliar, and therefore stressful environment. Are you the type to overcome them?

Enough questions. Working abroad is challenging, life-enhancing, and definitely worth doing. You can beat the problems if you're ready for them.

Let's look at the money.

Playing the self-assessment game

How do you react to the suggestion that you are more likely to succeed as an expatriate if you are naturally open-minded, outgoing, interested in people, confident, adventurous, fun to know, physically fit and full of common sense?

Full marks if you laugh.

Half marks if you agree – and think that, therefore, you'll be fine.

No marks if you agree – and despair because you don't match up.

In self-assessment, you get to the answers by catching yourself out. Job interviewers do the same. A trick is to take the final shortlisted candidates to lunch, one by one, at a restaurant serving an unfamiliar cuisine. You fail the test by searching the menu for something familiar. You pass by being open-minded enough to try something truly bizarre.

Try some questions.

When you were last overseas, whether on business or holiday, how much of the language did you pick up?

How much did you speak?

How often did you start a conversation in the local language? How often did the coversation switch to English half way through?

Were you relieved when it did?

When you ate out, did you find somewhere new every time, or return to a restaurant you'd tried and liked? Did you eat the local food?

Did you do so because you liked it, or because it was part of the 'foreign experience'?*

Exactly how glad were you to get home? What about your partner?

All of the above are questions that have been asked on briefing courses for expatriates.

And finally, think about the trick played on one residential briefing course for expatriates. After the culture, the language, the business usage, the history of the country, the several days of immersion, the soon-to-be-expatriate couple are invited to a party, to celebrate the completion of the course. They are not told that the party will be exclusively a gathering of nationals from their destination country, speaking the language, observing the customs, eating the food. Afterwards, they are each asked to reflect on their reactions as they entered the room.

Are you worried about how your partner is going to cope? Does your partner know that? Do you think your partner is worried about you? Why don't you ask?

---

* *Part of the process of settling in, which is discussed on page 48, is moving from that sense of coping with something essentially foreign, to feeling at home with your surroundings. You know you've arrived when things stop looking strange.*

Looking at the job offer

Factors to consider include the salary package, plus attached benefits, the effect that the job will have on your career in the longer term, and whether or not the contract will be sufficiently watertight to guarantee that when you get there, you'll find everything as promised. Note that an offer of a lot more money than you are getting in the UK does not automatically mean that you should take the job.

Assessing the salary package

In the UK, you decide to take a job because the money's better, and because it's a step up the career ladder. When you're offered a job overseas, the money is not simply a percentage on top of what you're getting now, perhaps quoted in another currency (see box on page 7), plus a bigger car and extra benefits. It's calculated according to a different set of criteria, some of which are local to where you're going, some of which relate to prevailing rates of pay and benefits for expatriates as a class of employee.

You must, accordingly, apply a different set of rules to assessing a salary package for another country.

1. Is the salary good enough?

Begin by totalling your package at present. Arrive at a figure for what you would be giving up by going. This should include your partner's salary and benefits. (Then adjust the figure by whatever subjective amount might cover the career cost of not going, if you think there might be one – see page 13.) This will give you a base-line figure.

So far, so normal. But this does not give you a figure to accept or reject, or indeed to seek to improve. Salary comparisons between the UK and another country have to be made on the basis of living-cost data.

Cost of living differences can be big. A London salary in Tokyo, for example, would give you something less than half the spending power you have at home. This is not because of the sterling:yen exchange rate, but simply because things cost more than twice as much in Tokyo.

Comparative cost of living information is not easy to obtain, and the first thing to say is that companies can get it more easily than individuals. Therefore, before looking for it yourself, ask your company's, or your prospective employer's, personnel department what sources they have.

They might, for example, be a member company of Employment Conditions Abroad (ECA also known as ECA International), an international human resource information service and consultancy which (as the name suggests) advises companies on what remuneration they should offer expatriate employees in different countries as well as providing information on accommodation, benefits, social security, law and tax. ECA don't work for individuals (except that they compile and sell annually updated Country Profiles – see page 16) and so you would have to go through your employer, and your employer would have to be a member company, to obtain comparative information.

The table provided by ECA gives percentage differences between the cost of a shopping basket of items in a number of countries, as at March 1995 (ECA updates its figures annually). This information should be used with care and depends on where in the country you're shopping as well as what you put in your basket. However, it does provide a first step in working out what you will need to maintain your spending power in your destination country.

Employment Conditions Abroad is at Anchor House, 15 Britten Street, London SW3 3TY, telephone 0171 351 5000, fax 0171 351 9396.

Another source of information is the Union Bank of Switzerland's free publication Prices and Earnings Around the Globe, which is updated every three years. The next is due in 1997 and a table of figures taken from the 1994 edition appears on page 7. Prices and Earnings Around the Globe takes Zurich as its base, and includes figures and commentary on prices, wages, taxes, rents, working hours, domestic purchasing power and the working time required to buy such items as a loaf of bread and a 'Big Mac' in upwards of fifty cities around the world.

Prices and Earnings Around the Globe may be obtained from UBS Ltd, 100 Liverpool Street, London EC2M 2RH, telephone 0171 901 3333, fax 0171 901 2345.

Eurocost, based in Luxembourg, provides quarterly, annual or bi-annual 'Cost of living comparison indices', plus rent surveys and spendable income tables, for around 140 places (cities and countries) around the world. These cost £100 for each place compared with your home base (in the UK, you are offered the choice of either Oxford or London as a home base), and are usually broken down into different types of expenditure.

Eurocost may be contacted at 1 rue Emile Bian, L-1235 Luxembourg, telephone (325) 40 48 06/7/8/9, fax (352) 49 57 13.

● Converting the salary

The standard calculation of an expatriate's basic salary should take the net home-country going rate for the job (you will prefer to take your base-line figure), and adjust it for cost of living if this entails an upward adjustment. To the resultant figure should be added an additional figure of between 5 and 25 per cent of home-country gross salary (use 10 per cent, which is standard). This additional percentage is the premium (the 'foreign-service allowance') that compensates you for going overseas (see page 9). It varies according to where you are going, whether the country is developed or third-world, European or not, English-speaking or not, etc. It is discussed further in the following section.

This calculation gives you the figure that should be your minimum acceptable salary after tax in your destination country. For the purpose of judging the offered salary, assume that you will have no remaining UK tax liability after you go (but see page 90). You can begin to work out your likely tax liability in your destination country (see page 124), but if your prospective employer cannot give you reasonably detailed guidelines on the tax treatment of expatriates in the country to which he is sending you – hesitate.

ECA's shopping basket

This is data calculated from ECA International's Cost of Living Survey conducted in March 1995. The cost of living indices from which the data are taken cover day-to-day living costs excluding housing and are based on comparing 'international' lifestyles reflecting an average of family spending patterns. Note that ECA's Country Profiles include shopping baskets, and cost £50 each.

UK	£100
Bahrain	92.9
Belgium	136.3
Denmark	168.6
France	133.8
Germany	139.4
Hong Kong	122.4
Indonesia	100.6
Israel	127.2
Italy	109.4
Japan	263.8
Kuwait	101.8
Malaysia	90.2
Oman	97.9
Portugal	104.6
Qatar	96.2
Saudi Arabia	90.7
Singapore	126.1
Spain	104.1
Sweden	142.7
Switzerland	182.7
UAE	96.9

Your employer's calculation of what to offer you should have begun, as above, from the home net figure, and arrived at the comparable destination net figure before any upward adjustment for tax. All this should have happened before you got the offer. The idea is that the net salary should leave you better off, or at least no worse off, than you would be in the same job in your home country.

If you do find yourself entering into a negotiation, you should know that British expatriates are generally cheaper to employ than German or US expatriates. An innocuous question such as, 'Did you advertise the position widely?' might bring in useful information at this stage. How international was the competition? Are you a bargain? Could you, therefore, ask for more?

In such a negotiation, it is a good thing to put your cards on the table. As discussed earlier, the 'best' expatriates are generally held to be those with stable and supportive home lives, and such people will inevitably face greater difficulty in deciding to uproot themselves.

From the employer's point of view, such people will be more difficult to employ, but more worthwhile in the long run. Some employers go so far as to pay an allowance to compensate for a partner's interrupted career; all of them are aware that the best expatriate employees are not necessarily the easiest to attract.

Note that no employer of expatriates will set out to calculate a salary leaving you worse off than you are now, any more than you would accept such an offer. If you are going somewhere with a significantly lower cost of living than in the UK – lucky you.

If the salary is not quoted in Sterling

As a general rule, it is better to have the salary quoted in a strong international currency such as US dollars rather than your destination country's currency. The bulk of your salary will tend to be paid outside your destination country (see page 22), and while the calculation of whether to accept the salary remains based on comparing your standard of living here with your standard of living there, you have the additional exchange-rate complication. Managing currencies is discussed in detail on page 146; the point to remember is that while you can live happily overseas in dollars, when you come back to the UK, you will have to convert back into Sterling. Note also that currency conversions can incur a Capital Gains Tax liability (see page 112 for a way round this).

If you are asked to suggest a salary

If you find yourself being asked to suggest an acceptable salary, whether because you are entering a newly created position or going to an employer not experienced in employing expatriates, you should complete the above calculation, add sums and benefits as discussed below and in the next section, and aim modestly high. Note that although such an invitation is not necessarily a bad sign, it's not good either.

Ask a number of questions. Are you joining a team, or will you be on your own? Are you joining a company, or working for an individual? According to what legal system is the contract drawn up and what is the procedure for resolving disputes? Generally, working for a multinational company on a contract negotiated in the UK is better than working directly for an individual on a contract drawn up locally by him. This is dealt with in more detail on page 15.

2. Will the salary stay good enough?

You will not have to look for small print to answer this question.

There is a movement among employers of expatriates to dispense with special treatment, and to pay the local overseas going rates for expatriate jobs. The movement is gaining ground, and its adherents point out that with international mobility now so common and so easy, it is anachronistic to pay a special rate to somebody who has simply moved from one country to another (and possibly achieved a better living standard in the process).

They also point out that all expatriates tend to 'go native' to some extent, so that sooner or later they are operating on the same cost base as the locals.

Paradoxically, this trend towards no special treatment for expatriates is most advanced at the upper end of the jobs market. Senior executives have similar responsibilities whatever their nationalities; the countries of origin represented in the higher echelons of a multinational company don't count for much. So why treat them differently?

Similar reasoning is beginning to percolate down the management structures of many companies employing expatriates. Increasingly, the going rate for the job doesn't depend on the origin of the person doing it. (The exception is where skills are not available locally and have had to be imported, so that there is an obvious reason for a premium to be payable. Even in this case, though, the distinction is skill, not nationality.)

The effect of all this is simple. Your prospective employer might offer you a figure inclusive of benefits that will cease to be payable after a specified time. This is because (as discussed below) the moving is additionally costly, but the living, once you've settled in, isn't.

If your salary package contains an element that will change with time, this will be spelt out in your contract of employment; one approach is to specify a time period after which a revised version of the contract will come into force (both versions to be spelt out at the time of initial signature).

Another, more generous, approach is to specify that any renewal of the initial contract will be on altered terms. Realigning a contract to local terms, however it is done, is called 'localization'.

The fact that your company proposes eventually to pay you the same rate as the local staff doesn't make any difference to your calculation; however, the 5 to 25 per cent gross addition (10 per cent standard) may not appear in your employer's calculations, or the percentage may be reduced, or varied with time. Take this into account from the start.

If you can't reach a basic salary figure above your acceptable minimum, maybe you've overestimated the value of your partner's career. If not that, maybe the moment has come to recognize that your partner's career is more important than yours.

But don't give up until you've answered another question.

3. What about the rest of the package?

You don't work abroad just for the money. You do it for a package of additional allowances and benefits as well. These may not increase your salary significantly in themselves, but the package should be accepted or rejected as a whole.

Also, it can sometimes be easier to negotiate for an additional benefit than for an increase in the basic figure; different budgets might be involved.

Your additional allowances and benefits might include:

- Hardship allowance/location allowance. This is to compensate for such 'hardships' as may be experienced through climate, culture, etc. The foreign-service premium often covers this element of the package, but for 'very foreign' countries an extra allowance may be paid, and accounted separately.
- Accommodation allowance. Some employers pay all or part of the cost of overseas rented accommodation, though not all regard this as additional to the foreign-service premium. You may use the employer's contribution to fund purchase of accommodation overseas, but see page 173.
- Relocation allowance. This will definitely disappear after a specified time. It's your setting-up cost in your new location. You should be able to negotiate a repatriation allowance for the other end of your contract as well.
- Removals allowance. This is another short-term item that should cover both ends of your overseas stay. On top of cost, you should ask whether the company makes regular use of a particular remover. See page 35 for more on removals.
- Relocation cost allowance. You may have to sell your house, your car, etc., at a disadvantageous time; you may have to pay storage costs for your furniture. This allowance may include a contribution to the legal costs involved in selling your UK property or those incurred in preparing it for rental.
- Accompanying spouse allowance. This notionally compensates for loss of earnings, but does not amount to a second salary.
- An allowance towards the cost of your children's education. You have a strong case for requesting this (stronger if your children are already in fee-paying education). It is impractical (though not impossible, see page 182)

for the children of expatriates to remain in the UK state system while their parents are working overseas. International schools are expensive; access to overseas state schools limited. It is therefore generally true that working overseas will oblige you to pay for your children's education (see page 183 for the related problem of eligibility for state help with the cost of UK further education). Note that if you are being asked to go at short notice, you may need to pay a term's fee in lieu of notice at your children's school; ask for this.

- Company pension contributions. You may prefer to do your own pension planning, and opt out of the company scheme. See page 180.
- Life and medical insurance contributions. See page 28. Company medical-insurance schemes do not necessarily cover the risks that will be encountered overseas, nor do they offer the levels of cover. Consider negotiating for the company's contributions to be paid towards a private scheme chosen by you.
- National insurance/social security contributions. As a general rule, these should continue in the UK, whether you pay them or the company does. See page 180.
- Terminal bonus. Generally, if a terminal bonus is paid in respect of employment overseas, it will not be liable to UK tax. But you should consider its value in the light of your overseas tax situation (see page 124); a bonus should be judged as a net amount.

4. Are there any additional benefits?

There are relatively minor benefits that matter a lot. They should be specified in the contract, and if they are not offered, you should consider the cost of their absence. Among them, of varying degrees of importance, are:

- Paid leave at regular intervals. This is one of the things you shouldn't take for granted. In some countries, the customary leave allowance is significantly lower than in the UK.
- Flights home. If you are likely to spend your paid leave in the UK, you should ask for, and may expect, a number of expenses-paid return flights home. You will certainly get one round trip, should hope for two or three, and ask for three or four. Your need, and the company's generosity, will depend on how far away from the UK you are working, and on what 'clout' the company has with the airline. The more tickets the company buys for its employees travelling on business, the greater the discount it can receive on all the tickets it buys.
- Children's assisted flights. You may receive a contribution towards the cost of flying your children to and from their UK boarding school for the holidays. If so, ask whether the company can help with the cost of escorted passage (page 81).
- Clothing allowance. If you're going to a different climate, you'll need

different clothes. So will your partner. This can be expensive. A specialist supplier can advise on what to buy for where, on which see page 38. See also page 123 for VAT-free export of such possessions.

- Company car. The UK system is not common overseas. If the company is to offer assistance with the provision of a car, ask whether a driver is included. This is standard practice in some parts of the world, where liability in disputes with locals can tend to be decided on the spot, on the basis of nationality. Ask whether the driver will be employed by you, or by the company. The latter is administratively more convenient.

- Cost of security. In some parts of the world, you may find yourself discussing security precautions (page 62). Ask whether the company will underwrite the cost of any necessary measures, and if so, what they are. As discussed later, it is wise to consider yourself responsible for your safety, and not necessarily to accept any company-provided measures as sufficient.

- The company should make a contribution to the cost of briefing and language-learning. You should establish whether the company makes regular use of particular consultancies, and ask about past 'graduates' of courses. They can be useful contacts, particularly those still in place. See page 30 for briefing and page 69 for language-training.

- Advice. The company may provide, or offer to pay for, advice on personal financial and tax planning. This is good, but you should ensure that the provision is structured so that you personally pay for your advice. The adviser(s) you use should be independent of your company. See page 147.

- Servants. In some parts of the world, it is normal to employ domestic servants. Your briefing should include handling them, and your package should include the cost of employing them.

- Note that in some circumstances, it can be more tax-efficient for an employing company to make ex-gratia payments to cover certain costs, than to structure them into a salary package.

5. Is the salary competitive?

From time to time, the *Financial Times* Recruitment Page summarizes research by employment consultants into executive salary levels around the world. These tend to indicate that comparable executives doing comparable jobs in other countries tend to be paid more than their counterparts in the UK.

The living-cost method of calculating an acceptable salary tends to work to the expatriate employee's advantage in both more and less expensive countries. It is the one used by prospective employers who do not choose the local-rate approach. Where it does not give a competitive result is where there are equivalent-rank expatriates from higher-cost countries of origin. This is why, on page 8, it was suggested that you should establish whether other-nationality candidates were also considered for the job.

But remember that you are going for a career-enhancing job rather than just a short-term good salary.

What effect will working abroad have on your career?

You can't always ask outright whether a contract overseas is intended to be the first of several, nor can you necessarily decide in advance whether you would like it be so. Any specification that the terms and conditions will vary after the initial contract rather than during it (see item 2 in the section above) is more likely to be precautionary than a statement of intent to renew your contract.

First point. Relocation to the UK can be as traumatic as going to work overseas, in both personal and career terms. After (say) three years, the UK is not as foreign to you as another overseas location would be (see page 189), but it is not going to be as familiar as you expect.

Second point. Substantial numbers (from 6 to 30 per cent; it varies from survey to survey) of returning expatriates do not remain with the employers who sent them overseas, after their return to the UK. They are not dismissed; they make their own decision to leave. This is cause for concern among employers of expatriates; they see it as a loss of their investment in the employee's skills, at the time when the employee, having now a wide breadth of experience and knowledge to contribute, is most valuable to them.

Importantly, from your point of view, the reason for 'repatriation failure' is most commonly held to be a failed reintegration into the company at home. Either the company has not thought through the further deployment of its expatriate employee after the particular assignment that took him (or in 25 per cent of cases, her) abroad is completed, or the returning individual, with changed experience, knowledge and therefore objectives, finds that the home company does not have as much to offer as it used to.

There is also concern at the 'double whammy' effect on the partner, of giving up career and connections to go overseas, and then having to give up overseas links to come home again. See page 189 for more on the traumatic effect of returning to the UK on both worker and partner. In the section on preparing for your departure, page 27, there is more detail on how to safeguard your long-term position with your company.

The career implications of a job overseas depend on a variety of factors, but primarily on the employer. You may find it useful to conduct a company search through a consultancy such as Instant Search at 4 George Street, Whalley, near Clitheroe, Lancashire BB7 9TH, telephone 01254 822288, fax 01254 822221, but you should think about more general questions as follows.

1. Are you being posted overseas by your existing employer?

If so, you should not have any difficulty in discussing the long-term implications of what you are doing. No employer can offer a guarantee of what will happen to you after the present assignment is completed, but you should aim to establish two things.

a. What's the point of your overseas assignment? This may seem obvious, but you will be in a better position in the long term if there is a positive rather than a neutral or negative reason for your going overseas. 'We want you to develop links with suppliers in the region,' for example, is better than 'The job has just fallen vacant and we think you're the man to fill it,' or 'The whole operation over there is in chaos, and we think you're the woman to put it right.'

The first offers you an opportunity to demonstrate your ability to make something from nothing (or more from less) and is a strategic objective. The latter two entail the risk that you will become so valuable to the overseas operation, or will be seen as such, that your further career development may be stunted. Neither of them is part of a long-term plan, either.

b. What is the longer-term plan for you? Your employer is sending you abroad either because you are a fast-track employee already seen as capable of running your own operation (it is in the nature of overseas assignments that you will be much more your own boss than you would be in the equivalent position back home), or because he needs somebody to go overseas and you're the ideal candidate. Are there future plans for you? It is not invariably the case that you could expect an unequivocally positive answer, but best practice in expatriate-employing circles is to give more explicit guidance to overseas employees than to stay-at-homes.

2. Is this a new job with a new employer?

If so, there will not be a place for you to reclaim when you return to the UK (if indeed the company is based in the UK), but you should ask the same questions as in (1.) above, or versions of them, with the objective of establishing whether the present contract offers prospects. In this situation, you may expect that you are being hired for the long term, albeit on a short-term contract, but the option lies with the employer as to whether or not your contract is renewed. The employer, therefore, has the advantage in a way that he does not with a job in the UK. Read the section on negotiating your contract on page 21. Your job security depends on the size (see below) of your employer and where the contract is negotiated.

The disadvantages of relative job insecurity are to some extent outweighed by the career advantages of becoming an 'international employee'. Mobil Europe Ltd conducted a survey in 1995 in association with Employment Conditions Abroad, in which questionnaires were sent to 500 companies either in Europe or with European subsidiaries. The questions asked covered their policy on and experience with expatriate employees in general, but one of the most striking results was that expatriate employees who are truly internationally mobile are at a premium. Younger employees are less likely to accept overseas assignments; married employees are far more conscious of partners' careers than they used to be; and only 50 per cent of current expatriate employees are prepared to give serious consideration to another assignment overseas, without placing restrictions on where they would consider going.

You should, therefore, take care to establish your long-term prospects with your new employer, or begin to think about taking steps yourself to develop your career in future. Whatever your skill, being an expatriate is in itself an additional skill. There is a section on networking on page 27, and suggested sources of further expatriate jobs on page 191.

3. Will you be effectively self-employed?

In this case, you are already working towards the modern concept of the 'portfolio career', in which the individual contracts to supply services to one, or more than one, employer. It is not unusual for experienced expatriates (though less usual for first-timers) to be 'employees' of a company they have set up themselves, or which they set up with the encouragement of a prospective employer, in a low-tax jurisdiction such as an offshore financial centre (OFC). The expatriate's company receives payment for the expatriate's services from the employer for whom he is working overseas. OFCs are discussed in more detail on page 131.

Your job security is not as complete in this situation as it would be with a direct employer, and you should ensure that you know the jurisdiction in which your contract was negotiated, and that you have legal representation there.

4. Will you be working for an individual, or for a non-multinational, non-UK company?

If your job offer is from an overseas company which is not internationally known, you should be careful. Expatriate employees are not always valued by such companies, and there can be situations where they are resented by the indigenous staff. Negotiate your contract carefully (page 21) and consider going alone at first. It may be sensible for your partner not to resign until you are securely in place.

This precaution also applies where you are going to be employed by, or employed to work for, an individual, however internationally well known or reputedly prosperous that individual might be. Such contracts can be unusually rewarding, but the wellbeing of foreign employees is not always necessarily a high priority with such an employer.

What about the country where you will be living and working?

A point to make immediately is that for most countries, work permits have to be applied for before arrival. For the working partner, this will generally be handled by or with the help of the employer, but partners should apply at least six weeks in advance.

Living in a country is not the same as going on holiday there. This is a piece of advice commonly given to people considering retiring abroad, but it applies just as much to prospective workers abroad, and doubly to non-working, non-retiring partners. If you know the country from visits, whether holiday or business, your experience is not necessarily a good guide.

Most established employers of expatriates will fund an advance visit by one or both partners, mainly for orientation but also for preliminary work on finding accommodation, etc., but such visits generally do not prepare for the shock of not only being away from your own language and culture, but also having to set up home and connections without even knowing, for example, whether the noise from the telephone is a dialling tone or the engaged signal.

Such visits generally take place after you have accepted the job. Use them for making expatriate contacts from whom you can get advice while you're preparing to come for good, and make a note of everybody's phone number while you're there. Get into the habit of asking such questions as 'Was there any preparation you should have made, that you didn't?' and even, 'Is there anything I should be asking you about?' at regular intervals.

There are various sources of information about living conditions in other countries. Start by buying one or more guidebooks for visitors, particularly those aimed at budget travellers. These will stand you in good stead anyway, because they tend to be good on such things as public transport, but in this context read through the general notes on culture and dealing with the natives. The sections on taking precautions and avoiding danger are useful indicators as well.

(On those subjects, the Foreign Office will issue guidance on other countries if you ring 0171 210 4197, but this is a service mainly meant for holiday and business visitors and is really concerned with dangerous countries, where the advice will be simple, brief, and either not to go or to take special care. A number to have in your diary if you travel widely on business, but useful in limited circumstances for only some countries.)

The Department of Trade & Industry (DTI) issues 'Country Profiles' at £11 to £15 per country, and 'Hints for Exporters' at £6 per country. Note that the £15 Country Profiles incorporate the relevant Hints for Exporters, although the £11 ones don't. As these are concerned primarily with doing business with the locals (and, for example, not offending against local customs) they can be useful. Contact DTI Export Publications, Admail 528, London SW1W 8YT, telephone 0171 510 0171, fax 0171 510 0197.

Corona Worldwide, also known as the Women's Corona Society, provides 'Notes for Newcomers' for more than 100 countries, at £5 per country, plus briefings for individuals, single men as well as women, and couples (page 31). The Notes for Newcomers provide 'everything one would need if one was going to the country, including living costs, housing, education, health, leisure, and useful addresses' and are a worthwhile investment; they have inserted, where approriate, such extra guides as 'Living in a Muslim Country'. They are available from Corona Worldwide at The Commonwealth Insitute, Kensington High Street, London W8 6NQ, telephone 0171 610 4407, fax 0171 602 7374. The fax is shared with The Commonwealth Institute, so faxes should be clearly marked for 'Corona Worldwide (The Women's Corona Society)'.

Until recently, Christians Abroad, 1 Stockwell Green, London SW9 9HP, telephone 0171 737 7811 ran a service putting intending expatriates in touch with a Christian recently returned from their destination country. This service has been discontinued but they do still issue an information pack that includes some useful addresses and a questionnaire in which you can ask for further information. The pack is intended for people who will be looking for work overseas in the aid/charity field, but it is free and worth adding to the collection. Note that churches can offer social contacts as well as a place of worship; Christians Abroad can offer contact details for churches overseas.

Among other sources of information on countries are Employment Conditions Abroad's Country Profiles, which contain useful addresses as well as other information under a variety of headings, and Eurocost's data on living costs, both of which were mentioned on page 6, as well as a variety of books (see page 23) and various specialist expatriate magazines (see page 232).

But reading about a country is no substitute for visiting it, or speaking to somebody who has been there, and if you have doubts about whether you could live in the country where your job is situated, turn to page 31, where briefing courses are discussed.

What effect will working abroad have on your family?

A word to the 'trailing spouse'

You may prefer 'accompanying spouse', but the implication of whatever term you like remains that the non-working partner's autonomy has been surrendered.

The really difficult thing about working abroad is being the partner of somebody who is working abroad. Not only do you have to say goodbye to your job, your friends and your family; in some countries you face the prospect of not being granted a work permit and therefore not being allowed to work. You end up running the home in the old-fashioned way.

Be prepared, therefore, for the shock of realizing that in the eyes of those around you, you're not your own boss, but somebody else's trailer. And don't forget that you need to use your freedom of action to develop interests and activities that will look good on your CV when you re-enter the UK jobs market.

The Dual Career Network

This puts 'trailing' partners in touch with each other, both in a particular location and worldwide. The quarterly Dual Career Magazine gives information and advice on training, business ideas and other subjects of interest. More information from Dual Career Network, Fenham House, Four Elms, Edenbridge, Kent TN8 6NE, telephone 01732 700555, fax 01732 864171.

The effect on your children

You will, of course, be thinking carefully about the effect a time spent abroad will have on your children's education and development. Those subjects are taken up in more detail on page 80. But the prospect of living abroad is as alarming for a child as it is exciting. Just as moving to a new house is the child's equivalent of moving to a new job, with all the attendant stress and anxiety, so moving to a new home, a new country, perhaps a new school, a new social world in which to find new friends and enemies, a new language and new games and customs, is the child's equivalent of something that even the most enviably competent adult will find difficult to handle. The big difference is that the child has no illusions about being in control of what's happening.

Particularly with younger children, what you intend to communicate, when you tell them that you're all going to live abroad, is not necessarily the message that is received. And children themselves don't invariably communicate back to you in ways that are easy to understand. Here are three suggestions.

1. Discuss this: do you tell them at all, and if so, how much? The first question will be easier to answer than the second, but remember to stress (not over-stress) the positives, and the similarities to home as well as the adventure-points about the new country. Tell the good points to each other, not always directly to the children.

2. Remember that you communicate more effectively by example than by what you tell them. Whatever you say, your attitude will come across – and not only while you're saying it, but at other times when they're thinking about it and tuned in to you.

3. If possible, allow several weeks for the telling; don't think that just because you've said it, the job's done. On a child's timescale, particularly a young child's, this conversation is going to take some time to work through. It will surface at odd moments, just going to sleep, in the bath, asking for reassurance, checking that some bothersome detail isn't really bothersome. (Is it, mummy?) Don't belittle their fears: if they're scaled-down versions of adult fears, remember that they're being faced by scaled-down adults, not you.

When you get there, the likelihood is that you will observe positive effects on your children's development. But you should watch for signs of stress, and pay as much attention to your children's assimilation into expatriate and local society as you do to your own. See page 73.

Telling your family and friends that you're going

Losing a child to a job overseas isn't exactly a bereavement, but it comes close. For your parents, elderly or not-so-elderly, the prospect of your going to another country for months on end, and possibly years, before coming back home even for a visit, can be frightening.

There is also a possible problem here for you. If you're the one with the job, your partner's parents have you to thank for taking their child away.

Okay, we're all grown-ups. The job's happened, the decision's been taken, and that's it. You'll come back to visit. It's not as though you're going to the moon. With modern communications, you're only a phonecall away. And anyway, you could fly home in a few hours.

No, you don't think that way. You explain it to them. You ask their advice. And above all, you remember that for both of you, families are a potential source of two things:

- Stress, or
- Support.

Whatever your relationship is now, do what you can to keep it at least as good while you're away.

Same with your other relatives, and your friends. But beware. The news that you're going overseas for a few years will bring in enough invitations to drinks, lunches, parties to take up all the time you have available for essential preparations.

There is a very good case for inviting everybody to

A VERY BIG PARTY

about ten days before you go.

And then, for the last week, keeping it secret that you haven't gone yet.

Taking the job
How it should happen

You receive a letter offering you the job. Whatever form the contract takes, whether it is a letter or a legal form of contract, it will most probably be a standard word-processed document into which your terms and conditions have been keyed in at a junior level in the personnel department.

You should read it carefully. This is for three reasons.

- You may have misunderstood the terms and conditions being offered to you.
- You may not have realized the extent to which the terms and conditions will change once you are established overseas.
- The terms and conditions may not have been correctly transcribed from the head-office memo authorizing that the offer be sent out to you.

The third of those reasons is not the least common. Particularly where you are being recruited by a new employer, and even where a recruitment consultant is mediating, there is the risk that the contract will not be checked by the person on whose authority it is being sent out. That person may not be the person who agreed the terms and conditions verbally with you. The contract may pass through several sets of hands before it reaches you.

It is up to you to check that the offer on paper is what you expected it to be. Once you've signed, it's too late to change anything. The salaries department will go by the contract.

Some consultants, for example Godwins International of Briarcliff House, Kingsmead, Farnborough, Hampshire GU14 7TE, telephone 01252 544484, fax 01252 522206, will advise on the legality of a contract of employment offered to an expatriate. Using such a service can be a useful precaution. [Note that handwritten alterations invalidate a contract.]

If you get a letter, it may read something like this.

Dear . . . ,

Further to our discussion, I have pleasure in confirming our offer to you of the position of Expatriate Employee based at our office in City, Country.

This letter sets out the terms and conditions of your employment. You should note that many of the terms and conditions outlined in this letter are designed to assist you and your family in establishing yourselves in City, Country, and that they are designed to take account of the additional short-term costs involved in transfer and resettlement. Your terms and conditions will be reviewed and may be altered after one year of service, as specified below.

Subject to satisfactory service, your employment shall be for a minimum term of [say] three years.

Your overseas salary will be £00,000 [or it may be quoted and payable in another currency] per annum for the three-year term payable from the date you take up the appointment and subject only to the normal annual salary review procedure of the company. Your basic home salary [if you are continuing to work for the same UK employer] will be reinstated should you return to the UK with any overseas review applied to it after adjustment to bring it in line with the UK review procedure.

Your title will be Deputy Director of . . . and you will report to the Director of . . . , Mr Name, who is also based in City, Country. You will have responsibility for . . . . Your hours of work will be . . . and you will be entitled to 25 days' leave per annum which may not be carried over.

In addition to your basic salary as above, you will receive the following fixed benefits which will not be subject to review after one year. [Pension, see page 180, health insurance, see page 174, National Insurance and social security, see page 180.]

[Other benefits, such as accommodation allowance, car driver, etc., which will remain for the whole three years, should be specified here. Refer back to pages 10–12.]

You will receive an overseas allowance of £00,000 in addition to your overseas salary as above. The overseas allowance will cease to be payable after one year.

[Other short-term benefits should be spelt out here. Refer back to page 12.]

The company will pay for a residential briefing course (page 31) for you and your partner.

Should it be agreed that your appointment will be renewed after the initial three-year term, these terms and conditions will cease to apply and you will transfer to local conditions.

Please sign and return one copy of this letter. Your signature constitutes acceptance of the terms and conditions of employment as detailed here [and/or agreement to vary your UK terms and conditions].

Yours sincerely,

Note that in addition to the terms and conditions, the contract of employment should spell out your responsibilities in detail, and the lines of command. This is particularly important where you will be working with non-British colleagues with whom you may not easily establish a rapport, due to cultural differences, or with whom even basic communication may be difficult at first. See page 56 for cultural matters and page 69 for language learning.

It is as well to have the working hours spelt out as well as your entitlement to holidays. There comes a point of seniority beyond which the official working hours become academic, but it is important to understand office routines, which may differ considerably from those in the UK.

Your employer should undertake to provide you and your partner with, or pay for the provision of, detailed briefings on your destination country. See page 31. Your employer should also provide guidance on your overseas tax treatment (page 90), and may offer guidance on the most tax-efficient way to receive your salary. As you will have to provide bank details when you sign your contract, a short section entitled 'How you should be paid' follows on page 22.

Questions you should ask

- Are you signing with the parent company, a UK subsidiary of a UK or overseas company, an overseas subsidiary of a UK or overseas company, or an independent overseas company? If things go wrong, and you find yourself in dispute, you need to know which legal system governs your contract. Note that different legal systems impose different basic terms and conditions to underlie the specifics being offered to you. Finding a lawyer in the jurisdiction where your contract will be enforced is dealt with on page 218.
- If you are signing with a government or its agency, your contract will be according to that government's laws. International organizations use the law either of your home country or where you're going.
- Does the contract specify any procedures for dealing with disputes? It should, and if it doesn't, you should have it changed. In most European

countries, a convention dictates that jurisdiction lies with the courts of the country where you normally work. If you normally work in more than one country, you're covered in the country where you were engaged.

- Do I understand all the terms and conditions? Are they in English? If not, and you ask for them to be translated (as you should), you should seek the employer's assurance, in writing, that the English-language version of the contract will be binding. You may find it necessary to seek a translation from a company such as International Translation Resources, 1 Dolphin Square, London W4 2ST, telephone 0181 742 7422, fax 0181 742 8080.
- Have I now got everything relevant in writing, and is it all binding? Am I relying on any spoken assurances from people who will not be travelling with me? You don't want to be caught in the middle of a dispute between recruiter and employer about whether they were authorized to fill the post. You don't want to find that the job was for three months, not three years.

How it might happen

You might get told on a Monday that you start in the Moscow office next Monday at 9am. The reason might be that the newly established Moscow office has brought in much more work than was anticipated, and needs new staff urgently.

This did happen to a married 28-year-old professional with a London-based multinational. Against all the odds, he prospered, and is now working for the same employer in Singapore. He never meant to work overseas, but now doesn't want to come back to the UK. Nor does his wife.

If something like this is happening to you, speed-read your way to page 46. Telephone Corona Worldwide at the number on page 16 and ask if they can organize a telephone briefing.

Then take a deep breath and press for a better job title and more money. And talk about what's likely to happen to you when you return from overseas.

How you should be paid

For reasons detailed in the section on financial planning in Chapter Three (page 90), you should generally arrange to be paid into a bank account in one of the British offshore islands (Jersey, Guernsey or the Isle of Man), with living costs paid into an account in your destination country. UK banks have branches in the offshore islands, and can open accounts with correspondent banks in most locations overseas.

This may be the arrangement suggested by your prospective employer. If not, you will tend to be supplying bank details when you sign your contract of employment, so would probably find it easier to suggest now than arrange later. Open your offshore account to receive your first salary cheque from your overseas employment, and get your UK bank started on opening your local account overseas.

Preparing for your departure

This section covers preparing your personal, professional, financial, tax, and other affairs for departure. The practical business of actually going – visas, removals, etc. – is dealt with in the section beginning on page 32.

Go by the rules

There are three rules of expatriate life. They apply to everything. They are:

1. Keep it simple
Working in another country, you have enough to worry about. You should think very carefully before taking the more complicated (and complicating) of any two options. In the context of investment particularly, you should not forget the enormous advantages of being able to sleep easily at night.

At the beginning, the simplest route to whatever you need is almost certainly the best. Preliminary advice, for example, can be obtained from your high street bank, who can also help with opening a bank account overseas, etc. The banks offer packages of services to customers going overseas, and these may include reduced-cost access to sources of advice as well as discounts on removals, health insurance, mail-order shopping, etc. Other sources of advice should be researched now, and are discussed on page 26.

2. Do it early
It is easier to be too late than to get something wrong. All your tax and financial planning should at least be considered before you go. You should begin to prepare for your return to the UK at least a tax year (6th April to 5th April in the UK) before it is due to happen. You should never defer thinking about any major change in your circumstances. In particular, you should get into the habit of checking, well before the end of the tax year, whether there are changes due next tax year that would be better done this year.

3. Keep the paperwork
Take every conceivable record with you when you go; you may take the originals, but duplicates may be safer in some countries. At the very least, take a note of where copies of records may be obtained. If you're leaving any records behind, make sure a friend or relative knows where they are so that they can be easily sent on. If you put them in a safe deposit box, don't you be the only one with access.

You should also keep a paper record of every transaction, communication with a tax authority, visit to the UK, etc., before and during your time overseas. Confirm telephone instructions in writing. Request receipts. Keep credit-card and bank statements. Based overseas, you are not well placed to carry on your end of any dispute that may arise, and you need to be able to settle it quickly, or provide a full briefing to a professional who will act on your behalf. Disputes have a way of arising just when the main facts have been forgotten.

Get it right from the start

General point: from the first, you should start scribbling down notes and queries. Questions don't automatically occur when you're in the presence of somebody who can answer them. Another general principle is: if you want to know something, ask everybody who might know. When you're talking to a professional or other adviser, perhaps a colleague who's there already, a good final question in any formal or informal consultation is, 'Is there anything else I should know?'

What follows are two checklists of everything you should aim to do between accepting an offer of work abroad, and checking in at the airport. The checklists vary according to the amount of time you have left before you go. First:

If time is short
You'll find that however much time you think you've got, you haven't got enough time for everything unless you start immediately. But if you're going at very short notice, and have no time at all, you should read this checklist through quickly, and the full one below, and then turn straight to the sections on British and overseas tax beginning on page 90.

- Then talk to your bank about moving your accounts offshore (more detail on page 131), and obtain your bank's briefing package for new expatriates.
- Then ask a friend, relative, estate agent or property manager to look after your property in the UK (page 170). You have a period of two weeks (usually; check your policy) after you have left your property vacant before your insurance will be affected. You should notify your insurer of your impending departure. Although the correspondence on this should be actively pursued, it need not be concluded before you depart. See page 172 for insuring an empty property.
- If your work permit and visas are being handled by your company, ask about a work permit for your partner. Note that in many countries, work permits have to be applied for before arrival. If you're going to have to apply in person for your work permit/visa, telephone in advance to confirm issuing times, and take with you some useful paperwork/reading matter to do while you're waiting. See the next item.
- Then obtain a copy of the relevant Country Profile from Employment

Conditions Abroad and other information as on page 6. Ring for sample copies of the expatriate magazines (page 232). Such copies can generally be obtained free. *Resident Abroad* offers the Expatriate Survival Kit at £10. This is a loose-leaf folder of briefing notes which also contains copies of Inland Revenue guidance notes and forms that you will need to complete before leaving the UK.

- Talk through your preparations with a close friend or relative in the UK. Nothing necessarily formal, but you need somebody who will understand what you're talking about if you ring later to say that you've forgotten to do something, or left something behind. Sometimes there is an argument for giving a close friend or relative (or your solicitor, or your bank manager) power of attorney to act in the UK on your behalf. This might apply, for example, if you have elderly relatives or other dependants whom you are leaving behind.

- Keep a record of the preparations you have made. Take it with you, with the rest of your paperwork, and notes on the preparations you should have made but didn't have time.

- Buy at least one phrasebook each for your destination country. While in the bookshop, check the travel section for books on your destination country. Books for low-budget travellers are more likely to contain useful information on public transport, the basics, etc.

   All of the above should be done while you are organizing removals (page 35), packing, and having injections (page 34). Remember that if you are going somewhere where you need a lot of jabs, you may not feel like organizing anything for a while after you've had them. Maybe make the doctor's appointment for the evening.

- Finally, at the last minute, whether you already know them or not, phone one or more of the people with whom you're going to be working overseas. Phone them in office hours if you don't have their home numbers. Tell them you're looking forward to working with them, say when you're going to arrive, and say that you and your partner are looking forward to meeting them. Keep going until you've got an invitation to drinks or dinner. It's good not to turn up as a total stranger; also good to know what a taxi from the airport should cost, and whether to tip.

If you have time in hand

Briefing and general preparation
- Do everything listed in the section above.
- Buy a diary or planner, work the preparations listed on these pages into a schedule.
- Find out what the company has to offer by way of briefing. There may be little more than an information package, but there may be a full-blown briefing package for you and your partner. See page 30.

- Get the names and numbers of your future colleagues overseas. Listen for anything you can pick up about them in conversation. If you are being posted overseas by your existing employer, find out who's been there, who knows people there. Start to formulate a networking strategy. If you can visit before going permanently, do so. Make social as well as professional connections.

- If you are going overseas for your present employer, you may report to a UK-based superior. You may have a UK-based 'sponsor' to look after your interests while you are away. But if you intend to stay with the same employer after your return from overseas, you should make informal as well as formal contacts to keep in touch with developments while you are away.

- Talk to your predecessor in the job overseas. If this is not possible, find out why not.

- Get a lawyer, accountant, etc., with knowledge of your destination country. See page 148.

Tax and finance

- Immediately start looking for sources of advice. More details on page 147. Your first moves should be to establish contact with your bank's expatriate division, and find out whether they deal with tax matters, or can recommend an accountant who will do so. Arranging your affairs for expatriation is, broadly, a matter of notifying the Inland Revenue of the details of your departure, and moving your assets offshore. See page 90.

- Obtain form P85 from your tax office, complete it and return it. This is the form on which you provide details of your employment overseas, and by reference to which you may be granted non-resident status for tax purposes by the Inland Revenue. See page 94.

- Submit parts 2 and 3 of your P45 to your tax inspector, as you may be entitled to a PAYE repayment for part of the year in which you go overseas. See page 98.

- Defer any capital gains until you are non-resident in the UK for tax purposes, and so not liable for UK capital gains tax. Defer any major capital gains until your first full tax year of non-residence for tax purposes. See page 112. This does not apply to the sale of your principal private residence in the UK, see below. If, on the other hand, you face the prospect of making a capital loss, do it before you leave. Losses may be offset against the tax liability on any other capital gains, but only if they occur while you are liable to capital gains tax.

- Establish the basis on which you will be taxed in your destination country (page 126). Note that although tax efficiency generally requires you to remove assets from the UK, you should not, as a rule, move all your assets to your destination country. This is partly for tax reasons and partly for asset-protection reasons (page 164).

- Take more than one major credit card with you. The limit on at least one of your credit cards should cover the cost of an emergency return to the UK. In due course, you may find it useful to have at least one US dollar-denominated credit card, and one in your destination country's currency. Note that you should change the billing address for your existing credit cards.

- If your contract of employment is due to begin shortly after the beginning of a tax year (6th April), consider bringing it forward, even if only by a week, so that you begin your period of absence from the UK during the previous tax year. You will be non-resident in the UK for tax purposes from the date of your departure, but this is only by concession, and your status will not be unequivocal until your first full tax year of absence.

- Open a bank account in your destination country before you arrive. Doing this via your UK bank (or another UK bank if yours hasn't the right connections) will give you the makings of a credit record as well as the necessary means of survival for your first weeks. Your bank account over there should have a balance equivalent to a month's salary in it before you arrive. If this isn't possible, even an empty bank account is better than no account, but don't introduce yourself by trying to go overdrawn on day one.

- Move your UK bank account(s) to the Jersey, Guernsey or Isle of Man branch.

- Find out from your bank, or by asking colleagues already 'in country', what are the accepted means of payment at your destination. Some countries function on plastic; some regard the production of banknotes as tanta-mount to an admission of involvement in drug smuggling. Find out what'll do nicely.

- Start planning your return to the UK. Your tax arrangements for return, and disposition of your assets, will have to be settled in the tax year before the tax year of your return. You should be aware of the need to plan early. Also, by factoring your return into your financial planning, you can begin to set realistic investment objectives (page 193).

- Start keeping detailed financial records. Your tax situation will depend on where you were, and when, and where you received money, and when, and where you entered into financial transactions, and when. Read Chapter Three for more on this. Keep evidence such as credit-card bills that will prove location and time. A chronological filing system, divided by UK tax years, is to be preferred.

Employment
- Take out subscriptions to the specialist journals in your field. If they are free, notify them of your new address. It is up to you to keep your skills up to UK standards for your return.

- Talk to your superior in the UK, or the personnel department, about maintaining formal contacts with the office back home. You should arrange to be on circulation lists for memos, staff publications, etc. You may be offered a formal 'sponsor' who will look after your interests while you are away.

- Back up the formal arangements with informal ones. There are sound professional reasons for keeping in touch, and even for having an idea of which other staff might be interested in posts overseas. The details are up to you, but don't be forgotten.

- It does no harm to let your counterparts in other companies know where you are going, before they find out that somebody else has taken your old job. They should know that working abroad will widen your skills base, experience, know-how and general employability.

- Don't miss out, for lack of asking, on any careers advice offered to non-working partners.

- It should not be necessary to take out insurance against the eventuality that your contract turns out not to be as you had expected and must therefore effectively be terminated early; however, such cover is available and you might wish to raise the subject when seeking insurance as in the section below. Note that credit card issuers offer insurance to cover payments in the event of loss of income.

Property
- Your home in Britain must either be sold, rented or left empty. If you think you will sell, you will need to instruct an estate agent immediately in the hope of selling before you go: empty properties are unappetizing. If you think you will rent, you may need to redecorate and should consult a property manager. Whatever you do, you should consider your insurance. More details on page 170.

- Generally, your principal residence in the UK may be sold free of UK Capital Gains Tax. It is, therefore, exempt from the point above about deferring capital gains until after you have left the country. Page 112.

- If you think you will buy property overseas, do not do so until you have spent time in the place where you are considering buying. Don't buy living space on a short-term contract of a couple of years. Property tends to be an immovable asset, and your plans may be slowed down considerably if you're trying to sell a property while managing your move back home, or to your next contract.

Insurance, health and medical matters
- You should obtain medical and general insurance for yourself and your family. Company schemes are not necessarily flexible enough to cover the risks encountered in an expatriate assignment, and you may find yourself organizing your own insurance on top of what the company has to offer. More details on page 174.

- All-risks personal insurance to cover you and your family while overseas may be available through the insurer of your UK property, although it will not be standard and will have to be requested as an add-on and paid for additionally, or you can contact a specialist in this field such as John Watson Ltd at 72 South Street, Reading RG1 4RA, telephone 01734 568800, fax 01734 568094.

- You should check immunization requirements for your destination country. See page 34 for sources of this information. You should obtain immunization certificates for every member of your family, and carry them with you when you go overseas.

- You should arrange for thorough medical and dental check-ups before you go. Obtain copies of medical records and any prescriptions (including for spectacles/contact lenses), and discuss with your GP the reciprocal arrangements for national health cover that may exist between the UK and your destination country. Obtain leaflets SA30 and SA35 from the Overseas Branch of the Department of Social Security (DSS) at Longbenton, Benton Park Road, Newcastle-upon-Tyne NE98 1YX, telephone 0191 213 5000.

- If you take regular medication, discuss with your doctor whether it is likely to be available in your destination country; any other names under which it might be sold; and any substitutes if it turns out not to be available. If you take serious prescription drugs regularly, be sure to have the necessary prescription with you when you go through customs.

National Insurance and social security
- If in doubt, keep up payments. A full national insurance payment record entitles you to UK welfare benefits as well as the UK state pension. There are reciprocal arrangements within the European Union and with some other countries whereby you continue to pay UK national insurance contributions for a period of one or more years while you are overseas, and receive local benefits as well as keeping up your contribution record in the UK. But it is sometimes the case that you find you must pay both overseas and UK national insurance contributions to be sure of benefits overseas now and benefits back home later. More on National Insurance on page 180.

Other practicalities
- If you are taking a car overseas, check that its insurance will extend to your destination country; otherwise, get insurers' addresses from your UK insurer or from the RAC at PO Box 499, South Croydon, Surrey CR2 6WX, telephone 0181 686 0088, fax 0181 667 1041, or the AA at PO Box 50, Basingstoke, Hants RG21 2EA, telephone 0345 500600, fax 0113 279018 (note that the same telephone number for the AA with a 0990 code is a recorded service requiring you to say one, two, three or four several times after tones).

- Should you give notice to your children's schools?
- Your change of address will have to be notified to any organization with which you have regular correspondence, particularly those that send you cheques. National Savings, for premium bonds, etc., is at Marton, Blackpool, Lancashire, F13 9YP, telephone 01253 766151, fax 01253 693182. See also the list on page 42.

Travel
- Who is booking your flights? You would be well advised to arrive in daytime on local time, and preferably at a time when you would normally be awake on UK time, if you can combine the two. Allow time at the other end for handling such glitches as not being met at the airport. Note that if you do need help, it is better not to introduce yourself to your new colleagues by ringing them at four in the morning.
- Travel with the address of the local Hyatt, Sheraton, Hilton and other international hotels. You may be moving into rearranged accommodation, but providing for temporary recourse to a hotel can be sensible. Note that in some locations, hotels are the centres of expatriate social life.
- If possible, make advance enquiries as to the cost of the taxi ride from the airport. This small detail can be comforting to know in advance.

Briefing

This should be for both of you, and it should not necessarily be limited to what the company provides. If you are unlucky enough to find yourself being sent abroad by an employer who does not fund a briefing course for both of you, you should take steps to remedy the omission as below. Briefing for one partner is insufficient, not least because the mood at a briefing course tends to encourage people to share their unexpressed fears, reservations and worries about what lies ahead.

Depending on how long you have before you go, and what challenges will face you when you get there, the choice of briefing courses ranges from telephone briefings and half-day sessions giving just the basics, to four- or five-day one-to-one intensive language-learning sessions with a native speaker. There are courses containing information on culture, business culture, social customs, politics, tax and finance, educating your children, and every other subject covered in this book. Prepare for any briefing by reading up on the country and noting questions in advance. If you find yourself on a briefing course with others going to the same country, you have the beginnings of a social and support network. Get phone numbers!

Generally speaking, it is easier to get your briefing via the company that is sending you overseas. This is not just because briefings can be expensive as well as worthwhile (£2,250 for five days of intensive language training, for example), but because some briefing organizations work for companies and not individuals. Some of them are set up explicitly to do this; some have simply made the commercial decision that companies are more lucrative customers than individuals.

If your company is committed to your success, it should be prepared to pay for your briefing. Note that there are courses for employers and human-resource directors who will be responsible for expatriate employees. It can be instructive to ask whether your employer has training in how to handle you as an expatriate.

The main sources of briefing for expatriation are:

- The Centre for International Briefing, Farnham Castle, Farnham, Surrey GU9 0AG, telephone 01252 721194, fax 01252 711283. Intensive briefings lasting several days, generally for company-sponsored delegates. Negotiation skills courses for different countries offered as an extra. Face-to-face language tuition. Country briefings are 'structured to take account of the delegate's own professional and personal interests'. There is a bookshop, and a useful library.
- Employment Conditions Abroad, Anchor House, 15 Britten Street, London SW3 3TY, telephone 0171 351 5000. Mentioned here because until recently, ECA ran company-sponsored courses and you may hear of these when you get overseas; ECA's training operation for individuals became a separate company, and is
- Going Places, 84 Coombe Road, New Malden, Surrey KT3 4QS, telephone 0181 949 8811, fax 0181 949 6237. Not to be confused with the travel agent of the same name, Going Places provides training courses for individuals, couples and company delegates, generally half-day or day-long, sometimes two days. Courses vary from country briefings to specific requirements; cost £550 for half and £900 for a full day, and are a more compact alternative to the Centre for International Briefing. From experience of both, the scheduled country-specific courses represent a very valuable opportunity to make contacts among the other delegates.
- Expatriate Management Limited, St Clement's House, 2 Clement's Lane, London EC4N 7AP, telephone 0171 280 7732, fax 0171 280 7733. Strictly speaking, this is a company handling the administration of expatriate employees on behalf of their employers, but director John Donegan organizes orientation and training courses as well. EML is like Going Places in that it is suggested by ECA to prospective expatriates enquiring about briefing.
- Corona Worldwide (The Women's Corona Society), The Commonwealth Institute, Kensington High Street, London W8 6NQ, telephone 0171 610 4407, fax 0171 602 7374. At a cost of 'probably a hundred and something, depending on what you want', Corona Worldwide will organize briefings (for men, women and couples) including a 'briefer' who has recently returned from your destination country, on health, security, culture,

moving, tax, finance, 'being a foreigner', etc. These can be telephone briefings if you have no time at all, or day-long sessions at a mutually convenient location. There are scheduled briefings and short-notice briefings as necessary.

Membership of the Women's Corona Society costs £10 per annum or is free for a year to any woman who has attended a briefing. Men can only be associate members, although this is changing and is not strictly adhered to in some overseas branches, for practical reasons (in Vanuatu, for example, most of the working-spouse members are women, so the 'male trailers' are allowed in). Note that Corona Worldwide provide an escorting service for children leaving UK boarding school and heading to the airport at the end of term (see page 81).

It is generally agreed that one of the things you should bring away from a briefing course with Corona Worldwide is a copy of the annual magazine, which contains useful addresses overseas as well as some illuminating write-ups of overseas postings.

In general note that briefing organizations commonly report that they find themselves briefing people who have done other briefings already. Briefing courses are a source of contacts, addresses, information and shared experience, and if you don't feel completely ready after one briefing – do another one.

The practicalities of actually going

Having accepted the job, sorted out your affairs and briefed yourself on your destination and how to approach being an expatriate, you need to get down to the practical business of actually going. This section is prepared with reference to the Expatriate Survival Kit, which is available at £10 from Resident Abroad, FT Magazines, Greystoke Place, Fetter Lane, London EC4A 1ND, telephone 0171 405 6969, fax 0171 831 9136, and other titles given in the further reading section on page 229.

You should prepare your departure under the following headings.

Work and residence permits

In the European Union, you will not need a work permit, but you will generally need a residence permit. Outside the EU, you will generally need both types of permit. Note that such permits should generally be applied for outside the country to which they apply.

You will also need a passport that will still be up to date throughout your stay overseas. You should have separate passports for each member of the family, and more than one passport if you are likely to be travelling between 'mutually exclusive' countries, ie Israel and some Arab countries.

Work and residence permits generally follow automatically from the offer and acceptance of a job, subject to various potential minor delays which will be dealt with by the employer (ie making a case that the job couldn't have been done equally well by a national in some countries), but the non-working partner may have difficulties gaining a work as well as a residence permit. It is generally a good idea to allow six weeks for work/residence permit applications, for both partners.

You should establish before you go whether you will be required to register as an alien when you arrive, and you should know whether your permits will need to be renewed annually. These points will generally be covered in briefings, or you will be advised by your employer, but you should note them as questions to ask.

Note that if a work permit is not forthcoming for a trailing spouse before departure, this is not necessarily final. There are circumstances in which permits can be granted after arrival. Note also that work may be found for trailing spouses in some surprising countries. There are, for example, women-only offices populated mainly by trailing spouses in some strictly segregated countries. This is, however, a matter on which you should obtain local advice.

Finding a place to live

You may be moving into a hotel at first, or straight into a company-provided house or flat. Wherever you live at first, you may well find yourself looking for longer-term accommodation, either because this was the arrangement or because you don't like the first place you move into. Where practicalities do not dictate residence on an 'expatriate compound', and where local conditions make a home-hunt feasible, your employer will generally leave you to find your own accommodation for the long term, whatever support or financial assistance may be provided.

The whole family may be travelling together, or the working partner may be going on ahead. Occasionally, the contract will allow for a commuting arrangement where only the working partner goes overseas, returning on some weekends and for holidays to a family that remains in the UK home for the whole assignment.

An idea of what accommodation is available in the category you are looking for, and addresses of agents, will be obtainable from country-specific briefings, or, for example, from ECA's Country Profiles. These go into considerable detail on the matter of poperty; the entry for Marseilles in the France Profile, for example, suggests that 'a better area for expatriates might be St Giniez – Ste Marguerite – La Corniche, situated between 3 and 10km south of the city. Both flats and detached houses are available and public transport reasonably good, a bus ride to the centre taking 20 minutes. Utility and service charges are normally included in the rent.' For Frankfurt in the Germany Profile, you are advised, 'The area preferred by many expatriates is in and around the Taunus hills to the north-west of the city, in such suburbs as Oberursel, Bad Soden and Kronberg,' which fits in with personal experience.

Immunizations and health

Start by talking to your GP or company doctor at the earliest opportunity. Note that not all immunizations are mandatory, and that some sources of advice (travel agents, etc.) will only tell you about the mandatory ones. Note also that different individuals are not necessarily suited by the same courses of injections or tablets, so that one partner may sometimes receive one course, while the other gets something different. One business traveller to South Africa was worried that he only had weekly malaria tablets, while his colleagues had daily. He consulted a local pharmacist, and was told, 'Yeah, weekly, but you got the Rolls Royce of treatments, while they got the standard jalopy' (his transcription of the conversation).

The World Health Organisation publishes an annually updated guidebook called *International travel and health: vaccination requirements and health advice*, at SwFr15.00 from WHO Distribution & Sales, 1211 Geneva 27, Switzerland. It is also available from HMSO Books, 51 Nine Elms Lane, London SW8 5DR, telephone 0171 873 9090 to order. Also available from HMSO is the Department of Health's *Health Information for Overseas Travel*, at £7.95. British Airways offers guidance from the British Airways Travel Clinic which are based at 35 Wimpole Street, London W1, telephone 0171 486 3665. The British Airways Travel Clinic at 35 Wimpole Street has further numbers, and advice in case you need immunization urgently, recorded as part of its answerphone message.

Perhaps the most comprehensive guide to the whole subject of health is *Travellers' Health: how to stay healthy abroad* by Dr Richard Dawood, which is updated regularly and published by Oxford University Press. It costs £8.99 and is available from bookshops or to order from Oxford University Press Distribution Centre, Saxon Way West, Corby, Northants NN18 9ES, telephone 01536 746337, fax 01536 741519. See page 53. Further useful information is available from the Medical Advisory Services for Travellers Abroad (MASTA) at The London School of Hygiene and Tropical Medicine, Keppel Street, London WC1, telephone 0171 631 4408, fax 0171 323 4547. MASTA's enquiry line is 0891 224100; tell them where you are travelling, and they will send you printed advice by first-class post (the cost of this is covered in what you pay for the call).

You may like to have a comprehensive health check, such as that available from BUPA's Health Screening Centre, Battle Bridge House, 300 Gray's Inn Road, London WC1X 8DU, telephone 0171 837 6484, fax 0171 837 6797, if the medical check-up you get from your employer doesn't satisfy you, or doesn't satisfactorily cover everybody going with you. Your GP can perform or refer you for a check-up, or you can obtain one through your medical insurer (see page 174).

Other general health considerations are as follows.

- You should have your eyes tested before you go, and take the prescription and a second set of spectacles/contact lenses. Insure them (page 28) and check that your phrasebook has the words for a conversation with a local optician. If you have kept old frames with old but not unusable lenses, there is no reason to leave them at home.
- See your dentist. Tell him how long you plan to be away. He may do things he might otherwise have deferred.
- If you take long-term prescription drugs, take a letter from your doctor explaining what you need and why you need it. For obvious practical reasons, a copy of this letter should accompany your drug supplies through customs.
- Take a note from your doctor giving details of any allergies you might have to medication, etc. This is doubly important if you have potentially life-threatening allergies, in which case you should beware that overseas food packaging does not necessarily include details of all ingredients.
- Contraceptives can be marketed overseas under different brand names from those used in the UK. Take your GP's advice, or contact the Family Planning Association at 27 Mortimer Street, London W1, telephone 0171 636 7866, or the International Planned Parenthood Federation at Regent's College, Inner Circle, Regent's Park, London NW1, telephone 0171 486 0741, fax 0171 487 7150.

There is further information and advice on health on page 53, and on health insurance on page 174.

Removals

Contrary to what you might expect, the business of removing one's goods from one country to another is rarely problematical. This is borne out in surveys run occasionally by *Resident Abroad* magazine, where the problems reported tend to be that too much, too little or the wrong things have been brought rather than that the removing process itself has gone awry.

Things do get broken, or sometimes lost, but the feeling tends to be that the service provided has been well up to acceptable standards. One expatriate reported a basement-full of incompatible electrical goods (hence the section on that subject below), and another, claiming to be an expert after six country-to-country moves, couldn't see why the magazine made 'such a fuss' about the subject. 'Things go, things arrive, that's the end of it.'

The headings under which to plan a move are what to take, how to find somebody to take it, and, generally, what you should do and what you should expect your remover to do. But first, think about

What should you leave behind, and where?

Divide your possessions into two categories: personal items and household goods. With valuables, you should check the terms of your insurance (page 28) whether you take them or leave them. Other personal items are a matter of choice depending on where you're going and the circumstances in which you will be living. Expensive jewellery and fragile items might be better in a box in a friend or relative's attic rather than in storage (see below) or on the move with you.

If you will be putting documents into safe custody with your UK bank, remember to arrange for somebody to be able to get at them while you are away. Of course the bank can send them to you, but it is better to know that you have access without the item being sent all the way to you, and then back. Solicitors, for example, sometimes insist on 'having sight' of a document before they will act (an example might be where the release of mortgage funds is subject to proof of identity on the property).

As to household goods, there are three main options – take, store or leave – and a fourth which is 'store until ready to receive'. The fourth can generally be arranged with your remover, who can take your possessions and deliver them when you've found your accommodation. You need first of all to be clear on what you will find when you get there. This is more than just being told that you will be offered 'fully furnished accommodation', or that the company will help with the rental of what will tend to be a 'vacant and unfurnished' property. Such terms have different meanings in different places. Read what's said in the accommodation sections of your country profiles and briefing notes. Ideally, consult future colleagues already in the country. If it's going to be unfurnished, does that mean that there will be a sink plumbed into the kitchen, or not?

Storage

For valuables, that means a safe deposit box. These are most readily available from your UK or offshore bank at rates from £50 per annum for a small box to around £3,000 per annum for a walk-in safe. Similar facilities are available from most foreign banks, but you may find it difficult to initiate a conversation on where valuables are kept unless you are an established customer. Therefore, approach your UK/offshore bank and ask them to make arrangements for you with a 'correspondent' foreign bank near your location (the bank, perhaps, where they will already have set up your account, see page 26).

For share certificates and other important documents that you will not be taking with you, you can give them to your UK bank for safe keeping for a fee around £10 per annum. Access fees for stored items with banks can be levied up to £10 a time. By granting limited power of attorney or simply by agreement with the bank arrange for somebody nearby to have access to UK-stored documents. Make sure that somebody has copies of all the paperwork setting up the arrangement.

With larger items, you have the choice of putting them into a storage warehouse near your home, or leaving them in your property. Note that insurance cover for a property left empty (page 172) will generally require that the property shows signs of normal habitation. In this case, furniture – tables, chairs, beds – should be left in place, and regular visits should be arranged from a neighbour or other 'responsible person' (this is a wide definition, but if you have truly irresponsible neighbours, consult the insurance company about possible arrangements with property managers – page 170 – or other parties; claims can be repudiated if visits turn out not to have been made). If you're going to rent your property (page 172), the tenants will probably not come with much property of their own.

Storage is a subject on which removers can generally advise. Many will offer a storage service. Your furniture should go into a storage warehouse near your home (you will find these in Yellow Pages if not from your remover or an estate agent, etc.), and it should be packed in order of unlikelihood of your needing access to it while you're away. You probably won't need anything (empty all drawers of important documents before packing up), but circumstances do arise where goods are needed. As with all storing and packing, make a detailed inventory of what's where, and take one copy with you and leave one with a friend or relative back home (or your solicitor or bank: in extremis, somebody can pick it up from them).

Safe transit

You can send valuables from and to the UK with an organization such as Securicor Network Europe, Unit B, Ponton Road, Vauxhall, London SW8 5BA, telephone 0171 622 2312, fax 0171 498 5357.

What should you take?

If your remover does not issue you with guidelines on packing, including advice not to include firearms, drugs and flammable materials as well as locally sensitive materials and suggestions such as to have ready paperwork for prescription drugs – you've got the wrong remover.

Ideally, travel light and budget for buying at least some furniture. When consulting future colleagues, ask whether there might be anything available from departing expatriates: there is often some kind of second-hand market in expatriate communities, for obvious reasons. You, too, won't want to take it all with you when you go.

With regard to furniture, you will have an idea of what is being provided, if anything, from your company if accommodation is being provided or subsidized, from your briefing course in any case. Furniture and household goods can be cheaper overseas, and more or less available, and this is a point to establish before departure.

To move the average entire contents of a three-bedroomed house will cost from approximately £2,000 to approximately £4,000, excluding insurance (see below) and VAT, depending on where you're going.

Clothes

Beyond a basic wardrobe, it can be a better idea to buy locally for a different climate where you can rely on finding shops. However, a specialist tropical outfitter such as Airey & Wheeler at 44 Piccadilly, London W1V 9AJ, telephone 0171 734 8616, fax 0171 287 3817 (the branch for large men is round the corner at 8 Sackville Street) can provide a hot-climate business wardrobe. Airey & Wheeler is a gentlemen's outfitter, but can recommend sources for ladies' clothes (one such recommendation would be their supplier the tailor Mr Keith at Peter Simple Ltd, 83-84 Berwick Street, London W1, telephone 0171 439 9834; Mr Keith is described as 'a very fast worker, faster than you'd find in Hong Kong').

Note that your new wardrobe can be supplied direct to your remover if you are going beyond the European Union and so taking advantage of the Retail Export Scheme (page 123).

Electrical goods

As a general rule, anything made by a company with service facilities in your destination country may be taken with you, with exceptions as below, but you would probably be better off taking only the minimum of electrical equipment with you.

There will be a list of other-country service agents in the paperwork that came with the appliance (if you can't find it, visit your local dealer or ring the company in the UK). If the voltage is different (see table) you should establish first that the appliance's voltage can be adjusted, either by you or by the servicing agent (again, contact dealer or company).

However, electrical appliances are affected negatively by being moved, and it is a common experience to find that electrical equipment big enough to have been packed and shipped (page 35) simply doesn't work when it gets there. Mending, and establishing which little piece of circuitry has been jolted into inaction, can be expensive. You will probably find, when you visit your local dealer, that you could have bought the same appliance more cheaply there than in the UK.

Televisions and video recorders will need retuning at least to work in another country, and may be entirely incompatible with the local system. Computers are notionally international, and many are supplied with alternative cables to connect them to non-British sockets. However, transit is hazardous for such sensitive equipment, and you should

    a. consult the manufacturer before shipment on whether it is feasible to carry your computer that distance to that destination, and whether it will be compatible with local electrical standards (ask for the service department), and

b. use the manufacturer's original packing if at all possible. You should also back up all important data onto discs travelling separately.

Don't bother taking washing machines, etc. If they're not installed in your accommodation (and they may well not be – do you leave the fridge behind when you move house?), you will be able to get them locally, probably more cheaply than in the UK. Buying locally makes for more simple servicing arrangements.

This is a subject on which to ask questions of an expatriate already established in the country. Better still, if you can talk to your predecessor in the accommodation, do so.

It is as well to plan for an unpleasant surprise when you move into your accommodation, particularly if you are likely to be arriving at night. Some expatriates are lucky enough to find everything working, milk in the fridge, and a welcoming note from an expatriate neighbour. Some aren't. Arriving after a long journey, you will not be in your most resilient of moods.

Nor will you be feeling particularly competent. You may have decided, rightly, that a set of screwdrivers, pliers, insulating tape and a few lengths of wire might be useful accessories to have in your travelling kit (not too much wire; you don't want to look like a bomb-maker). But if so, bear in mind that foreign electrical connections and circuits can look strange to the untrained eye, and the familiar 'blue neutral, brown live, green earth' routine won't work for a two-pin socket where the wires are unexpected colours.

Sample overseas main voltages

The mains voltage for your destination country will be included in the country information sent out by, for example, Employment Conditions Abroad (see page 31).

Australia	230 volt 50 Hz
Canada	120 volt 60 Hz
China	220 volt 50 Hz
France	220 volt 50 Hz
Hong Kong	220 volt 50 Hz
Italy	220 volt 50 Hz
Japan	110 volt 50/60 Hz
Malaysia	230–240 volt 50 Hz
Netherlands	220 volt 50 Hz
New Zealand	230 volt 50 Hz
Russia	220 volt 50 Hz
Singapore	230–240 volt 50 Hz
USA	120 volt 60 Hz

If you have to perform emergency electrical work when you arrive, in that there are wires hanging out of the walls and no lights, you would probably be better advised to spend the first night by candlelight (pack candles and a book of matches as well as a torch) than prodding around unfamiliar circuits with a screwdriver.

Such electrical maintenance should be carried out by a local electrician recommended by a fellow expatriate. Find the fusebox early on, as well as the mains. Turn things on cautiously at first. Look for loose or frayed wiring.

Your car

If you have a car already, you can take it with you for your own use (not for resale) because personal effects (ie, the things you're already using in your day-to-day life) can be imported free of duty. Shipping cars is no different from shipping anything else. See page 122, and obtain form V561 and leaflet V526 from Customs & Excise at Thomas Paine House, Angel Square, Torrens Street, London EC1V 1TA, telephone 0171 865 3000, fax 0171 865 3105.

However, you should find out what a car would cost to buy once you're overseas. Right-hand drive is inconvenient in a left-hand drive country, and in any case your car's specifications may not be acceptable in your destination country. Information on this can be obtained from the car's manufacturer or from the AA or the RAC at the addresses given on page 29.

There are those who suggest that the best option is to plan to sell or store your UK vehicle and, once you're overseas, to buy a second-hand car that you won't reimport. Storage can be arranged with companies such as The Autostore, PO Box 833, Sawston, Cambridge CB2 4UE, telephone 01223 872879, fax 01223 872983 or Manor Car Storage, PO Box 28, Clavering, Saffron Walden, Essex CB11 4RA, telephone 01799 550022, fax 01799 550021. You should check that the company offers insurance and maintenance (including MOTs) and a delivery service to and from UK airports, and that your car will be stored indoors, in non-humid conditions.

Pets

This is a difficult one. It is possible to take animals to many countries, but their treatment according to local culture will not be the same as at home. Dogs are considered unclean in some Muslim countries, and most domestic animals will be uncomfortable in other climates. You will need a vet's certificate of good health to travel with an animal, and should check import restrictions (and remember the six months that your pet will have to spend in quarantine on return to the UK). Specialized containers for animals are available from removal companies and pet shops.

If you can lodge a dog or cat with family and friends for the term of your absence, that might be best. There are long-stay kennels such as quarantine kennels, but this is not a realistic option for an absence of years. The Royal Society for the Prevention of Cruelty to Animals (RSPCA) at Causeway,

Horsham, West Sussex RH12 1HG, telephone 01403 264181, fax 01403 241048 will advise on animal shelters and sanctuaries, as will your local vet or pet shop. If you are hoping to sell or give away your animal, try local schools as well as the newsagent's window, local newspaper, vet and pet shop.

Passports for Pets

This organization can supply information on vaccination guarantees which may allow pets to be imported into certain countries without quarantine. Write to Passports for Pets, 44 Little Boltons, London SW10 9LL.

A practical point

Somewhere easily accessible in your luggage, whether removed or carried, should be scrubbing brushes, plastic bowls, non-flammable and preferably non-liquid cleaning agents, etc. Kettles, unbreakable vacuum flasks such as are available from camping shops, plastic mugs, plates and some cutlery are all worth having easily accessible when you arrive. Do not pack for removal, but have with you, candles, matches, torches, etc.

Choosing a remover

There are official and unofficial ways of doing this. Contact the British Association of Removers (BAR), 3 Churchill Court, 58 Station Road, North Harrow, Middlesex HA2 7SA, telephone 0181 861 3331, fax 0181 861 3332 for a list of three names of members in your area and a useful folder of guidance notes; or alternatively, ask for a recommendation from your company or from colleagues already in your desination country. However you get your remover, he should be a member of the BAR, which is affiliated to the international association of international removers, FDI.

It is not difficult to find removers because they compete keenly with each other. The Yellow Pages, for example, are full of half- and full-page advertisements for removers, and any estate agent or property manager will be able to offer names.

Choosing between removers is more difficult. You should establish that they have experience in moving goods into your destination country, rather than just that they are prepared to take on the job. Ask when they last went there (and follow up with which town they went to). Ask whether they have any guidelines on moving into that country (beyond general observations about packing and customs restrictions). An experienced remover will have contacts in the country and know the quirks of customs at your point of entry.

Get several quotations. Get a detailed explanation of what is involved – in other words, what they've quoted to do. Above all, get an explanation of what happens at the other end, and a contact name. It is as well to use a company with an international reputation so that in case of a snarl-up, customs will give your shipper benefit of the doubt. But follow the rules that a company unable to get you a quotation will generally not be motivated enough to get your belongings through on time.

And clarify the date on which you can expect your belongings to arrive in the country, and the date, subject to customs clearance, on which they will be delivered to your residence (check that the terms include delivery at the other end). You will find that many removers have scheduled shipments to countries; if you are going beyond Europe, the term for the service you need is a 'deep-sea removal'. Note that air freight is more expensive than sea freight, and is probably better used for urgently needed goods only, in combination with slower sea freight.

Insurance

'All risks' insurance is more expensive than 'total loss' insurance, but worth having. This is because all risks allows you to claim for minor breakages, etc., while total loss only covers the one eventuality it describes. It is as well to give some thought to the valuation of your goods for insurance purposes.

You will probably be asked to pay for your removal in advance. It is worth taking out the BAR's International Movers' Mutual Insurance (IMMI) which insures the completion of your move.

Inventories

Make your own, and agree it with the remover. Do not vary from it when you pack up your belongings, without reference to your remover. Have your copy ready for unpacking.

Value Added Tax

Note that if you are travelling beyond the European Union, and using the Retail Export Scheme (page 123) to buy and export goods VAT-free, you can arrange for your purchases to be delivered directly to your removers. This removes one administrative headache from the business of leaving the UK.

Last minute checks and checklists

Ideally, check this section with at least a fortnight to go before you move.

People to tell

- Bank
- Building society

- Insurance company/ies
- Tax inspector
- Mortgage company
- School(s)
- Doctor
- Vet
- Social security
- Removal company
- Estate agent or property manager
- Driver and Vehicle Licensing Centre (DVLC)
- Customs
- Milkman
- Retailers
- Magazines
- Employer(s)
- Season ticket issuers
- Water company
- Telephone
- Electricity and gas
- The Post Office
- Your next of kin in the UK
- Same for your partner
- Your solicitor
- Your accountant

Things to do

- Make a record of your preparations and, for example, where everything is packed; attach to this a list of useful addresses
- Pay off credit cards so that you have spending power available for necessities
- Find out the numbers to ring if you should lose your credit cards; confirm that the UK numbers are appropriate from overseas
- Buy everything you will need from the 'Other things you'll need' list
- Obtain packing materials for fragile or valuable items
- Find certificates and other documents
- Review standing orders, direct debits, etc.
- Circulate your new address
- Contact your UK and offshore bank regarding methods of giving them instructions long-distance; faxed, e-mailed or telephoned instructions will require a password
- Copy documents that you will not take as originals, and arrange safe-deposit storage for valuables not coming with you (page 36).
- Ring 0800 444844 for the Royal Mail's Mail Redirection Service

and make informal arrangements for redirecting arrived mail, ie leave several large SAEs with a friend

- Have the house keys copied and appoint a keyholder
- Notify the local police that your property will be empty, and of the name and address of your keyholder.
- Drain water tanks, etc., and go through your house's heating systems, stopcocks, etc., with your keyholder (subject to the conditions of your insurance, page 170)
- Confirm flights, and ring overseas colleagues-to-be to confirm times of arrival
- Drain or use up fuel or oil, particularly from items to be packed
- Send back the rented TV
- Tell the water, gas, electricity and telephone companies
- Settle any accounts with newsagents, shops, etc.
- Cancel the milk
- Cancel/take out subscriptions to journals and magazines
- Have business cards printed with the local language version on the back; have similar cards printed for your partner in case he/she gets lost
- Get the name of a lawyer in your destination country (page 148); also get the address of the British embassy or consulate
- Write down useful phrases such as 'How much is the fare to [your accommodation address]?' Also note important destinations; your pronunciation might not be accurate at first. Both partners should have copies of such notes.
- Work out a rough-and-ready formula for converting the currency so that you can, in haste, decide whether you're being asked for £50 or £5
- Note the emergency numbers at your destination (page 63)

Documents you'll need

- Passport
- Tickets
- Copy of your contract and contact details for your overseas employer/colleagues
- Inventory and paperwork for your removed possessions
- Visas, work and residence permits
- Birth and marriage certificates
- Reading matter, distractions for the children
- Medical certificates, prescriptions
- Immunization certificates
- Overseas bank details, offshore bank details, UK bank details
- Copies of correspondence confirming your overseas bank account

- Travellers' cheques (Sterling, US dollar or local currency according to destination)
- Credit cards
- Driving licence, permit
- Car insurance (check with AA/RAC whether this will be valid; same source for insuring overseas)
- Phone directories (page 194)
- The address of your accommodation overseas
- A city map for overseas
- Phrase books and dictionaries

Other things you'll need

- UK and foreign currency (including as small denominations as possible for taxis and tipping)
- The keys for your luggage
- Keys or details of how to get into your accommodation overseas
- Business cards and contact details of colleagues in the UK and overseas
- Office telephone lists
- A sheet of numbers to call if things go wrong when you get there; you're not met at the airport, you can't find/get into your accommodation
- Medical insurance cards and contact numbers (page 177)
- Several passport photos for each member of the family; six minimum
- Your business cards. Always travel with these; they establish your bona fides.
- Your Christmas-card list of friends and relatives
- A supply of British stamps for sending SAEs etc.; International Reply Coupons are not always readily available, nor are they as simple for the recipient
- Addresses and phone numbers of local hotels
- The facilities for immediate cleaning of the bathroom and kitchen
- A small plastic bowl, rubber gloves
- Battery versions of shavers, etc.
- Sunglasses, sunhat, mosquito repellent, sun cream, long skirts and long-sleeved blouses; warm clothes
- A small first-aid kit (clearly marked as such) including analgesics, insect repellents, anti-diarrhoea treatment, oral rehydrating salts, crepe bandage, sterile gauze, and various sizes of fabric plasters, scissors and tweezers, water purification tablets, suntan cream (high factor)
- Family photograph albums; mementoes
- A loo roll

- International plug adapters, several; at least one should allow you to plug in a UK three-pin plug; also take a few UK three-pin plugs
- A screwdriver and basic toolkit
- Corkscrew, bottle opener, picnic plates, mugs, non-electric kettle that can double as a teapot, knife, fork, spoon, instant coffee, unbreakable thermos (from camping shops), short-wave radio, tin opener, teddy bears, toys, good books, magazines, a portable chess set.
- Notepads and pens, pencils
- A torch, batteries, candles and a few books of matches
- A moneybelt, preferably of the variety that is simply a belt with a zip on the inside to give access to the space beween the top and bottom layer of material. Moneybelts that look like moneybelts are useful carriers, but regarded by pickpockets as likely to contain valuables. Moneybelts that look like shoulder holsters should be reached for carefully in some countries.
- One or more portable alarms

Last words of advice

If you will be travelling far enough to be vulnerable to jet lag, start to adjust your sleeping hours towards your destination pattern by one hour at night at least a fortnight in advance, as far as is possible. Do not do this at the expense of sleep, ie don't force yourself to get up early if you haven't been able to go to sleep early. Cut down on alcohol, and ideally, do not drink in the week before your departure. It is a very bad idea to schedule your leaving party so that you might have alcohol in your blood, or indeed a hangover, when you travel. Drink water on the plane; colder liquids are absorbed more quickly.

Assume that you will not be met as arranged when you arrive. This is a commonly reported experience, and an eventuality to plan for, however cast-iron your arrangements. In extremis, travel to the local Sheraton, Hyatt, whatever, and take it from there. If you're staying at a hotel and they can't seem to find your booking, remember that it isn't the reception desk's fault. Showing a business card at the earliest opportunity (ie, to confirm the spelling of your name) is a good way to establish your credentials.

If you travel from the airport by taxi, one standard rule is to confirm the cost of your trip in advance. At the airport, have in your pocket the likely amount in small bills if possible, plus a small sum for any porters, etc. Nobody carries your bags out of generosity. Business travellers with little luggage moving fast through the concourse are generally the ones to follow to the official taxi rank.

'It can be very difficult to get either Marmite or Bovril. Take a supply with you. I always get people to bring it out when they come and visit me.'
Teacher, Berlin.

CHAPTER TWO

THE FIRST YEAR ABROAD

'The best thing about working abroad is that as a full-time foreigner, you're accepted into the social life, but in a non-competing way. You don't have to take sides.'
Businessman, Antibes.

'I wish I'd known earlier about the network of clubs, societies and groups which conduct themselves with quite a lot of secrecy. It took months of empty evenings before I found out that there really was a lot going on if you knew where to look and who to talk to. Even if you're not a joiner, it pays to get out and about and be involved with the social scene. In the absence of public entertainment the only sort you're going to find here is the home-made variety.'
Teacher in the Middle East, who met and married his British wife, a nurse, while out there.

Get this year right, and the rest is easy. The first year is when you make the plans that will see you through your expatriate years and beyond. It is a time of discovering unforeseen opportunities and facing up to unexpected difficulties. It is, above all, a time to remember that life is supposed to be fun, too.

Immediate action plan

If moving into accommodation, find the fusebox, find the mains, find stopcocks for water and gas, and work out how the drains run. Be the first member of your family to try all the plugs, switches and electrical appliances. Check that wiring is not frayed

Be ready for emergencies that arise out of unfamiliarity with the country. Children might look the wrong way before crossing the road, or try to pet wild dogs

Check locations of hospitals, surgeries and medical units. You will have received information from your medical insurer (see page 174); supplement this by asking questions of your local contacts

Confirm 'book knowledge' of your location with local contacts. A roadmap bought in London, for example, can't give you the latest roadworks. Guidebooks can be wrong, or general in a way that is misleading for your location

Make contact with a family and friends back in the UK, and with colleagues and future friends here overseas

Register with the British Embassy and with the local authorities

Look for social contacts as a matter of urgency (see 'Settling in'). Find the important noticeboards at the earliest opportunity. Find the British/American/International Club(s), the British/American/International School(s). Ask local hotels for details of future social activity. Seek local advice on such matters

Don't buy anything expensive until you've tried second-hand sources among expatriates

Obtain the local phonebook if you don't have it; start to assemble your own local address book. Begin to 'network' socially and in business

Settling in

However optimistic you may have been in the weeks prior to your departure from the UK, however carefully you may have weighed up the pros and cons of life overseas, you will find yourself unable to start as you mean to go on. The first weeks of expatriate life are a time of stress, tension and second thoughts. But don't worry. That changes.

When you arrive

You will feel euphoric. Then you will feel depressed. Then you will think seriously about packing up and going home. You will find fault with the locals and their customs. Then you will have a good day, and realize that your depression has come to be a habit, and that underneath it, you're not really depressed any more. Then you'll cheer up

This whole process takes anything between a month and three months, sometimes longer. It's such an established pattern of behaviour that a graph showing its progress (up, down, gradually up, level) circulates among personnel managers. In a company with a lot of expatriate employees, you might sometimes detect that an apparently informal chat is in fact aimed at finding how far you've got along the graph.

The beginning of the end for the down phase is triggered when you begin to get a handle on the situation. You're not quite beginning to think in the local language yet, but you've got all the phrases you need to get you through the day. Your travel passes have arrived for getting to and from work, you've understood the public-transport system, and you've begun to know your way around the local market. You no longer buy everything at the expensive glossy supermarket where it's easy because you don't have to ask for anything.

And the children are beginning to chide you for the slowness of your integration. They speak a mix of both languages, and seem all of a sudden to be enjoying school.

Getting through this first stage depends on first of all recognizing that it's happening, and then sharing the experience. You and your partner should resist the temptation as far as possible to compare the situation with how much better it was back home, but you should discuss this rather than think about it separately.

Note also that any pattern of conversation in which you begin to compare each other's experience is to be avoided. It is necessarily the case at this stage that one of you spends the whole day managing the home, getting the utilities connected, etc., and one of you spends a hard day at the office. You probably both need more support than you're getting. 'Looking after each other,' said one expatriate, 'is give and take without too much of the take.'

Practical matters

While you're both making your way up and down the emotional rollercoaster, you will need to spend some time concentrating on the more mundane details of your arrival.

When you get there, register with the British High Commission, Embassy or Consulate. Her Britannic Majesty's government may not devote much of its time to ensuring that your local colleagues allow you to go about your business without let or hindrance, but it is sensible to ensure that the local British authorities know you're there for several reasons.

- In the event of serious emergency such as civil disturbance, war or revolution, the Embassy will activate contingency plans to evacuate the British community, if this should become necessary. It will notify voluntary and unpaid 'wardens' among the British community and provide them with names and addresses of all registered Britons in their respective areas of responsibility. The Embassy will communicate any evacuation plans via its wardens; only by registering do you get on the list for assistance, and when you register, the Embassy will tell you who's your local warden. (Note that if you are evacuated, you will have to pay for your flight.)
- If you are arrested or otherwise fall foul of the law, whether you are at fault or not, the British Consul will arrange for you to have legal representation. His intercession will not be aimed at 'getting you off', but at ensuring that you receive fair treatment. Note that, as is obvious, the British Consul can only intervene if he is notified of your predicament; this is why it is important, in more sensitive locations, for expatriates to notify each other of where they are, where they are going, and when they should arrive. The early appearance of the British Consul might persuade the local police to drop a minor charge.
- The British Consul will register births, marriages and deaths; is empowered to provide notarial functions; will replace lost passports.

- The British Consul will be able to advise you, if you do not already know, on where and whether you should register as a foreign resident with the local authorities.
- The British Embassy will have a mailing list for invitations and functions (in a small British community, you will be more likely to be towards the top of this; the same will be true if you come to play any semi-official part in the community, ie, secretary of the British Club).

You will find the makings of a not-necessarily-office-oriented social life (see below) via the British Club, the International Club, the American Women's Club . . . any expatriate community has its set of clubs. Find them via the noticeboard at the Embassy, or through office connections, or – a source not to overlook even if you haven't got children – through the British School or the International School. Note that social life in a British community overseas, particularly beyond Europe, tends to focus on different venues from those in the UK. In the Middle East and Asia, for example, hotels are important centres of social activity.

Anecdotal evidence from successful expatriate couples suggests that the best legacy of the first month is a relaxed attitude to such situations as when, for example, A was in a meeting that he couldn't leave when B phoned to say that the removers wouldn't unload the furniture without a payment, but that wasn't in the contract, and anyway, A had taken the credit cards and the money with him, and . . . so on.

Other anecdotes tell of the missing document. There are too many permutations on this one, but suffice to say that your first move should be to agree a place to keep the paperwork, and stick to it. Take more paperwork than you think you could possibly need for all your encounters with official-dom, and be patient.

An early discovery is that expatriate life involves both partners in office-related socializing. Be aware not only that the first invitations will include both of you, which is a good thing, but that you will be expected to reciprocate. It is rare to find an expatriate community that does not do at least a proportion of its socializing at home, whatever the local culture may say about using restaurants. Take care not to get so dependent on the people you meet first, that you exclude the possibility of meeting others, or of meeting locals. The second year can be a process of unmaking the friendships of the first; don't make too close ties.

Reciprocal club membership

Clubs tend to have reciprocal arrangements with other clubs elsewhere in the world. A list of these is usually available from the club secretary, as is a letter of introduction allowing you to claim reciprocal membership rights in another club.

Sometimes, a small British club with little more than a bar and a tennis court will turn out to have reciprocal arrangements with a London club which include the right to book a room. Clubs tend to be less expensive than hotels. The East India Club in St James's Square, for example, has many reciprocal arrangements with overseas British clubs.

Interpretation

Your preparations might include having to speak to non-British colleagues and other parties overseas before your language-learning has got properly under way. If they don't speak English, you should know about telephone interpretation services such as Language Line.

This began as a charitable effort to assist UK ethnic minorities. Now it helps British companies operate in overseas markets, and is accessible by anybody with a credit card. It includes a text translation service. Further information from Language Line, 18 Victoria Park Square, London E2 9PF, telephone 0181 983 4042 (interpreters on 0181 981 9911), fax 0181 983 3598.

Emergency numbers

These are not as familiar to the locals in other countries as they are in the UK, and in some places the emergency system is not as developed as in the UK. In some countries, you have to prepay an emergency call, ie, by quoting a credit-card number to the operator. You are advised to check the numbers before you need them, and to seek expatriate advice on whether or not they work. An informal emergency-number system using fellow expatriates as emergency contacts is worthwhile as an additional precaution in some countries; carry the number of the British Consul.

Note that 112 is the European Union's emergency number in addition to national numbers.

Europe	Fire	Police	Ambulance
France	18	17	15
Spain	00	091	regional
Portugal	115	115	115
Germany	112	110	110
Switzerland	118	117	144
Italy	113	113	113
Belgium	100	101	100
Cyprus	199	199	199
Austria	144	144	144
Greece	166	100	166
Turkey	077	077	077
Holland	0611	0611	0611

Sweden	90000	90000	90000
Iceland	112	112	112
Hungary	05	07	04
Czech Rep.	150	158	155
		(154 for road accidents)	
Denmark	112	112	112
Luxembourg	112	113	112
Norway	110	112	113
Finland	112	112	112
Russia	01	02	03
Poland	998	997	999
Asia			
Japan	119	110	119
Korea	119	119	119
China	119	110	119
Hong Kong	999	999	999
Thailand	191	191	191
Singapore	999	999	999
Indonesia	113	510	119
		(118 for road accidents)	
Malaysia	999	999	999
India	No national number		
Pakistan	No national number		
Nepal	110	110	110
Taiwan	119	110	119
Australia	000	000	000
New Zealand	111	111	111
Middle East and Africa			
Bahrain	999	999	999
UAE	998	999	999
Saudi Arabia	0997	0997	0997
Israel	100	100	100
Egypt	122	122	122
Iran		6403688	
South Africa	999	999	999
Kenya	999	999	999
Nigeria	199	199	199
Lebanon	16	14	16
Liberia	114	115	113
Mauritius	999	999	999
Americas and Caribbean			
Bahamas	919	919	919
Barbados	113	112	115
Canada	911	911	911
USA	911	911	911
Mexico	06/08	06/08	06/08
Argentina	100	101	107
Brazil	Varies by city		
Chile	132	133	2224422
Bolivia	119	110	371234
Venezuela	171	171	171

Looking after yourself

This section is divided into three parts. First, you must maintain your health and fitness. In an unfamiliar country, eating unfamiliar food, resisting unfamiliar diseases and, at first certainly and later perhaps, dealing with the debilitating effects of stress (see below), your physical wellbeing requires more attention than it would in the UK. Note that health insurance is dealt with in detail on page 174.

Secondly, you must avoid 'cultural hazards'. These are the mistakes you risk making, and the offence you potentially give, by acting in the way that comes naturally. Different cultures have different body language, different gestures, different ideas of what constitutes polite behaviour. You succeed more completely if you fit in than if you are written off as an impolite foreigner who doesn't know any better. (Note that some body language is subliminal: if you naturally stand too close, or touch people – on the shoulder, say, during conversation – where touching is not the custom, you risk being avoided as odd without anybody realizing that it's just because you are foreign. This works both ways, and you should examine your attitudes to your local colleagues.)

Thirdly, you must avoid more overt threats to your wellbeing. This is more straightforward, except that danger overseas is potentially greater because, as a foreigner, you are less likely to recognize danger signals, and because in dangerous places, foreigners are potential targets.

Health and fitness

Your body has built up resistances and immunities to the potential sources of upset that it encounters in the UK. Wherever you go overseas, you will find yourself more liable to suffer both minor and major infections, etc., for the reason that your body needs time to build up a new set of resistances (the same will be true when you return to the UK, proof against all overseas nasties but certain to catch a cold within days of your arrival).

Your lower resistance applies to the food as well as to the ailments. It will last at least as long as settling in, because the causes of disorder needn't be exclusively physical. Combined with the inevitable stresses of a new and wholly unfamiliar environment, it is a powerful argument for healthy living. Just as partners need to devote time to each other, so you need to make space in the day for keeping fit. Playing tennis, therefore, is a better way of making friends than staying out late drinking.

But the serious approach to health needs to divide the threats into two groups, as follows.

- Low-profile risks. These are the ones you don't necessarily see coming. The food, the stress, the lowered resistance. One expatriate joked that she 'ate an apple a day to keep the doctor away, but I made a mistake, I forgot to peel it first.' If you're not in the habit of looking after yourself, remember that your susceptibility to the ailments of modern life – heart attack, high blood pressure, etc. – is potentially greater for the first months of your time overseas.

- High-profile risks. On the health front, these are the life-threatening diseases that you don't encounter in the UK, and for which you will need additional protection by injection or other means. AIDS as well as malaria, cholera and typhoid come under this heading; if you are going to a less developed country, or if your job will entail your visiting such places, ask your employer or your insurer about local arrangements for obtaining clean blood for transfusion (see below). Air evacuation – flying out to a hospital that is up to Western standards – is dealt with on page 179, as is the problem of communicating that you have cover and can therefore pay care bills when your problem is that you are unconscious.

Remember that whatever the threat to your wellbeing, whether it is major, minor, health-related or otherwise, you should take care:

1. not to place yourself in a state of vulnerability, ie, by travelling unprotected; and
2. to be ready in case the threat comes to you. This is the more important, in that it is less readily appreciated. A high incidence of a life-threatening disease does not mean that it is limited to the indigenous population. Not all expatriates are as careful as they should be; your colleagues are not necessarily taking the same precautions as you are, nor are contacts from other companies. There is one documented case of a high-ranking British expatriate executive who concealed his suspicion that he had become HIV-positive on a business trip to the Pacific Rim. He concealed it from his doctor, and from his wife. His suspicion was justified.

The World Health Organisation's *International travel and health: vaccination requirements and health advice* includes a chapter on risk avoidance. Among the headings under which precautions should be taken are:

- Travel. 'In the age of jet travel, international travellers are subect to various forms of stress that may reduce their resistance to disease'
- Bathing, whether in fresh water or sea water
- Bare feet. Keep your shoes on. But in some climates, examine them for snakes and scorpions before putting them on. This does not mean sticking your finger in to check that they are empty
- Altitude. Find out how high your overseas location is; high places can exacerbate heart problems
- Heat and humidity
- Sun. Wear a hat. In terms of ultraviolet radiation, dark days overseas might be brighter than dark days in the UK

- Insects
- Animals. Familiar animals such as dogs and cats can carry unfamiliar diseases when they are overseas. Don't pat anything, even if it's stuffed. Note that inadequately treated leather goods – belts, purses, wallets, etc. – can carry anthrax.
- Accidents. Particularly motor accidents. Chillingly, the WHO guidebook comments, 'A traffic accident in an area that is not well served medically is more likely to be fatal.' Your own good driving is not necessarily a guarantee of safety
- Food. 'Diarrhoea affects an estimated 20–50% of all travellers.' But beware typhoid, polio, hepatitis and parasitic infections. Watch for unpasteurized milk, uncooked food, unpeeled fruit and vegetables, eggs and ice cream. Cooked food should have been freshly cooked – ie, it should still be hot (not just warm). Check 'sell-by' dates, if any, on packaged goods. Beer and wine are usually safe, as are carbonated soft drinks. Take a supply of water-purification tablets if the destination requires it, and take local advice on replenishing supplies. Coca-Cola is widely held to be kinder than most alternatives on a suspect stomach
- Sex. Anybody who might, as the WHO guidebook puts it, 'place themselves at risk of infection' should be equipped with the necessary means of preventing the exchange of bodily fluids. Condoms, etc., are not necessarily available everywhere, and anyone who seeks to escape infection by not going that far should note that many emergency services now use physical barriers (small plastic sheets fitted with one-way valves called 'isolaides') before attempting mouth-to-mouth resuscitation. This is why you should take care when dealing with
- Other people's accidents. Enough said
- Medical treatment. This is not included as a heading in the WHO guidebook, but drug-taking, blood transfusions and the use of unsterilized syringes, etc., are discussed at length. Note that twenty minutes' boiling is required to sterilize a syringe, and that a doctor's authorization for its use should be carried with any personal stock of medical equipment. Blood used for transfusion should have been screened for HIV, hepatitis B and syphilis.

There is another threat to health that affects expatriates disproportionately, and not only working expatriates. It is

Stress

Whether or not you think you suffer from stress, you should know that if you experience any of the following symptoms, you probably do. Stress leads to physical illness, and can have a negative effect on your personal and business relationships. You cannot always adjust your lifestyle to remove the causes of stress, as when, for example, you are working on an important business project, but you should aim to have 'quality time' away from any identifiable sources of stress, even if only for an evening or a weekend.

Symptoms of stress are:

- Changed sleep patterns: you can't get to sleep, but you wake up early and stay awake
- Changed leisure patterns: you're no longer as interested as you used to be in your leisure pursuits
- You're eating significantly more, or significantly less, than is normal for you
- You're drinking more than is normal, and a drink is becoming your way of winding down at the end of the day (over-reliance on coffee is the corresponding symptom at the beginning of the day)
- You're tired
- You find it difficult to concentrate, and sometimes can read paperwork without taking in its meaning
- You don't see issues clearly, and find decisions less easy to make
- Minor setbacks are disproportionately irritating
- People are irritating; you are more easily annoyed
- You turn irritations over in your mind, unable to set them aside
- You are cynical and find it difficult to be enthusiastic about the job
- You are worried, anxious or apprehensive without being able to identify a reason
- You have lost your sex drive

Stress is dangerous because the sufferer can't get outside it to deal with it. This is why getting away from the causes of stress, by going out/staying in for an evening, or by going on a short holiday, is a good idea. Note that a stress-release break should not involve too much booking, arranging and organizing for the sufferer.

Another approach to stress is to retake control of one's situation by such simple means as beginning the day by listing things to do, and the order in which to do them. Such lists should always include one or two items that can be struck off immediately, but those that seem most tedious or difficult should be confronted first. The sign of recovery from stress is when you smile as you pick up your list at the beginning of the day, and replace 'Monday' at the top with 'Tuesday'.

Cultural hazards

It is a truth widely acknowledged these days that detailed etiquette guides can do more harm than good. If you have a list of things to do, such as eating with your right hand and not showing anybody the sole of your shoe, you are in danger of forgetting that these are just examples and not the whole story.

Good behaviour in an unfamiliar culture is not a matter of doing a few odd things and otherwise behaving as you would at home. Anywhere on earth, the purpose of good behaviour is to ease social (and business) transactions. This is best achieved when each party acts in a way that the other will understand. If you do the right things, but self-consciously, the chances are that you will communicate your unease. Better than that would be to convey the right general attitude. If you can do that, you will find that the specifics of good behaviour (as set out below) start to make sense, and in due course, come naturally.

Therefore, the route to success in a foreign culture is to act according to a few simple principles as follows.

- Local customs, manners and forms of behaviour are worthy of your respect. They make at least as much sense as, for example, shaking hands and saying 'How do you do?' without expecting an answer.
- Generally, social customs have evolved for good historical reasons (shaking hands: you put the other party at ease by giving him the opportunity to hold your sword arm).
- They are normal behaviour. You are the odd one out.
- They are unconscious. Your host is not twisting round to hide the sole of his foot, it just comes naturally.

The right attitude is nine-tenths of success. If you can incorporate into it all the specific details of local correct behaviour, you are, frankly, made. This is because Westerners are familiar visitors to most cultures in the nineties, but many of them don't get it right. Western behaviour is tolerated (after all, most cultures set great store by respecting the guest), but a visitor who shows understanding and respect as well as a guidebook familiarity with what to do with his hands is a rare and welcome exception.

So here's how to behave. The advice is divided by region, and not every region is included specifically, but read all of it wherever you're going. Non-Western cultures are far more similar to each other than any one of them is to Western culture.

1. In Asia

- To speak of the 'Far East' is tactlessly Eurocentric. You are in Asia.
- Superstition (which is not a term you should use to describe it in local company) is part of life in many Asian cultures. 'Feng shui', which is variously spelt in Western texts and which means 'wind and water', is, for practical purposes, the art of having everything in the right place to appease whatever forces of nature and supernature might otherwise be offended. In Hong Kong, for example, the office blocks in Central are designed so as not to obstruct the path of the dragons who live in the mountains behind to their drinking water in the harbour in front.
- Fatalism is also a common attitude to life. This shows itself in a variety of ways. If you are meant to get from the airport to your accommodation, for example, you will do so. This might be the attitude of the person who is

supposed to meet your flight; he will therefore regard your destiny as more important to the success of your journey than whether or not his car meets you at the airport.

- It is a very serious mistake to believe that when you encounter the apparently irrational, either superstitious or fatalistic, you can convey a Western attitude by talking the matter through. As explained above, better to appease the dragons than insist on what you think is common sense. You are, in local terms, wrong about that.

- Present your business card face up, using both hands. Your card will be printed on both sides; the upside is the one in local characters. NB: Try your card out on a local colleague before you present it to an important customer. Just to be sure it hasn't been embarrassingly misprinted.

- Read any business card when it is presented to you. This is a mark of courtesy; you are impressed by the individual's qualifications and job title. The time you should take to read a card varies from country to country (longest in Japan, ten seconds is a good average); what matters is that you are pleased to receive the card, and that you don't immediately put it away when you are finished. Let it linger in your hands. Checking pronunciation and commenting on details shows interest if it is not forced.

- Generally, the surname is written first on a business card; thus, Mr First Second Third is to be addressed as Mr First, not Mr Third.

- Carry a supply of business cards on social occasions. Better to carry them unnecessarily than to commit the faux pas of not meeting business card with business card.

- Find out how your name is likely to be written. This is important (in China particularly) where characters used to write your name will have meanings of their own.

- If in doubt, dress more rather than less formally for both business and social occasions. You will lose significantly in the eyes of your local counterparts if you are dishevelled, overheated, untidy or underdressed for the occasion. Don't be the first to remove your jacket at a business meeting, in case you're the only one to do so.

- You may not receive direct instructions from your local superiors; at least, when you do, you may not immediately recognize them. Indirectness is courtesy in many business relationships. Express the view that it would be good if something were done rather than tell somebody to do it. If it is not done properly, better to let your disappointment become apparent, than directly to reprimand your subordinate.

- Observe the order of seniority at a large business meeting. Disagreement is better effected by the technique of 'agreeing and adding'.

- Western influence varies from country to country; do not make the mistake of imagining that an apparently 'westernized' business contact is westernized under the surface.

- Seniority does not necessarily coincide with age; be circumspect when it does not, and generally respect age as well as seniority.
- Do not lose face or cause another person to lose face. Do not lose control or respond in kind to a loss of control.
- If your business methods are not getting results, change them. Watch your fellow expatriates. Remember that loudest is not most effective; the opposite is more likely to be true.
- In general, be conscious of the body language of locals roughly equivalent to you in status, age, etc. Copy it.
- Keep your socks in good condition. If there are shoes in an entrance area, take yours off and expect to be offered slippers. Do not wear these outside.
- Do not eat everything on your plate.
- In general, do as others do. Do not stand out. Keeping face is generally the same thing as keeping in conformity with your fellows.

2. *In Arab countries and north Africa*

- Holy day is Friday; Moslems pray five times a day, every day, facing Mecca. During the month of Ramadan, Moslems do not eat, drink or smoke between sunrise and sunset. You should not be seen to do so either.
- Always shake hands on greeting an Arab; do not be in a hurry to let go; do not ask an Arab about his wife's health, but about his family's health. When sitting with an Arab, do not show the soles of your shoes.
- Have your business card printed in Arabic as well as English. It is not necessary to bring a small gift to a first business meeting, but if you do so, do not let it be refused, and do not expect it to be opened there and then.
- Business meetings with Arab hosts will tend to follow a familiar Western pattern; this is because Arabs have grown used to Westerners' ignorance of Arab etiquette (as above). It would do you no harm to get it right. If invited to sit by your host, sit where indicated even if somebody else has to vacate the chair. The order of precedence runs downwards from the place at the right of the host; to avoid confusion, observe this in your own team. Strict etiquette requires that the meeting begins with general conversation (silence is not necessarily a bad sign); you drink more than one cup of coffee with your host, indicating by a shake of the cup when you have had enough. Then you get down to business.
- Use your right hand for everything.
- Do not admire anything that you are not prepared to be given. Arab hospitality rests on the principle that the visitor should be able to regard the host's possessions as his own, and this can lead to difficult consequences
- If invited to a social gathering at an Arab's home, reply in writing, preferably in Arabic, and arrive punctually. Leave shortly afer the coffee at the end of a meal, and send a small gift when writing to your host to thank him for his hospitality. This should be a gift to the host and not to his wife.

- Generally, Arabs are tolerant of Western failures to observe their ways of behaviour. This, however, does not mean that you can break the local rules with impunity.
- Women should dress soberly, avoiding short skirts and sleeveless low-cut tops. One can work out one's own dress code with experience, but note that a Western woman who is considered to be underdressed can meet with hostility in public places.
- Do not drink or be in possession of alcohol except in countries where you are absolutely sure it is allowed. The practice in some expatriate circles of importing such items as hops, malt, sugar and yeast and making one's own potions is, frankly, dangerous, and not only to the digestion.
- There is a ban in many Arab countries on publications showing pictures of women who are not properly clothed. You should note that the definition of 'properly clothed', and the offence, is in the eye of the beholder; that the penalty can be imprisonment; and that many Western magazines and newspapers routinely publish photographs that would offend an Arab. If you subscribe to any Western publications, find out if they come in a see-through envelope (the subscription staff of a genuinely international magazine will understand why you are asking this question). If in doubt, obtain them pre-censored from a retail outlet such as a super-market.
- There is also a ban on publishing caricatures of Arab Royalty or other leaders. This, too, can be inadvertently transgressed with serious conse-quences. A subscriber to a British financial magazine spent three nights in prison and was only rescued from severe punishment by the intervention of the British Ambassador. He had been stopped for a minor driving offence, and the magazine had been open on the passenger seat, to a cartoon showing a caricature that resembled a member of the Royal family.
- Never talk politics with an Arab.
- If your passport has an Israeli stamp in it, get another one. If you're in Israel, get a second passport for Arab countries.

3. In southern Africa
- Generally, behave as in north Africa, as above.
- Never talk politics. Show respect (remove headwear) when in the presence of a photograph of the head of state.
- Avoiding eye contact is a way of showing respect.
- If an instruction is given but not carried out, assume that this is not a sign of inefficiency, but indicative that the subordinate is seeking a way to disagree that will save face for both parties.
- Take local advice when travelling, and if in the company of the guide, stay with the guide. Note that in many countries, your dress and appearance should be conservative. Long (below the knee) skirts for women, short (off the collar) hair for men.

- Remember that the family is the key social unit, and that this carries through into business. Relationship-building is your priority at first.
- A confrontational attitude is not the way to succeed in the long term.
- In difficult situations, stay calm, stay confident.

4. In Europe

- Behaviour in Europe is generally 'westernized' in business circles, but this does not mean that you can overlook the need to observe local customs and cultural differences between countries. As a resident, it is a better approach to look for differences and behave with them in mind than be reassured by similarities.
- Official and actual working hours vary widely across Europe, as do attitudes to them. Turn up on time at first, and go by your colleagues' behaviour, not what they say.
- You will offend, socially as well as in business, if you are mistaken about punctuality. Take local advice on this. In France, Belgium and Germany particularly, you should be on time; in Spain and Italy, you should not.
- The Germans are formal in their behaviour, though not necessarily in their dress. It is a safe generalization to make about Germany, Austria, Belgium, Switzerland and the Nordic countries that meetings include little small talk and socializing in general is kept for after working hours. Socializing can be lively, but you will be marked down for being late the following morning.
- In Germany and Belgium particularly, shake hands on meeting and parting. In general, note body language and respond in kind. Note, however, that in tactile countries where close contact such as kissing is a social practice, it may not be appropriate to greet the opposite sex in the way that you greet your own.
- Most European countries divide into regions, and customs can be regional rather than national. Be circumspect.
- Queueing is a British habit.
- In France, most socializing occurs outside the home. You need not follow this rule, but a careful choice of restaurant is better than a half-unpacked, half-decorated home if you are making friends and influencing people in the first months. It is a general rule in many European countries that appearances and other formalities matter in social life, even among friends.
- In general, it is good to arrive for a social occasion with a small gift for the host or hostess (generally the latter); be more formal than you would in the UK, and do not offend by attempts at humour which use irreverence or indeed self-deprecation. Chocolates or flowers (not chrysanthemums, well-wrapped, an easily manageable quantity) are appropriate gifts; anything alcoholic is a mistake.
- Reply in writing to written invitations; send thank-you notes.
- In eastern Europe, you will find the dictum useful that 'business is personal'. This is by contrast with the supposed Western notion that

'business is business' (which, in practice, is rarely useful). Build relationships as well as contractual obligations.

- Throughout Europe, but particularly in eastern Europe, do not talk politics. If western politics come into the conversation in eastern Europe, it is likely that a compliment is intended rather than an in-depth discussion.

Avoiding danger

In most parts of the world where there are expatriate communities, you are most likely to receive a warm welcome, or at worst indifference, from the majority of the local population with whom you can come into contact. Where expatriates are rare, the welcome tends to be warmer, and some expatriates have reported being treated as though not being a native was a condition deserving sympathy.

But the fact remains that an expatriate is an outsider, and outsiders tend to be a focus for any tension that might arise in the community. As a resident expatriate, you are more likely to find yourself the focus for racist, nationalist, political or irrational resentment than a tourist. This is because tourists are a transitory modern plague with money to spend, while expatriates may be seen as threatening local culture with their imported ways, taking local jobs, money, etc.

Bear in mind also that the employer you represent is a potential focus for resentment, either by virtue of nationality, or because of the industry in which the company is engaged.

As with health (page 53), it is sensible to make a division between low-profile and high-profile risks. The former are a more general category, and apply wherever you are going. Simply remember that you stand out, and that you are not necessarily as 'street-wise' as you would be in the UK. Crime varies from culture to culture; be vigilant, especially in public places.

If you are going to a potentially dangerous location, there are some general precautions you should take, and some specific points that are dealt with under separate headings below.

The general precautions are:

- Don't stand out more than is unavoidable, by your appearance or behaviour, and avoid any conspicuous displays of wealth. This applies in the reception areas of hotels and other semi-public places, as well as on the street.
- Vary your daily routines, at weekends as well as on weekdays. This advice is generally taken to mean that you should vary your route to work, which can be surprisingly tiresome to do. Vary the route, and equally important, don't vary it predictably.
- Stick to the areas you know. Better to let your knowledge of the town, city

or indeed country evolve slowly than go exploring down unfamiliar back streets.

- Remember that you are most vulnerable to attack when between places of safety, ie, leaving a car to enter a building. In these situations, your attention will tend to be distracted. You should remove any cover such as bushes that might be used by an attacker from around the entrance to your home.
- You should plan journeys, etc., so that your arrival at dangerous places does not happen at dangerous times, ie, don't pass through unsafe parts of town late at night.
- Have a wallet that you can hand over easily, without reaching as if for a weapon. This should not be a 'dummy wallet' with practically nothing in it, and you should not carry two wallets (a moneybelt that is not obviously a moneybelt can be useful).
- Travel with emergency numbers; get into the habit of informing your fellow expatriates where you are going, and when you will arrive. Get into the habit of checking that other expatriates have arrived safely.
- Learn at least one other British expatriate's home phone number as well as the official numbers for use in an emergency. The principle is that somebody outside official circles can attempt to speed up efforts on your behalf.
- If you encounter anything out of the ordinary or suspicious – loitering strangers, for example – report them to the police and mention them to other expatriates.
- Make sure that your car cannot be tampered with.
- In the event of serious civil disturbance, it is better to be in a group of expatriates than to be alone, and better altogether to be at home listening to the World Service and waiting to hear from your local warden (page 49) than to be out.
- Build up a cache of emergency supplies, and turn a room in your house into a lockable safe haven to which you can retreat in case of attack (but have escape routes in case of fire). One expatriate in a southern African country reported spending periods of weeks at a time sleeping inside the front entrance of the house, behind the heavy front door.
- Talk to the members of your family about these precautions, and work out contingency plans.
- When planning, remember that what tends to happen is what you don't expect. Also plan for your not being present to co-ordinate your family's response to an emergency.
- Your contingency plans should include places to meet if you are unexpectedly separated, and, for example, times at which the one of you not lost will be at a given phone number or location rather than out looking.

A consultancy that advises companies on the dangers that may face their expatriate employees, and offers guidance on how to face those dangers, is

Control Risks, 83 Victoria Street, London SW1H 0HW, telephone 0171 222 1552, fax 0171 222 2296. Note that degrees of risk in different expatriate postings vary over time. Control Risks issue tables ranking countries by their danger to expatriates, and these appear from time to time in the expatriate magazines.

A number of specific considerations with regard to your own safety now follows. But remember that the most valuable protective measure is a cautious approach, and that a list such as this cannot be exhaustive. There may be other dangers.

Crisis preparation and management

Have water, food, drink, house and vehicle fuel, radio batteries, medical supplies stored in advance. Better, as a general rule to stay at home than to risk excursions. Listen to BBC World Service news on your short-wave radio/satellite television. Be clear in advance on plans for communication with your local warden and British Consulate. The resident Western news media are also worthwhile contacts to develop in a developing crisis. Keep in contact with other expatriates; discuss contingency plans together. If going out, tell another responsible expatriate (not only your partner, if he/she will have the children to look after) where and why you are going and how long you will be, and arrange to contact each other when you return. If you are the responsible expatriate in such a situation, never assume or be persuaded that anything is 'probably okay'; at the very least, your responsibility is to contact the local British authorities on your friend's behalf. For emergencies, have light and portable 'emergency bags' ready; do not be separated unless unavoidably from your documents; have your documents readily accessible, not packed away. If you are in a group of expatriates, stick together as a family and do not be separated from the rest of the group if this is avoidable.

Domestic security

You will tend not to move into accommodation that has not been equipped for security to at least a basic local standard.

However, your attitude should be that what is unknown is potentially dangerous. Lock up tight at night, seek immediate advice from fellow expatriates on this subect, and remember that in many countries you are guarding against animals and insects as well as intruders.

Mosquito screens, etc., are there for a reason; get into the habit of using them.

Home and hotel security

Attack alarms are widely available and easily portable in a handbag or pocket. Inexpensive movement alarms (some of which, for example, are video-shaped and designed to be inserted into a video recorder to shriek if it is picked up by a burglar) are also available and can be hung on the inside handle of a bedroom door.

Weapons

Do not carry any weapon that you are not prepared to use to the full. A mugger or other attacker will not be deterred by the sight of a knife or a gun; the opposite response is more likely. Self-defence courses generally advise flight rather than fight.

If you do decide to carry deterrents beyond simple noisemakers, some expatriates suggest carrying the locally available varieties rather than things brought from London. This is because an attacker will react unpredictably to something he does not recognize.

The best weapon against mugging is an easily accessible wallet with some cash in it. In dangerous situations, feigning incomprehension or stupidity is a better way to gain time than resistance. Remember that a mugger is likely to be better at violence than you are, and has less to lose.

Cultural problems of men and women

Western women are generally assumed to have more problems than western men in unfamiliar foreign cultures, but this is not necessarily true everywere. It can be at least as dangerous, for example, to seem to harass, as to be harassed. Remember that the most dangerous mistakes are those that you cannot foresee, rather than those you can find written up in any guidebook. Above all, both sexes should maintain a circumspect attitude. Do not talk to a member of the opposite sex, or make eye contact, unless you are confident that you are not communicating more than you intend.

'Armed response' and self-preservation

In a city where there are signs promising an 'armed response' to intruders, the social life tends to take place at semi-public places such as hotels and restaurants. There is certainly no dropping in unannounced at people's homes, and you should take local advice from more established expatriates and local colleagues as to any 'no go' areas and particular precautions that you should take. Local knowledge will include latest incidents, and will be better informed as to whether these are isolated or indicate new grounds for caution.

As a newcomer, you should be aware of your ignorance and seek to brief yourself at the earliest opportunity. If there is anything to know, it will probably be readily forthcoming.

But note that different places offer different risks, and that behaviour that would count as 'streetwise' in one location might not work in another.

Note also that places superficially the same as home are not similarly safe or dangerous as at home. Bad mistakes can be made just as easily in a European city as further afield.

Note that in many cultures, the outsider is generally in the wrong.

Politics

Do not discuss local politics. In many places, you should not ask the locals even the most innocuous questions about politics. To do so will be taken as a sign of dangerous naiveté, and you will be avoided in case you do anything even stupider.

The appearance of espionage

Commercial espionage is more lucrative these days than the political variety, and this means that business people are particularly vulnerable to espionage, and to charges of espionage. At the same time, political realities can change, and being helpful to representatives of the regime, whether you realize what you're doing or not, can suddenly turn into a crime against the state.

In practical terms, this means developing a habit of caution in your dealings with local business people and contacts, particularly those who act in a 'facilitator' role, and especially those from state and close-to-state entities. Business meetings should happen in offices or in recognized business settings such as hotel meeting rooms.

You should also be careful in your dealings with representatives of companies from other countries.

Be wary of social conversations that turn towards business even if you do not think your job is particularly sensitive. Note that ignorance is no defence, and that the appearance of involvement in espionage can be as dangerous as the reality.

Bribery and corruption

Bribery is a mistake, both at work and elsewhere. Job situations have arisen in which individuals have had to be provided with an incentive to proceed, but such incentivizing, where it falls short of illegality in local terms, is much better undertaken with written authorization from higher up in your company, and thus after consultation. Respond in general terms, and as a rule, don't complete any such deal at the first meeting.

Circumstances occur in which expatriates avoid difficulty by happening to have stored a banknote in with their identity papers, but these are no more common than those in which similar precautions have led to charges of attempting to corrupt an official. If you are with a more locally experienced colleague who offers a bribe, keep your distance; you may need to be free to report his arrest to the British authorities.

If a situation develops in which a bribe is clearly the intended result, a useful form of words is to ask whether there is a fine to pay, or if there is a way of speeding up procedures. But generally, bribery is better left to others.

Communications technology

Some regimes, China and Iran for example, ban satellite dishes. While you will tend not to be able to buy such equipment in such a country, remember that the intention is to curb the dissemination of Western ideas. If you propose a gathering around your radio or television to see/hear a British event such as a cup final, it might be tactful not to invite any local colleagues (or at least, to accept their refusals easily), and not to draw attention to what you are doing.

If your job will involve a lot of travelling around the world, and therefore faxing and otherwise communicating from hotels, you should know that just about anything is cheaper than a hotel telephone.

More importantly, fax communications through a hotel fax are not necessarily reliable or secure. With a sensitive communication, prearrange an acknowledgement of receipt, and perhaps a code for the substance of your message. Some expatriates insist on seeing the fax go through.

A hotel in Hong Kong routinely photocopied every document it was asked to fax, even those marked confidential, so it could refax if necessary without disturbing its guests. A disaffected ex-employee tried to sell a bundle of this private and commercially sensitive material to a local newspaper, revealing that there was more in an unlocked filing cabinet.

If you plan to communicate by modem from your own technology while travelling, take a set of miniature screwdrivers plus electrical tape and a few lengths of telephone wire (from any electrical shop) as well as adapters. The seasoned business traveller knows that the wires in telephone systems are compatible even if the sockets sometimes are not.

Note that modern telephone exchanges do not replace old ones, but run alongside them. If you get a bad line from Uzbekistan, for example, ring off and try again. The routing of your call through a new or old exchange is a matter of chance.

The 'information superhighway' is widely accessible. It can be much easier to send an e-mail than a fax, because fax technology stopped developing in some countries when e-mail arrived.

Dangerous purchases

Quality control standards are not as high in some countries as they are in the UK. This applies to food, electrical appliances and toys as well as everything else. Anything which might be dangerous should be handled with care.

Things not to buy

There is a big market in gadgetry such as bugging and anti-bugging devices, long-range microphones, cameras concealed in briefcases, etc. It is unlikely that you as an individual will have a legitimate use for such equipment, although some companies will want to protect commercially sensitive information by its use. If you might find yourself in possession of such equipment, think about how you might explain its discovery. See also the section above on giving the appearance of espionage.

More seriously, there is also a market in equipment that purports to reduce telephone and electrical bills by interrupting or slowing down the pulse between your appliance and the meter. Such devices are found in the small ads of some magazines. If you can find one that works, consider whether it is illegal before connecting it.

There are also small ads for facsimile identification documents that resemble passports, ID cards and driving licences. In rare events where you might wish to conceal your identity and/or nationality, such as if you are threatened with kidnap or violence in dangerous locations, these might have some limited value if you are not also carrying your genuine papers. But you are more likely to be shot for spying than you are to need false papers.

Note that it is not illegal, nor particularly difficult, to obtain a second passport if your travels will take you to mutually exclusive countries such as Israel and certain Arab countries. Contact the Passport Office at Clive House, 70–78 Petty France, London SW1, telephone 0171 799 2290, or pick up a passport application form at a post office, or respond, if you'd like to do it more expensively, to one of the sensationalist small ads that you will find only too easily.

Animals

In some parts of the world, it is necessary to prepare your children for the treatment of dogs and cats and other animals that are domesticated in the UK but not locally. Warn younger children not to attempt to stroke animals wandering the streets or found in the wild. With very young children, particularly in places with large animal populations, avoid reading too many bedtime stories involving friendly lions. Children's videos can need reinterpretation, too.

All animals are potentially dangerous, pack animals like dogs and chimpanzees doubly so. If you find yourself alone in the presence of more than one dog, don't hurry away quickly enough to persuade them to chase you.

In extremis, it is better to remain still than to try to outrun an animal. But animals are unpredictable, and 'playing dead' is not a sure-fire method of self-preservation. If you are definitely about to be eaten, the alternative is to confront the animal with as convincing a threatening display as you can manage.

But it is better not to get into that situation in the first place.

If you have children enthusiastic for pets, take local expert advice (ie, ring the local British school) before filling the house with unidentified rodents and strange lizards. If you do take possession of an animal while overseas, you will not find it easy to reimport it to the UK. Perhaps best to be pragmatic and choose something with a life expectancy shorter than the term of your contract.

Learning the language

Everywhere, you will be told that it is important to learn the language. But the whole world speaks English, and it is possible to get 'advice fatigue' on this subject. How much of the language do you really need to speak, and isn't there, surely, a stage of reasonable facility at which you can give up?

From the beginning of your time overseas, you will find that your attempts to speak the language pay dividends; this is particularly true in a country where the language is difficult or not widely spoken outside its borders. To attempt to speak a language, especially where it is difficult, is to pay a compliment. You might, as one expatriate in Poland half-jokingly reported, always buy two or four of something because you cannot pronounce the local word for 'three', or you might (an expatriate in Spain) find that you have been asking, 'Can I hit you?' rather than 'Can I pay you?' But in general, 'mastering the art of communicating with difficulty', as it has been called, is worthwhile. Always be careful with the pronunciation of anything that expresses friendship or the wish to see more of somebody, in case they start to undress.

Basic words and phrases are not enough for a posting of several years. Persevere in your attempts to begin conversations in the local language even if the locals constantly switch into English. This is important for a number of reasons.

1. You can't rely on English to work with everybody. Even though they speak English, they're going to notice after a few months if you don't speak the language. If you are administering local staff, you will be at a disadvantage.

2. When a sensitive negotiation switches into the local language; that's when you most want to understand. The same is true of conversations between local and language-proficient expatriate colleagues.

3. Your local counterparts may not be able to convey the nuances of what they mean in English; worse, they may not realize their inability, and so may assume you understand.

Where there are interpreters, there are sometimes exchanges such as, 'Shall we tell him about . . . ?' 'No, don't mention that, just keep reassuring him.' Your interpreter can hardly translate that, and may not want to. Better to understand for yourself.

You should also recognize that languages in general are an important skills base for an international employee. Your grounding in the local language will be provided as part of the briefing procedure before you arrive (see below), and you will find that living and working among native speakers is the best language course you can get, but to be limited to English and whatever is spoken locally is potentially a handicap, now as well as in the future. You may encounter a Spanish-speaking Mexican, for example, and discover that the only language you have in common is French.

Pre-departure language training

It is a commonplace to say that different methods of learning a language suit different people. But it is also common experience that living there is the best training of all. This suggests that contact with native speakers is what you need most.

But you should think about what parts of the language to learn before you go. Concentrate not only on getting by, but also on finding out about polite forms that do not occur in English (the choice between *tu* and *vous* in French, for example), and on business usage (including negotiating styles and other near-language considerations).

Examples of language courses designed for soon-to-be expatriates are those provided by the following companies.

- Audio-Forum, 2/6 Foscote Mews, London W9 2HH, telephone 0171 266 2202, fax 0171 266 2314.
- Language Studies International, Woodstock House, 10–12 James Street, London W1M 5HN, telephone 0171 499 9621, fax 0171 491 0992.
- Linguarama, Queen's House, 8 Queen Street, London EC4N 1SP, telephone 0171 236 1992, fax 0171 236 7208.
- The Centre for International Briefing (page 31) has launched its 'Language Plus' programme of intensive one-to-one tuition with a native speaker in any of 25 languages. The programme is 'suitable for executives, either on long- or short-term assignment, who need to hit the ground running', according to the Centre's Stephen Sweby.

Continuing to learn once you're there

Languages should be an ongoing study for an expatriate, and when you are overseas, you will find that not only the local language is useful. There will always be occasions when you cannot communicate a point in the local language, and you may find that something other than English is a common resort. You will also listen to your fellow expatriates speaking a stream of one language in which words and phrases of English and other languages are interspersed. Language is a medium of expression, and needn't depend on the words of just one phrasebook only.

Whatever local facilities are available, distance-learning of languages comes in a variety of forms and from a variety of sources, of which the following are examples.

- The Linguaphone Institute, St Giles House, 50 Poland Street, London W1V 4AX, telephone 0171 287 4050, fax 0171 434 0451, will provide home study courses
- CERAN, Avenue de Château 16, 4900 SPA, Belgium, telephone 32 0 87/77 41 64, fax 32 0 87/77 36 29, lays on intensive but enjoyable residential courses of several days' duration at which it is forbidden to speak anything but the language to be learned.

Doing the job

To some extent, this section encapsulates points made elsewhere in the book, on personal, cultural and career considerations. But there are some other points to bear in mind when you arrive for the first time at your place of work overseas.

Your expatriate colleagues

To work with expatriates is to find yourself a member of a club with its own rules, privileges, advantages and disadvantages. Newcomers bring information and news of the wider world, and are a source of variety in what might be a small and closed community. They provide an opportunity to widen the social circle, and you will find yourself enjoying a 'honeymoon period' socially as well as professionally. This has the clear advantage that help and advice are only too readily available. The experience of needing support in unfamiliar surroundings is something that all expatriates share.

But small communities have their politics, and while it is comforting to be so welcomed, don't overreact. Don't let yourself be tempted into 'taking sides', and remember that these are the people with whom you will have to live for the next however many years. Keep your distance, in your mind if not in your day-to-day behaviour.

Note that the biggest potential divide in any posting is between the locals and the expatriates, not between different nationalities of expatriate from broadly equivalent cultures.

Your local colleagues

You may find your local colleagues, of whatever seniority, somewhat disconcerting at first. This is because cultures differ from each other at the most basic level. You act according to a number of more-or-less subconscious assumptions about how to deal with other people; they are not shared locally. For example, you will have an idea of how far away to stand from somebody with whom you are conversing; their idea will be different and as you might back away they might edge closer. You will have an attitude to physical contact between individuals; it can be as disconcerting not to be touched on the arm, or embraced, or to have your hand shaken, as it can when these things happen too frequently.

Reflect on your dealings with any non-British colleagues in the UK; you may recognize that, in an undefinable way, there was something non-British about their behaviour.

The locals do not read books about how to deal with expatriates, and they are probably less prepared for their dealings with you than you are for them. Recognize that your behaviour is subtly foreign to them as well as overtly so, and think twice before taking offence at any apparent slight. They think you're strange, and in their country, they're right.

Dealing with head office

If you are expatriated from a company in another country, particularly one in the UK, you may sooner or later find that the people at head office 'just don't get it'. This is because they don't have any perspective at all on local conditions, while you are coming to be aware that things aren't as simple here as they look from outside.

Remember that you have a career beyond your present posting, and that 'going native' is a process that happens by degrees. You should maintain detachment from your posting, and keep your eye on the 'bigger picture'. Your local expertise is an asset, and part of what you have to offer the company, but present it with care.

Incidental duties in the UK as a factor in your tax planning are covered on page 106; keeping in contact with UK colleagues with whom you will work again is discussed on page 28. Such activities as attending board meetings in the UK, going on training courses in the UK with UK-based colleagues, and arranging visits from UK-based colleagues, are to be encouraged.

For professional purposes, keep a measure of detachment as you settle in and assimilate yourself to local conditions.

Family matters

As everybody settles in and assimilates and learns the language and makes friends, so do new pressures and influences make themselves felt. One can't live in a different culture, even as an outsider, without changing to some extent. This is likely to be beneficial in the long term, in the sense that one's horizons broaden and one's understanding and self-knowledge deepen, but there are some points to bear in mind, particularly in the first year.

You and your partner

Concentrate on your shared interests rather than those you have separately. An expatriate community tends to be sociable, and to be amply supplied with organizers of social activity. This is a good thing, particularly in the early months when you need a support network, but the downside is that each of you can be drawn out of the family unit into a social circle that does not necessarily bolster your home life. If only one of you plays tennis, for example, or Mah Jong, this is the time for the other to learn.

And make time for each other. The box below gives an idea of the cost of taking your partner out to dinner in a selection of cities.

Dinner for two

This information was collected by ECA International in March 1995 as part of its annual Cost of Living Survey (survey information becomes available in the following September); see also the commentary to the table 'ECA's shopping basket' on page 7. Note that it is a percentage comparison with the UK figure given in sterling.

Tokyo	100.21
Copenhagen	61.72
Hong Kong	57.20
New York	51.64
Paris	45.88
Rome	42.83
London	£42.73
Singapore	41.32
Los Angeles	38.75
Mexico City	37.91
Beijing	30.18

Your children

Bring new experiences into the family unit. Entertain your children's friends and enter into activities with other parents. Before taking a young child to a local schoolfriend's birthday, check what the local customs are regarding presents, dress, games, party bags, etc., and brief your child on what to expect. Above all, do things together as a family; support each other.

In general, children are better at being expatriates than adults once they are past the language barrier. But remember the basic rule that however wide the range of new experiences now open to your children, and however beneficial to their all-round education this posting might be, you must provide them with a stable and secure base from which to go out into the world. You should make a priority of establishing routines at home, and the family should have its meals together as far as possible. Note that to replicate UK family routines in an overseas posting, you may need to exaggerate them somewhat in the opening stages.

Particularly in the first months of your posting, organize family activities for the weekends. And throughout your time overseas, have it as an item in your diary to organize things regularly that you can do together as a family.

Education is dealt with on page 80. Because one potential effect of expatriation on children is that their education is disrupted, it can be worthwhile contacting the World-Wide Education Service (WES), 35 Belgrave Square, London SW1 8QA, telephone 0181 866 4400, fax 0181 429 4838 for information on home schooling either as a complete alternative or a supplement to school-based teaching.

Your parents

The age at which expatriate postings tend to occur in a career is also the age at which parents begin to make the transition from representing a source of care and support for their children, to needing it for themselves. If you have elderly or infirm relatives in the UK, you should know about such organizations as The Grace Care Advisory Service, 35 Walnut Tree Close, Guildford, Surrey GU1 4UL, telephone 01483 578160/304354, fax 01483 452936.

Christmas, birthdays and shopping by mail order

It is easy to send hampers to friends and relatives in the UK for Christmas. All the expatriate magazines (page 232) run features on mail-order gift-giving by expatriates from October onwards (allowing time for the post from overseas), and these are enthusiastically supported by large and small mail-order companies. Large London stores such as Fortnum & Mason also participate, as do suppliers of shirts, ties and other potential gifts.

Additionally, the mainstream UK 'lifestyle' magazines such as *Good Housekeeping*, *Country Living* etc., run regular (in some cases monthly) one- or two-page directories of mail-order suppliers, and these are widely available overseas, if expensive. A selection of companies providing mail-order services may be found on page 201.

It is less easy, and in some cases impossible, to get the same range of goods sent overseas from the UK. Food and drink generally don't travel, and postage costs can be high. Fortnum & Mason, for example, charge minimum carriage of between £12 for Europe and £17 for 'rest of world' for small items; larger objects or combinations of items can cost upwards of £125 to send to the rest of the world.

If you are likely to be sending mail-order items around the world, think first about local restrictions. It would be tactless to send whisky, for example, to an expatriate business contact in Saudi Arabia.

Marmite

You can get Marmite and other food unavailable overseas from a company called Goodies by Post, PO Box 285, Guernsey GY1 1WR, telephone 01481 722868, fax 01481 714234. A survey of its readers by Resident Abroad magazine with Avis Rent-a-car confirmed anecdotal evidence that Marmite was what expatriates missed most (see the quotation on page 46), and so an entrepreneur plugged the gap in the market.

Getting the shopping done for you

A company called Global Presents, Unit 16, Talina Centre, Bagleys Lane, London SW6 2BW, offers The Shopping Service Catalogue, which is published every six months. It contains goods from the major London stores, which the company will send for you to any address in the UK or overseas (subject to customs, etc). Telephone 0171 731 3000, fax 0171 731 1219.

Phoning home

There are companies that will offer you substantial savings on international phone calls. One such is Connect International Discount Services, Dr. Poelstraat 14, 6451 EM Schinfeld, The Netherlands, telephone and fax 0031 45 527 1031.

Visitors from home

They will be out of their depth, and they will need your time and attention. If their journey has been a long one, they will have booked for a stay of several weeks, and however pleased you are to collect them from the airport, remember that to them, this is a fortnight's holiday.

There is a case for not having visitors in the first month or several months of your time overseas, when you are stressed and tired, and need peace and quiet and mutual support in the evenings rather than constant encouragement to go out.

Often, it is the first visitors from home who bring home to new expatriates how much they have adapted. Seeing your location through your visitor's eyes is to be reminded how different it is from the UK. Once you really are settled in, this can be encouraging.

The downside

There are two possible fates that befall expatriates. One is that the spare room is always full. Visitors, however sensitive, can fail to realize that they are just the next in a long line, and quite apart from the amount of free time you have to spend looking after friends rather than each other, there is the expense of catering for them.

The other possible fate is that only the people you don't want to see manage to find the time and money to come to stay.

It is as well to be ruthless with visitors. Issue invitations only if you're serious, and arrange visits for when you are not likely to be pressured at work. Tell them what to bring: things you can't get locally, but also driving licences for hire cars, for example.

When visitors arrive, have town plans and entertainment guides ready. Suggest trips to see local landmarks, and feel comfortable about declining to come along because you've seen the sights already. Visitors are entitled to your company during the day at weekends only.

Lend them bicycles (not the car). Tell them that they really must visit the delightful little market where you shop for groceries. Above all, keep them busy, even when you can't be with them.

Meet your partner at lunchtime so as to have time together.

The upside

Visitors from home remind you where your long-term life is lived; they can stop you getting too sucked into the expatriate life. Alternatively, they can remind you how lucky you are to have got away from all that. They can bring it home to you that actually, you don't want to go back.

They can bring Marmite and Cooper's Oxford Marmalade. They can bring eyewitness reports of how your relatives and friends are really getting on. If they come from the world of work, they can update you on office politics.

But more importantly, they can supply a perspective on the community in which you're now living. Big issues and irritating personalities can be returned to their proper insignificance by an outsider's cool view.

Handled properly, visitors from home can be simultaneously a relief from the pressures of expatriate life, and confirmation that you did the right thing by coming overseas.

Holiday and working visits to the UK

All visits to the UK have potential tax consequences, and these should be thought through in advance, as below. But this section is primarily concerned with the more enjoyable practicalities of returning to the UK.

Working visits

If you are likely to visit the UK in the course of your duties, ie to attend a board meeting or otherwise report back to headquarters, first read the section on 'incidental duties' on page 106.

If, as the non-working partner, you accompany your working partner on such visits to the UK, you have the more straightforward consideration of how many days you will be spending in the UK, in total, in the tax year.

With that sorted out, you can begin to think about making arrangements for the non-working part of the visit. This is covered under the next heading.

Holiday visits

Your first consideration is the number of days you will be spending in the UK, in total, in the tax year.

After that's sorted out, the first discovery expatriates make is that unless they plan carefully, they do not get holiday time to themselves if they return to the UK. This is for the simple reason that they've been away so long, everybody wants to see them.

Your annual holiday will not seem so generous if you have to combine it with 'duty visits' to the family. Some expatriates think of their real holiday as the one they spend overseas, and their trips to the UK as an opportunity to catch up with relatives, friends, the upkeep of their property, etc.

This is a pity. Always, when you go back to the UK, insert gaps into the schedule where you can enjoy yourselves. This means not expecting to spend the whole time in your home town. Your property, if you have retained one and not left it empty, will have tenants in it and you will end up with friends or family, or in the local hotel (the whole question of what to do with UK property is taken up on page 170).

To be properly methodical, you could arrange your visits for the gaps between tenants at your UK property. But a better idea is to get away completely at the beginning, middle and end of your visit.

But first, you need to think about

Car hire

Car-hire companies are enthusiastic advertisers in the classified pages of expatriate magazines (page 232). Their rates are competitive with each other, and the first rule is not to hire from the company with the lowest advertised figures before establishing what is and what isn't included. The cost of hiring a car is made up of so many components – mileage, insurance, etc. – that it is easy to produce a small number by putting practically everything in the extras. Always say you're an expatriate when you're booking; there are discounts not available to ordinary travellers.

Many expatriates do a lot of driving on visits to the UK, visiting relatives and friends, and so will need a high mileage allowance. If they're going long distances, they'll need something big enough to be comfortable. Don't waste your time on luxury cars; go for something familiar. If you commit yourself for a week's hire on a cheap deal, the eighth day will be highly expensive. Ask whether you can return the car early for a refund, or exchange it, if you don't like it. Do you have to return it to where you hired it (and how are you going to travel, however short the distance, from the return point)? Don't forget to drive on the left.

Pay by credit card as the credit-card company is then liable to you for satisfactory performance of the car, etc.

Make sure the deal includes breakdown insurance and that you have the necessary telephone numbers for assistance. Are you a temporary member of the AA/RAC? (You do know, don't you, that the small arrows on the barriers alongside motorways point to the nearest emergency telephone?)

Prod the spare tyre, check the toolkit, don't leave it until you return the car to complain that the petrol tank wasn't full; there may be a leak. Check the recorded mileage when you pick up the car.

Most important of all, get detailed instructions on how to collect the car when you arrive at the airport. Does the car hire company have an office at the airport? Which terminals? Is it open twenty-four hours? Will they know you're coming? What if your plane's delayed? Where will the keys be if the office isn't open? Where will the car be?

A selection of car-hire companies may be found on page 203.

Where to stay

This is generally not a problem for most of any trip to the UK; you will tend to have too many choices rather than too few. But plan ahead to spend at least some of your time away from friends and relatives; this is why you were advised in Chapter One to bring a copy of a UK hotel guide overseas with you. If you didn't, here are some suggestions. Note that if you want to get away from friends and relatives, it is wise not to stay within easy driving distance of anybody who might issue an invitation to lunch.

Hotels
The expensive, short-term option. There are country-house hotels like Bodysgallen Hall, Llandudno, Gwynedd, North Wales LL30 1RS, telephone 01492 584466, fax 01492 582519, or Middlethorpe Hall, Bishopthorpe Road, York YO2 1QB, telephone 01904 641241, fax 01904 620176, if you decide to spoil yourself, or London hotels like Brown's Hotel, Dover Street, London W1X 4BP, telephone 0171 493 6020, fax 0171 493 9381, for post-arrival, pre-departure. Trouble is, these days, many hotels seem to set their rates for expense-account visitors. If you're looking for smaller hotels, or such atmospheric alternatives as, for example, country pubs like the Royal Oak Inn, Withypool, Somerset TA24 7QP, telephone 01643 831236, fax 016243 831659, or hotel/restaurants like the Seafood Restaurant, Riverside, Padstow, Cornwall PL28 8BY, telephone 01841 532485, fax 01841 533344, you can get information from the British Tourist Authority, Thames Tower,

Black's Road, Hammersmith, London W6 9EL, telephone 0181 846 9000, fax 0181 563 0302.

Among the other possible alternatives are

National Trust properties

These are a good idea if you've spent a long time in very unBritish surroundings, and want to get a real feel for home. Some properties are remote, and some require a spartan attitude, but there are a lot of them. The catalogue is available from National Trust (Enterprises) Ltd, PO Box 536, Melksham, Wiltshire SN12 8SX, telephone 01225 791133, or telephone 01225 791199 for bookings (bookings from overseas on telephone/fax 01225 790617).

Serviced flats

These are more like pieds-à-terre than hotels and are most commonly associated with visiting London. A serviced flat is what it sounds like: a flat which can be booked for a period of time, which is 'serviced' in the sense that laundry, etc., is taken care of. Serviced flats are priced for the longer term visitor – weeks or months rather than days – and you would tend to book one for the whole of your stay, and use it as a base for visits elsewhere in the UK. A serviced flat is, therefore, best suited to a combined business and holiday trip.

Information on serviced flats may be obtained from the London Tourist Board, 26 Grosvenor Gardens, Victoria, London SW1 0DU, telephone 0171 730 3450, fax 0171 730 9367. Some serviced-flat companies are Dolphin Square Hotel & Apartments, Dolphin Square, London SW1V 3LX, telephone 0171 834 3800, fax 0171 834 8735; NGH Apartments Limited, Nell Gwynne House, Sloane Avenue, London SW3 3AX, telephone 0171 589 1105, fax 0171 589 9433; Wedgewood Apartments, Chenil House, 181 King's Road, London SW3 5EB, telephone 0171 823 3397, fax 0171 376 5653. Information on serviced flats outside London may be obtained from the British Tourist Authority at the address given under 'Hotels' above.

Education

You have two principal alternatives. As discussed below, your children can board in the UK, or they can move to schools overseas. Either way, you will have to pay for their education, and planning for this is taken up on page 182.

The first rule of educational planning, at whatever stage, is that what is right is what suits the child. The second rule is that a second opinion, particularly an informed second opinion, is worth having.

What you will need first, therefore, is

Educational advice

This is available from sources such as Gabbitas Educational Consultants, Carrington House, 126–130 Regent Street, London W1R 6EE, telephone 0171 734 0161, fax 0171 437 1764, or The Independent Schools Information Service (ISIS), 56 Buckingham Gate, London SW1E 6AG, telephone 0171 630 8793, fax 0171 630 5013, or Oasis, Arunvale House, 10 Kingsmead Road, Broadbridge Heath, West Sussex RH12 3LL, telephone 01403 269378. In general terms, such advisers will aim to clarify what your child needs, to provide you with the names of schools that will meet those needs, and to support you in the process of choosing between them.

You will need advice on a number of specific points as follows.

- If your children are not yet at school age, you will seek advice on nursery education overseas, and its compatibility with the UK curriculum when you bring your children back to the UK again.
- If your children are already at day school in the UK, you will need to know about UK boarding alternatives, and overseas alternatives.
- If your children are already at UK boarding school, you will need to weigh up the relative advantages of leaving them where they are, against taking them with you.
- If this is a 'crunch time' academically, with exams looming, you will need to discuss the possible disruption that your move will cause to your children's education, even if they are secure in a UK boarding school and you propose to leave them there.
- You may wish to discuss ways whereby you might support your children's education at at home, in which case you will be referred on to such organizations as the World-Wide Education Service (WES), who were mentioned on page 74.

In addition to these, there are general points of advice that are equally applicable to stay-at-home and potentially expatriate parents. These will include:

- Academic suitability. Children will perform better at a school which suits their natural aptitudes rather than one offering the education their parents think they ought to have. An A grade in an arts subject is more useful in the long term than an E grade in Economics.
- Personal suitability. There are all kinds of schools for all kinds of children, and you should seek an educational environment which will be conducive to learning. The gentle coaxing of one school might suit a bookish child, for example, while the emphasis on discipline at another might be more effective for a tearaway.

Note that there are several thousand private schools in the UK, and almost certainly at least two potentially suitable international schools within easy range of your destination overseas. The change in your circumstances is a significant change to the background of your children's lives. Whatever plans for their education you have already made, this is a time to review them.

First worries

The answers to the three most commonly asked questions about going overseas as a parent are as follows.

- If you leave your children at a UK boarding school, you will not be leaving them alone in this country. You must appoint a guardian – a relative, preferably, and there are professionals, as below – who can perform such duties as visiting the school, checking up on academic performance, watching the occasional school match, and, if necessary, signing consent forms if medical treatment becomes necessary and you are unobtainable in time.

  You must also make arrangements for your children to be escorted to or from their flights at the beginning and end of term, half term, etc. Schools can generally help with this, and it falls within the scope of most guardianship services. Airlines, also, make provision for unaccompanied minors, and should always be notified in advance when a child is travelling alone (this is something to mention when booking, and again when confirming the flight arrangements).

  That said, this is a subject on which it is wise to have fallback arrangements. The best combination is to have a relative who will accept the need to provide a familial presence at such things as school matches, visiting weekends, etc., with a full-time professional guardianship service providing a full service as well (make sure guardian and relative are in contact with each other, and that the professional guardian accepts full responsibility for providing a full service). Guardianship is provided by such organizations as Gabbitas, above, and Joanella Slattery Associates, 63 Grosvenor Road, Tunbridge Wells TN1 2AY, telephone 01892 515875, fax 01892 520825. Mrs Slattery formerly ran the Gabbitas service, and has considerable experience in this field.

  Additionally, you should know that Corona Worldwide (see page 31) provides an escort service between schools and airports, as does, for example, Universal Aunts Ltd, PO Box 304, London SW4 0NN, telephone 0171 498 8200, fax 0171 622 1914.

  Always clarify the arrangements you make with your children's school, and confirm the circumstances in which they will accept a guardian's instruction.

- There are British schools overseas, in which you will find many other children of expatriate parents, and many of these use English as their primary language of instruction. There is a strong case for saying that a period of education overseas is powerfully beneficial for a child, and that the experience of learning with British, American, German, French and other-nationality children is very positive.

● British, European, American and other international schools overseas offer a range of curricula, and it is not difficult to find an education that will be compatible with the UK curriculum, so that reintegration at the end of your contract will not be too difficult. See below.

Choosing a school for your children

There are three groups of schools from which to make your choice. They are as follows.

Independent boarding schools in the UK

Often loosely referred to as 'public schools', this category includes a wide variety of different non-state schools offering a wide variety of different approaches to education. They are not all as expensive as commonly supposed, and if your child has a particular ability (in music, for example), you should enquire about scholarships. Bursaries – effectively, reductions in the fees payable – can be made available to parents who meet particular criteria (which differ from school to school). The Assisted Places Scheme, which will help with tuition fees but not boarding accommodation costs, is means-tested and unlikely to be applicable here.

With independent schools, you have the choice of single-sex or co-education, and the argument in their favour is that being fee-paying, they can raise the money to buy in the best teachers and the best educational facilities (it is a commonplace of independent school parenting to find that your children have access to more up-to-date computer technology than you have).

When choosing between independent schools in the UK, you should visit the school, and notice in particular: the quality of the living accommodation; the response of the children to the teacher who is showing you around (and/or the attitude of the child who shows you around to interrupting teachers' lessons); what the evidence of your own eyes tells you about the distribution of resources between arts, sciences, sports, etc. You should consider the attitude and accessibility of the Head, and the general atmosphere of the school.

State boarding schools in the UK

These are a UK alternative to the expense of a private education. State boarding schools charge for accommodation only; tuition is free. This means an effective halving of the total cost (guide figures: £6,000pa rather than £12,000pa).

The state-boarding sector covers a variety of schools, including single-sex, co-educational, totally boarding and mainly day. Some of the schools are grant-maintained, and others funded by their local education authorities.

There is a list of state boarding schools on page 208. In theory, every child entitled to a UK state education (effectively, any child holding a UK passport) may claim a place at a state boarding school, as may children of the EU, but in practice places are limited and sometimes locally resident children or others with a special claim (ie children of service families), may be given priority.

The rules for choosing between state boarding schools are the same as for independent schools. Further information is available from the State Boarding Information Service (STABIS), 43 Raglan Road, Reigate, Surrey RH2 0DU, telephone 01737 226450, fax 01737 226775.

British and International schools overseas

In general, British schools offer a British curriculum, American schools offer an American curriculum, and international schools offer a variety of curricula to children of a variety of nationalities. But this distinction is not clear-cut, and you should view all of the alternatives within range before making a final decision. Schools other than British schools can offer a British curriculum, and there are non-British qualifications, notably the International Baccalaureate as below, that are compatible with further education in the UK.

When considering a school overseas, find out the language of instruction and ask whether there are procedures in place for monitoring the assimilation of new arrivals. Establish what records will be provided of your children's progress when they come to return to the UK system. Also note the names of the board of governors, as this will be likely to include the names of other expatriates if the school is well used by the British community.

Given the nature of the communities that they support, it would be surprising if British and other international schools were not adapted to accepting new pupils at any stage of the academic year, as they are. Some, however, have waiting lists, and it is important that you should decide as early as possible whether you will be likely to want to take your children overseas to school.

Sources of guidance include the Council of European Schools in the European Community (COBISEC), c/o The British School of Brussels, Chausée de Louvain 19, Tervuren, Belgium 3080, telephone 32 2 767 47 00, fax 32 2 767 80 70, which has 27 member schools in the European Union, and the European Council of International Schools (ECIS), 21 Lavant Street, Petersfield, Hampshire, GU32 3EL, telephone 01730 268244, fax 01730 267914, which provides information on schools and further education institutions (see below) worldwide.

The International Baccalaureate (IB)

This is a pre-university qualification, the course for which lasts two years, and which can be taken in place of A levels. It is accepted by British universities for entrance.

The International Baccalaureate Office in Geneva states the aim of the IB as being 'to improve and extend international education and so promote international understanding; to facilitate student mobility and provide an educational service to the internationally mobile community; and to work in collaboration with national educational systems in developing a rigorous, balanced and international curriculum'.

In keeping with such aims, the IB avoids the early specialization inherent in choosing two or three A levels; IB students study six subjects, three or four at 'higher' level and the rest at 'subsidiary' level, and take a 'theory of knowledge' course. They must also engage in 'CAS activities' (ie, Creativity, Action and Service) and submit an extended essay (effectively, a thesis) on one of their six subjects.

The six IB subjects are: two languages (one or both to include the study of selections from world literature); the study of 'individuals and societies' (history, geography, economics, philosophy, etc.; experimental sciences; mathematics; art/design, music, computing, Latin or Classical Greek.

Note that the IB is accepted as an entrance qualification by both UK and overseas universities.

Further information on the IB may be obtained from the International Baccalaureate Office, Route des Morillons 15, CH – 1218 Grand-Saconnex, Geneva, Switzerland, telephone 41 22 791 0274, fax 41 22 791 0277.

Further education

The procedures for applying to further-education institutions in the UK are outlined in the UCAS Handbook, which is available free from the Universities and Colleges Admissions Service (UCAS), Fulton House, Jessop Avenue, Cheltenham, Gloucestershire GL50 3SH, telephone 01242 222444. Turn to page 182 of this book if you have children who will be reaching the further-education stage at or around the time of the end of your contract overseas.

The procedures for applying to further-education institutions in other countries may be found in the ECIS Higher Education Directory, which is available from ECIS at the address given above and on page 182.

Voting in British and European elections

When you move overseas, you retain the right to vote in British local and general elections, and in European elections. Your right to vote lasts for up to twenty years after your departure, and is subject to your declaration that you do not intend to leave the UK permanently.

You vote in the constituency where you were last registered as a voter before you left the UK (new voters also register where they were last resident in the UK). You cannot vote in person, for obvious reasons, but nor can you vote by post. This is because polling cards and ballot papers cannot be sent overseas. You must therefore find a UK resident who is eligible to vote, who can cast your vote for you by proxy. Note that your proxy may cast your vote by post from another constituency within the UK.

To claim your right to vote as an 'overseas elector', you must first register with the electoral registration officer in your constituency, and make an 'overseas elector's declaration'. The form on which to do this may be obtained (although stocks have been known to run out) from a variety of official sources, including British Embassies and Consulates, British Council offices, the Home Office and the electoral registration officers themselves, but your wisest move might be to contact one of the British political parties.

There are two good reasons for this. First, the political parties have a clear incentive to help you, not least because in two constituencies in the 1992 general election, the number of overseas electors registered exceeded the winners' margins of victory, so the overseas vote quite possibly clinched it in both cases, and secondly, because the political parties can provide you with a proxy if you would prefer not to burden a friend or relative back home with the task.

Both the Conservatives and Labour have organizations set up to promote the overseas vote among expatriates, and the Liberal Democrats offer assistance through their Campaign Department. Addresses below.

Note that unless you are looking for a proxy, you do not have to approach the political party for which you intend to vote. There is nothing to stop you applying to more than one source for your overseas elector's registration form.

The deadline for registration as an overseas elector is 10 October (15 September in Northern Ireland) for the next year's electoral register, which comes into force on 16 February and remains in force for all elections until the following 15 February. Anecdotal evidence from expatriate sources suggests that you should allow at least a month, preferably more, for your form to be sent to you, from any source.

No representation without taxation

Expatriates were first given the right to vote in 1985. Then, it lasted for five years after leaving the UK.

At first, the take-up rate was slow. Britons working overseas were wary of the requirement that they should declare their intent eventually to return to the UK, and wondered whether this might affect their tax position.

Such worries were mistaken. Future intentions only become relevant with regard to inheritance tax, which depends on domicile (page 117). If you're getting into avoiding inheritance tax by giving up UK domicile, you're way beyond taking an interest in British politics.

In the face of concern that people might be giving up their newly awarded democratic right to vote because of a mistaken fear of its tax cost, the Inland Revenue indicated that it would not take into account overseas electors' declarations when assessing UK tax liabilities.

This still stands. You do not complicate your tax position by claiming the right to vote in British and European elections.

Making an overseas elector's declaration

Get the form from whichever source you prefer. You will need to know where to send it when you've filled it in. The form has a suggestion. 'If you do not know the registration officer's address, send your application in an envelope addressed to The Electoral Registration Officer, Town or City [where you were last resident], County, United Kingdom, or . . . in Northern Ireland, to The Chief Electoral Officer, 3rd Floor, 65/67 Chichester Street, Belfast BT1 4JD, Northern Ireland.'

Communications from government offices often seem to aspire to this mix of approximation and extreme precision, but rarely is it achieved as cleanly as here.

If you're not from Northern Ireland and you're late filling in the form, or it hasn't reached you until the last minute, the exact address is obtainable from your local town hall in the UK (if its phone number has accompanied you overseas – see page 209), or from one of the political parties, or from official sources such as D Division at the Home Office, which handles electoral matters. D Division may be contacted on 0171 273 3347, but they're a last resort: don't ring them at a peak time, and expect to spend a long interval waiting on hold, listening to silence. Alternatively, write to D Division at The Home Office, 50 Queen Anne's Gate, London SW1H 9AT.

(Remember, at this point, a basic principle: if you want to know something, ask everybody who might know it.)

On the form, once you've got it, you will be required to state:

- that you are a British citizen;
- that you will not be resident in the United Kingdom on the qualifying date (ie, 10 October or 15 September) for the register on which you are applying to be included;
- when you ceased to be so resident; and
- that you do not intend to reside permanently outside the UK.

New electors are required to send a photocopy of their birth certificate, and for them, there is a section to be completed by a parent or guardian.

You will be required to sign your declaration, and date it. Curiously, dating it is a legal requirement stipulated in the part of the Registration of the People's Act 1985 which extends the franchise to overseas electors. Don't forget to do it.

The electoral registration officer will write back to you confirming that you're on the register. If you don't hear, write again, enclosing a photocopy of your original form clearly marked as a photocopy.

Note that in spite of the legal requirement to date your declaration, your twenty years start to be counted from the qualifying date. Note also that 'residence' in this context is a simple matter of whether you've left the UK by the qualifying date; it has nothing to do with the tax-related status spelt out in the first part of Chapter Three beginning on page 90. The electoral registration officer's only concerns are to give you your one vote, once, and not to give a vote to anybody who never had it and shouldn't have it.

Your declaration is made with reference to one year only. You will have to repeat the process again next year. This is the same as for UK-resident electors, and you will receive a reminder in the post, with a fresh form on which to make a fresh declaration, in June or July.

Expatriates in British politics

There is a perception that expatriates are motivated by money, and that by going overseas, they have given up their right to take an interest in their home country's affairs. The counter-argument is that many of them are earning valuable foreign exchange, and all of them are projecting Britain's image abroad.

Most expatriates find such politicized discussion of their motives tediously simplistic. But expatriates are a significant force, now that they have the vote. The Foreign Office keeps records of the numbers of Britons registered with consular authorities overseas. On 6th April 1995, there were 10,831,243 recorded British expatriates. If you write to your MP and you don't get a quick response, mention that.

Appointing a proxy

You can do this straight away, by filling in your proxy's name and address in the section provided for the purpose on the form, or you can send the form to your proxy to be filled in and forwarded on your behalf. If you are in contact with a political party, the whole process can be done for you.

It is more important to get yourself on the register of electors than to get a proxy sorted out. Don't hold onto the form while waiting to confirm that a proxy is prepared to act for you. Detach the proxy section and send it on later.

A proxy can act for more than one overseas elector at a time, but not more than two unless they are close relatives of each other. Looking at it the other way round, this has the effect that one proxy, perhaps a relative or friend back home, can act for your whole family.

You should remember that although you have to renew your declaration annually, your proxy will remain in place until you cancel the appointment. If you do cancel, you don't have to offer a replacement immediately, but you won't be able to exercise your vote until you do so.

Remember also that the whole of any re-election period is predictated on the assumption that voters change their minds.

You may consider it wise to appoint a proxy who can be relied upon to do your bidding, not one who will only ever vote for one party. It is not unknown for overseas voters to replace one party's activist with another party's activist, and then to try to reverse the change. Whoever's holding the vote when the music stops gets to choose which way to cast it.

British political parties abroad

The British political parties all maintain a presence abroad, and these can be a source of social connections in a difficult posting as well as a place to find like-minded people if you're interested in politics.

Whether or not you'd get involved in a local political association's events in the UK, get the appropriate addresses for your overseas location from the parties in the UK, as below, and expect to find a somewhat more social approach to life than you would back home. (Also, among the stalwarts, a somewhat more black and white appreciation of the political issues of the day. Expatriates joke that the one place not to bring up politics is at a British political association meeting.)

Depending on where you are, you may not find all the political parties represented, but if you do – you can confidently expect to see the same faces at each party's parties. The list of forthcoming fixtures at a British political association overseas doesn't over-accentuate the purely political, by any means. The food is often better than it would be in the UK, though, as is the conversation.

The British political parties are:

Conservatives Abroad
Conservative & Unionist Central Office
32 Smith Square
London SW1P 3HH
telephone 0171 222 9000, extension 2728 or 2308

Labour International
The Labour Party
150 Walworth Road
London SE17 1JT
telephone 0171 277 3362

Liberal Democrats Campaigns Department
4 Cowley Street
London SW1P 3NB
telephone 0171 222 7999

House of Commons general information is available on:
0171 219 3000
and parliamentary information is available on:
0171 219 4272

CHAPTER THREE

FINANCIAL PLANNING

'Prices can go down as well as up. Past performance is not necessarily a guide to the future.'
The UK's standard wealth warning.

First, you need to get out of the British tax system

Wherever they've gone, there's one tax system that all British expatriates have in common. It's the one they believe they've left behind – the British one, administered by the Inland Revenue.

When you're becoming an expatriate, however long you're going to be away, the first thing you must do is sort out where you stand vis-a-vis British tax. No other financial planning can usefully be undertaken until you have done this.

Why? Because if you go the right way about becoming an expatriate, you can remove most, and sometimes all, of your liability to British tax while you are away. As we shall see later, by going to live in another country you do not necessarily replace your UK tax burden with that other country's tax burden.

No worthwhile financial planning leaves in place an unnecessary tax liability, nor does it incur one either. This is why you have to think about British tax first, and your destination country's tax second, and only then turn your attention to the disposition of your finances.

But before you get to any of that, you need to know how the British tax system works. Then you need to understand how the Inland Revenue operates.

The British tax system and the Inland Revenue

To state the obvious, the British tax system is extremely complex. This is because British tax 'law' is an accumulation of statutes, precedents, legal judgements reversed on appeal, changes of the rules by the Inland Revenue, and annual interventions by the Chancellor of the Exchequer at Budget time.

The system is complex because it has to be comprehensive. It has evolved over centuries, and over that time it has adapted and expanded to cope with every conceivable variant on a taxpayer's circumstances. As taxpayers have changed over the years, and new circumstances have arisen, so have new tax laws and practices been introduced to deal with them.

This means that behind every general rule, and statement of practice, there lies a vast abundance of cross-referenced small print that may have to be taken into account in assessing any individual's tax position, it is not small print in the sense that it is hidden or concealed, except in the sense that a tree is hidden when it is part of a forest, but it is small print all the same.

So unless it is dealing with the simplest of taxpayers, the Inland Revenue cannot just apply the general rules across the broad range of cases. With such detailed and interlocking provisions at its disposal, it has to go further, and judge each case on its merits – or, more accurately – on its precise details. This has two important consequences.

First, the Inland Revenue will not commit itself to providing detailed answers to tax questions in advance. There are just too many variants on every conceivable question, and too many relevant details that might not get mentioned.

So beyond general guidance (see the next section), the Inland Revenue won't help you to know for certain whether or not you're going to incur a tax liability.

Secondly, the job of working out the precise application of complex rules to detailed cases inevitably tends to become a process of interpretation. As one accountant specializing in expatriate tax affairs observed, 'there's the written-down part, and there's established practice, which is how they actually do it.' What matters most is the interpretation, not what's written down.

The thing about interpretation is that it is conducive to discussion. Inland Revenue people like talking to tax accountants, some of whom are ex-Revenue gone over to the private sector, because they speak the same language. When misinterpretations happen, as they do, they get corrected because somebody whose judgement is respected draws into the discussion a piece of small print that has hitherto been overlooked.

And for that, you need an expert. You need expert advice in advance, on how not to incur undue tax liabilities in the first place, and you need an expert thereafter, to handle your relationship with the Inland Revenue. Also to watch for misinterpretations, yours and theirs.

Expert advice, information, and how to use this chapter

So you need to take expert advice. That's easier to suggest than to do, and there's a section on finding, evaluating and using advice on page 147. But first, you should know that the general guidance you can get from the Inland Revenue itself is extensive.

This chapter is written with particular reference to Inland Revenue guides IR20 *Residents and non-residents* and IR58 *Going to work abroad?* You will find a full list of relevant guides, and how to get hold of them, on page 229.

The guides are free, and useful. They are as simple as they can be, given the complexity of their subject matter. Although they don't get automatically updated every time Inland Revenue practice changes, they're useful background. They suggest contacting any Tax Office or Tax Enquiry Centre for further information. 'Or,' they say, 'you can consult a professional adviser.'

Take the hint. Take advice from somebody who knows all the small print and knows enough about you to work out which bits of it will apply.

Don't deal with the Inland Revenue on your own. Read what follows, and all the other information you obtain, as a preparation for a meeting with your tax adviser. And if you're thinking about the cost of advice, start thinking about the possible cost of not taking advice.

Now let's talk about tax liabilities.

UK income tax rates for 1996/97

If you are liable to pay UK income tax, the rates after personal allowances (for which, see page 108) are:

20% up to £3,900
24% from £3,901 to £25,500
40% over £25,500

The three fundamentals of British tax for expatriates

When planning your departure from the British tax system, there are three fundamental tax concepts that you must understand. These matter whether you are taking up a job abroad, or accompanying a partner and not expecting to go into employment. Briefly, they are:

1. Residence

If you are resident in the UK for tax purposes, and working in the UK, you will be liable to British tax on your earnings and other income and any capital gains, wherever any of these arise. As an expatriate, you may qualify for 'non-resident status' if your period of absence from the UK lasts for more than a whole tax year (see the section 'Establishing non-resident status' on page 94), and so may be released from liability to British tax on all your income and capital gains with the single exception of your UK-source income while you retain non-resident status (this ceases to be true when you reach the tax year in which you will return to the UK, see 'Capital Gains Tax' on page 112 and the 'Returning to the UK' checklist on page 105. If your absence from the UK will not cover a whole tax year, see 'The foreign-earnings deduction' on page 100. For an exception to the general rule as stated here, see 'Incidental duties' on page 106);

What is the UK for tax purposes?

For tax purposes, the UK is England, Wales, Scotland and Northern Ireland (out from the shore to a distance of 12 nautical miles). For tax purposes, the Channel Islands and the Isle of Man are not part of the UK.

What is a tax year?

A UK tax year runs from 6 April in one year to 5 April in the following year. References to, for example, '1996/97' in this book or any other source dealing with tax and finance, are to the tax year 6 April 1996 to 5 April 1997. Note that some overseas tax jurisdictions have a tax year running from 1 January to 31 December, and some have other variants. This comes up in the section on dealing with your possible liability to overseas tax which begins on page 126.

2. *Ordinary Residence*

If your period of absence from the UK will last for at least one tax year, you may qualify as 'not ordinarily resident' in the UK for tax purposes as well as non-resident. You are non-resident in a single tax year; you are not ordinarily resident over a period of more than one complete tax year (although both statuses will normally apply together, from the date of your departure from the UK – see 'Establishing non-resident status' on page 94 and 'Extra-statutory concessions' on page 100).

It is Inland Revenue practice in cases involving departure to work abroad for more than one tax year, to treat individuals as not resident* and not ordinarily resident as though the two statuses were indivisible from each other. Indeed, in most circumstances they are.

Your ordinary residence is relevant in British-tax calculations if, by virtue of the number of days you have spent in the UK in one tax year, you become resident in the UK for that tax year only, while being already not ordinarily resident for a longer period of tax years of which the (perhaps inadvertently) resident year is one (see 'Establishing non-resident status', and also 'The remittance basis of British taxation' on pages 99–100).

The third fundamental tax concept you must understand is:

---

* *In common usage among tax practitioners, 'not resident' describes the condition of having 'non-resident status'. 'Not' and 'non' are interchangeable in this context. Another minor quirk is that although the phrase 'not resident and not ordinarily resident' is always given in full, 'non-resident status' can often be used interchangeably with it.*

3. Domicile

This is separate from residence and ordinary residence, which tend to occur together, as explained above. Residence and ordinary residence are established by reference to the length of your absence from the UK. Your domicile, however, is something much deeper. It is established, for tax purposes, by reference to a long list of factors arising in your circumstances and your behaviour; for our purposes, it is sufficient to say that your domicile is the country that, in your heart of hearts, you regard as your home. Broadly speaking, if you intend ultimately to return to the UK, and if you think of yourself as British (or English, Scottish, Welsh, Northern Irish), you are domiciled in the UK. UK inheritance-tax liability depends on domicile, and is dealt with on page 117; other UK tax liabilities are assessed according to residence and ordinary residence. (See also 'Giving up UK domicile' on page 120).

In preparing your finances for expatriate life, your first objective is to become not resident and not ordinarily resident in the UK for tax purposes. How do you proceed?

Establishing non-resident status (and what happens if you can't)

First, you must meet all the Inland Revenue's conditions for non-resident status, or more accurately, be able to show that you will be able to meet them. The conditions vary according to whether you are going abroad to work, to accompany your working spouse, or to accompany your working non-spouse. If you don't meet the conditions, you may still be able to release yourself from liability to UK tax – see item 6 below.

Whether you meet the conditions for non-resident status or not, if you hope to change your liability to British tax when you go abroad, you must communicate with the Inland Revenue. This should be done well before you leave the UK – see item 4 below.

The conditions for achieving non-resident status are as follows:

Residence and ordinary residence; what are they?

Surprisingly, neither 'residence' nor 'ordinary residence' are defined in the Taxes Act. Their meaning is inferred from successive judgements in tax cases. The Inland Revenue's statement of its own practice is that the terms should be given their 'ordinary meaning'.

1. When you are leaving the UK to work abroad

If you are leaving the UK to work full-time abroad under a contract of employment, you will be treated as not resident and not ordinarily resident if you meet *all* the following conditions.

● your absence from the UK and your employment abroad both last for at least a whole tax year, and

- during your absence any visits you make to the UK
  - total less than 183 days in any tax year, and
  - average less than 91 days a tax year (the average is taken over the period of absence up to a maximum of four years).

You have to meet *all* of these conditions to be treated as not resident and not ordinarily resident in the UK for tax purposes. Not just some of them; *all* of them. The Inland Revenue's guidebook IR20 *Residents and non-residents* (see page 108) stresses that point by repeating it, so this book will too.

You will hear the 183-day and the 91-day conditions described as the 'six-month rule' and the 'three-month rule' respectively. The Inland Revenue counts in exact numbers of days; so should you. Days of arrival and departure are not counted in adding up visits; nor are days spent in the UK because of exceptional circumstances beyond your control, such as your illness or that of a member of your immediate family.

It does not matter whether you come and go during the tax year, or make one visit; all days spent in the UK in a tax year are added together.

The point is made several times in this chapter that you should keep detailed records of everything that might be relevant to your tax affairs. That point is doubly true here: keep ticket stubs, diaries and credit-card records relating to visits to the UK.

Note that the 183-day/91-day conditions do not apply to the tax years in which you leave and return permanently to the UK. You gain non-resident status from the day after the date of your departure, and you become resident again from the date of your permanent return to the UK.

Available accommodation

You may hear 'available accommodation' mentioned as a factor in determining UK residence or non-residence. Take no notice. The availability of accommodation in the UK, whether owned or rented property or just a room kept empty by a friend or relative, was a factor in residence questions until 1993, when the law was changed to make it irrelevant. If somebody mentions it to you, ignore the rest of their advice as well.

---

2. When you are an 'accompanying spouse'

If you are married, and you are what the Inland Revenue calls an 'accompanying spouse' (and common parlance among expatriates describes as a 'trailing spouse', as discussed on page ix) because you are not going to work abroad yourself but are accompanying your husband or wife who is going to work abroad, you may also be treated as not resident and not ordinarily resident in the UK for tax purposes.

(You are granted these statuses by concession – for which, see 'Extra-statutory concessions' on page 100.)

If your spouse meets the conditions set out in (1) above, and you accompany or later join your spouse abroad, you will be treated as not resident and not ordinarily resident in the UK for tax purposes if you meet all the following conditions.

- you are absent from the UK for a whole tax year, and
- during your absence any visits you make to the UK
  – total less than 183 days in any tax year, and
  – average less than 91 days a tax year, as above

The further comments made in (1) above also apply here.

3. When you are accompanying, but not a spouse

If you are leaving the UK for a period of tax years, but can show neither a contract of employment nor a spouse who has one, the Inland Revenue will look for other evidence to prove that you're really going.

Such evidence might include the fact that you're the regular partner of a departing expatriate, but that might not be enough on its own – after all, your commitment to absence might not be as great as your partner's. You could split up, for example (which is also true of spouses, but let's not get in too deep here. Remember that spouses too are assessed independently for non-resident status).

More conclusive evidence would include giving up your job, giving up your (no doubt shared) home and committing yourself to overseas accommodation. You might also get onto any pre-departure training being offered to your partner (actually, you'd be a fool not to – see page 30).

The point here is that there is no simple set of rules to test whether a person is leaving the country for real; every case is judged on its merits, so whatever evidence is available is the evidence that is used.

If you can demonstrate that you are really going, the Inland Revenue will regard you as provisionally non-resident from the day after the date of your departure. Normally, this provisional ruling is confirmed after you have lived abroad for a whole tax year.

If you cannot offer reasonably conclusive proof of your intention to depart, and if, for whatever reason, the Inland Revenue does not accept that you are becoming/have become non-resident, you will be treated as provisionally resident in the UK for up to three years; that is, the Inland Revenue will postpone its decision on changing your tax status for up to that long. In this situation, you will continue to receive British tax allowances and reliefs (see the section under that title on page 108) and your tax bill will be adjusted when the final decision is made.

If you have read the spouse's section above, you will reflect that having provisional non-resident status is much the same as any other kind; that is, you have to keep it up to keep it. Calling your status provisional is just the Inland Revenue's way of reminding itself to keep a slightly closer eye on you.

Whatever you are, working expatriate, spouse, non-working non-spouse, your status will only apply if you keep to the rules. See item 5 in this section.

Case history: Separation can be fun

Miles had arrived a week early for their holiday in the UK. His old college had been having a reunion, and his wife Barbara had been happy to let him attend that on his own.

'I don't want to sit for a whole evening watching you lot talk about people I never met,' she said, 'You go on ahead and I'll join you the day before we're due at my parents'.'

Now, after two weeks of visiting Barbara's parents, sister and cousins, Miles was ready to take her home. It was their last night in the UK, and they were spending it at an hotel in London prior to catching the flight from Heathrow tomorrow.

The phone rang. 'Miles? It's Connie. Remember me? Barbara's old friend from art school. I heard she was in town and I was going to invite her for a few days' shopping around the West End.'

'Actually, Connie,' Miles began, 'I have to go back because I've run out of time. If I don't get out of the UK by tomorrow night, I'll be liable to British tax again.'

Barbara had been listening on the other line. She cut in. 'Connie, I'd love to see you. I'm assessed separately for tax from Brian, and I've got a whole fortnight before I have to leave. We could start in Bond Street; do you know, I haven't a thing to wear. Oh, the sales don't start until two weeks' time. Never mind; good clothes are worth it however much you pay . . .'

Alone on the plane home next morning, Miles remembered that he'd left all three of their credit cards, including the gold one, in Barbara's handbag . . .

4. Telling the Inland Revenue that you qualify for non-resident status

If the Inland Revenue don't know that you're going overseas, they're not going to know that your tax status might be changing. If they don't know that, they're going to send you a tax return just as they did last year.

If they do that, and you're already overseas, you're going to have a busy time corresponding with them, and getting whatever new status they might concede backdated. In short, you'll be buying a lot of stamps.

Far better to get the whole thing sorted out well in advance. Allow time, if you have it, for exchanges of correspondence. In a perfect world, you should allow an absolute minimum of six weeks.

Contact your tax office. You'll find the address on your Notice of Tax Coding, along with the various numbers you should remember to quote. Or contact the Claims Branch (International Section) at St John's House, Merton Road, Bootle, Merseyside L69 9BB, telephone 0151 472 6000.

You will be asked to complete form P85, which in appearance and layout is a variant on the standard tax return. When returning it, you should request confirmation of your non-resident status.

You should also send in parts 2 and 3 of your P45, as going overseas part-way through a tax year will probably lead to a PAYE repayment.

Telephoning the Inland Revenue

Don't call long-distance at a peak time. You will hear a recorded request to enter the extension number of the person you're calling, if you have it. Then silence. Then the ringing tone, then the General Switchboard. Have your National Insurance number ready, and ask for the department you want. If you've got a question and don't know who's best to answer it, ask for General Enquiries rather than spelling it out. General Enquiries, too, are better at passing you on to the right department than providing answers themselves.

If you're lucky, you'll end up talking to an enthusiastic specialist who will not only spell out the rules, but also quote the Taxes Act, etc., in which they may be found. If that happens, make sure you get the extension number for next time.

---

5. *Failing to sustain non-resident status and the nightmare scenario*

You cannot demonstrate conclusively that you meet the conditions for non-resident status until you can show that you have been satisfactorily not-resident and not ordinarily resident for a period of at least one tax year.

But it would be impractical to go on paying UK tax while non-resident, for the simple reason that if you are working abroad, you will tend to be resident elsewhere and so liable for another country's tax (non-UK tax liabilities are covered in the second part of this chapter, which begins on page 126).

So, by concession, the Inland Revenue treats you as having non-resident status from the date of your departure from the UK, subject to your demonstrating that you will meet the conditions detailed in 1, 2 or 3 above.

Fine. But the fact of your having non-resident status, whether this is formally provisional or not, makes you an interesting case, in the eyes of the Inland Revenue. They don't want you to pay more tax than you legally should, but they don't want you to pay less tax either, and you're likely to be paying very little, if any. The affairs of 'once and future taxpayers', as they have been described, tend to get more closely scrutinized than those of stay-at-homes.

If, for whatever reason, the Inland Revenue determines that you have not met all the conditions for non-resident status in one or more tax years of your absence, you will receive a tax bill shortly after you return to the UK.

This does happen. It happens to expatriates who have broken the rules. It also happens to expatriates who (a) have met all the conditions for non-resident status, or (b) believe that they have met all the conditions for non-resident status.

The Inland Revenue is capable of getting things wrong. But so are you.

If this happens, you will need immediate expert help to sort it out. No argument: you will. Indeed, if you've got this far without expert help - go back to the section headed 'The British Tax system and the Inland Revenue' on page 90.

You will also need a filing cabinet. A tax bill on your return might refer to a couple of years back. You will be much happier if you can find, for example, the credit card slip that proves your presence in a shop over there when you were alleged to be visiting family over here.

Can you prove that you're going? Could you prove that you've gone? Will you be able to prove that you stayed away?

If you become resident in the UK for tax purposes in one tax year (ie, by breaking the 183-day rule), but you remain not ordinarily resident for tax purposes for the longer period of tax years of which the UK-resident year is one, your tax liability will be assessed on:

- the remittance basis of British taxation

This also applies if you return to the UK at the end of a contract, and become resident for tax purposes, but take up another contract overseas soon enough to avoid ordinary residence. See also 'If you decide not to stay in the UK' on page 190.

The remittance basis applies to sums you remit to the UK in your UK-resident tax year; these become subject to UK tax. Fair enough. But if you are taxed on the remittance basis, you will also be liable for UK tax on remitted overseas income from investments or any trade or profession (ie, if you are self-employed) *in the previous tax year* unless the source is new. A source becomes new if you 'bed-and-breakfast' your investment; that is, sell and then immediately buy again. Bed-and-breakfasting appears again among the measures to take before finally returning to the UK, on page 188.

You will also be taxed on the preceding-year basis on any 'constructive remittance'. This is a category without a strict definition: if you are making payments to the UK in respect of a UK mortgage, or even a credit card, or even if you pay a UK-based travel agent for flights to and from your overseas location, you are making a constructive remittance.

There are good reasons to avoid breaking the 183-day rule during your time overseas, and the remittance basis of British taxation is one of the best.

Extra-statutory concessions

Occasionally in this chapter you will find the words 'by concession'. They refer to the established Inland Revenue practice of allowing 'extra-statutory concessions'; that is, of relaxing the rules in cases where to apply them would be either impractical or otherwise undesirable. This doesn't mean that individual tax inspectors can make up their own minds as to whether or not to tax you. The available extra-statutory concessions, which you will find listed in Inland Revenue guide IR1, may not be part of the statutes, but they're very much a settled part of the system.

Emergency returns to the UK

By concession, the Inland Revenue will normally disregard days spent in the UK for unavoidable reasons such as serious illnesses in your close family. This does not mean that you can disregard the 183/91-day and other rules. If the unavoidable visit comes at the beginning of the tax year, do not exceed the limit with an avoidable visit at the end; rearrange your affairs. As one tax accountant put it, 'a visit is unavoidable if it's unavoidable.' If you have the option of worrying about the tax implications before you go, your visit is not unavoidable.

---

6. If you're not going away for long enough to qualify for non-resident status

If, by reference to the conditions outlined above, you decide that you are going to remain resident and ordinarily resident in the UK for tax purposes, you may still be able to extract yourself from liability to British tax on your earnings from working overseas. You do this by means of

● The foreign-earnings deduction

This is a deduction of 100% of the tax payable on your foreign earnings, normally including terminal leave pay, commission, bonuses and expenses allowances.

You qualify for this if, while remaining resident and ordinarily resident in the UK for tax purposes, you are absent from the UK for a 'qualifying period' of at least 365 days between any two dates. Note that you do not have to be working for the whole of your absence abroad. Leave taken from your work abroad, including terminal leave, counts towards your qualifying period provided it is spent abroad.

However, you do not have to stay outside the UK for the whole of the 365 days. Return visits to the UK may count as part of the qualifying period (ie, the 365 days may include some days spent in the UK) if

- no single visit to the UK lasts for more than 62 consecutive days, and
- 'the total number of days you have spent on visits to the UK during the qualifying period is not more than one sixth of the number of days in the period beginning with the first day of the qualifying period and ending with the last day of the period you spent abroad after that return visit'.

That second condition is a direct quotation from the Inland Revenue's leaflet IR58 *Going to Work Abroad?* It is known as

- The one-sixth rule

It means, in effect, that you have to know how long you will spend abroad after a visit to the UK, before you can work out how long that visit can be, to count towards the qualifying period.*

Suppose you work abroad for	30 days
the return to the UK for	10 days
and then work abroad for	19 days

You will, therefore, have worked abroad for 59 days in total. But 10 days is more than one-sixth of 59 days, so you cannot begin counting your qualifying period until the end of that particular absence from the UK.

But if you are planning a subsequent visit to the UK, at least you have the first line of the calculation. That, and the third line – the time you will spend overseas after the visit – dictate the length of the visit you can make to the UK.

If you know that after you have visited the UK, you will spend, say, 30 days abroad, you have:

work abroad for	19 days
the return to the UK for	?
and then work abroad for	30 days

So you will work abroad for 49 days. The calculation to work out how long you spend in the UK is, therefore:

$$49/5 = 9.8$$

---

* Note that the 62-day and one-sixth rules do not apply to merchant seafarers and aircrew. See the sections on pages 105 and 106.

Fractions must be rounded down. You can, therefore, spend nine days in the UK. This works because the rounded-down nine days are less than one-sixth of the total number of days including the nine.

If you restrict your visit to nine days, you can count your qualifying period as beginning with $19 + 9 + 30 = 58$ days.

Note that if you are in the UK at midnight at the end of a day, you count as having been in the UK for that day.

Note also that the calculation of your next visit, which will begin, according to the example above, 30 days after you return from your previous visit, will begin with 58 days in the first line. Once a period has qualified, it is counted as a total, whether the qualifying days within it were spent in the UK or overseas.

But remember also that your qualifying period must be continuous. Those 58 days count for nothing if they're followed by a non-qualifying period.

● The foreign-earnings deduction and British tax allowances

You may be resident in the UK for tax purposes, but with the foreign-earnings deduction, you do achieve a 100% reduction in your liability to British tax on your overseas earnings. You retain your UK tax allowances. You may offset these against any UK or foreign income you may have in addition to your tax-free foreign-earnings. See the section 'Tax allowances and relief' on page 108.

If you think you will qualify for the foreign-earnings deduction, you will naturally need to know about

● Claiming the foreign-earnings deduction.

If your employer is sending you abroad to work on a foreign contract, tax will continue to be paid under PAYE. However, if your Tax Office has enough information from both you and your employer to believe that the foreign-earnings deduction is provisionally due, they will ask your employer to pay your earnings without deduction of tax.

If the position is judged to be sufficiently uncertain, your Tax Office will not authorize payment of your earnings without tax. In this situation, you will have to claim the foreign-earnings deduction on your return.

Note that if you are going abroad to work for a foreign employer, and PAYE is not possible, normal procedure would be to send you a quarterly (or less frequent for a shorter absence) bill for any tax payable, with any adjustment being made after the end of the tax year.

The foreign-earnings deduction must be claimed in the first instance by you, not your employer. Write to your tax office, giving

● your National Insurance number
● your employer's name and address

- your date of departure from the UK
- your expected date of final return
- the dates of any intended/planned visits to the UK during your time abroad.

Note that you do not have to stick to your planned list of visits, but you must keep a record of your actual visits.

Your Tax Office will confirm the information you provide with your employer.

Note that whether you get the foreign-earnings deduction in advance or retrospectively, the final decision on whether it was due will only be made after your return. If you got it in advance, you risk receiving a large tax bill if your calculations about visits to the UK were wrong. Expatriates who have been grated the foreign-earnings deduction tend to be enthusiastic collectors of ticket stubs, receipts, credit-card records.

Look-through legislation

Dispositions of assets made with the single purpose of frustrating an otherwise legitimate tax liability can, under the UK tax system and others, be made subject to 'look-through' provisions. This means that the situation is assessed as though the cunning move hadn't been made. In other words, it's a waste of money to pay an over-clever accountant who is obsessed with defeating the tax authorities to the exclusion of other objectives. Three terms to remember are: avoidance, which is legitimate; evasion, which is not; and avoision, which is the former shading too far towards the latter.

Unofficial experts

The expatriate world is full of experts who don't know what they're talking about. Tax advisers talk about clients who have taken steps on the basis of what they have been told by another expatriate over drinks, who have thereby expensively wrecked their tax planning. Decide on an adviser, and stick with your decision. Remember also the point made in Chapter One (page 27), that in the advice business, you only have legal redress against an adviser who gets it wrong if you have paid for his advice.

Special cases

What has been said so far will enable you to get an idea of where you stand vis-a-vis British tax. But some expatriates aren't treated according to the normal rules outlined above.

First, two special situations, and then the categories of British expatriate whose UK tax treatment varies, or potentially varies, from the norm.

● If you are self-employed

The rules for establishing non-resident status are the same for self-employed as for employed individuals. However, if you do not have a contract of employment to show the Inland Revenue, you have one fewer item of evidence to support your claim for non-resident status. Your status will be granted provisionally, or it may not be granted until three years after you have left the UK. The comments under 'If you are accompanying, but not a spouse' apply to you too.

● If you are thinking of going overseas without a contract, to look for employment

The possibility that you might fail to find overseas employment means that your own intentions are provisional, and consequently that any status you might obtain from the Inland Revenue will be provisional. The comments under 'If you are accompanying, but not a spouse' apply to you too.

You should also bear in mind that there are strong arguments against going first, and looking for the job second. Not least, that many countries require applications for visas and work permits to be made before you arrive (see Chapter One, page 32). There is more on the subject of finding jobs overseas on page 191.

There are categories of expatriate who receive special UK-tax treatment. These are:

● Crown servants and members of the armed forces

Broadly, your employment as a Crown servant overseas will be treated as if it is occurring in the UK (just as embassy premises overseas are part of the UK), and taxed accordingly. This also applies to members of the armed forces.

But only your employment will be treated as occurring in the UK. If you meet the conditions for non-resident status (or the foreign-earnings deduction), your UK-tax treatment in respect of any other income, etc., will be as outlined elsewhere in this chapter.

Contact the Inland Revenue's specialist office for further information. Public Departments (Technical Unit) Foreign Section, Ty-Glas, Llanishen,

Cardiff CF4 5WN, tel 01222 753271. Give your National Insurance number and details of your overseas employment.

- Employees of the European Union and other international organizations

Your tax treatment depends on whether you are abroad on a 'seconded basis' or by virtue of being employed directly by the international organization.

If the ultimate source of your salary is the British government, whether or not payment to you is made via the international organization for which you work, or its agency, you will be treated as a Crown servant overseas, for which see above.

If you are employed directly by the international organization, without reference to your home government, you will be taxed by the UK according to whether or not you qualify for non-resident status (or the foreign-earnings deduction).

Contact the Claims Branch (International) for further information, at St John's House, Merton Road, Bootle, Merseyside L69 9BB, tel 0151 472 6000. Give your National Insurance number and details of your overseas employment.

- Oil and gas workers on rigs offshore of the UK

The UK for tax purposes includes British territorial waters. It also includes the British sectors of the gas/oil exploration fields around the UK. Your tax position will depend on whether or not you can establish and maintain absence from the UK as thus defined.

Contact your Tax Office, if your employer is UK-resident, or, of your employer is not UK-resident, the Foreign Group, HMIT Centre 1, Queensway House, East Kilbride, Glasgow G79 1AA, tel 0131 552 28733. Give your National Insurance number and details of your overseas employment.

- Merchant Navy seafarers

If you're going to be away from the UK for long enough to qualify for non-resident status, whether at sea or making voyages from a foreign base, your treatment for tax purposes will be as outlined in the relevant sections earlier in this chapter.

But if you are UK-resident when not at sea, and your voyages begin and/or end in the UK (irrespective of intervening stops at ports overseas), you should note that your entitlement to the foreign-earnings deduction on long voyages will not be based on the 62-day and one-sixth rule outlined earlier in this chapter. For you, the applicable allowances are 183 consecutive days and one half of the qualifying period.

However, notwithstanding the apparent simplicity of the previous sentence, this is a complex area. If, as a UK-resident merchant seafarer, you hope to reduce your UK tax liability, you would be well advised to seek prior clarification of your position from the Inland Revenue Marine Section, HMIT Cardiff 6, Ty-Glas, Llanishen, Cardiff CF4 5TW, tel 01222 753271. Give your National Insurance number and details of your overseas employment.

You should also read the section on 'Incidental duties' below.

- Aircrew

In some ways, your UK-tax treatment will be similar to that accorded to merchant seafarers – except, of course, that there is no equivalent of a long voyage in an aeroplane.

Your residence status will, therefore, tend to be decided according to whether you are based outside the UK and stay there for long enough to qualify either for non-resident status or for the foreign-earnings deduction (by the 183-day/one-half rules applicable to merchant seamen).

A complication arises where you visit the UK in the course of your duties. This is taken up in more detail below under the heading 'Incidental duties'; briefly, if you carry out a part of your work in the UK that is not merely 'incidental' to your work overseas, you will be charged UK tax on the proportion of your salary that you receive for doing it.

You are treated as UK taxable for non-incidental duties from the moment you arrive in the UK. Aircrew are taken to arrive/depart at the moment they touch down/take off. This should mean that if you land an aircraft at a UK airport, you will pay UK tax on what you receive for taxiing it to its berth, or for telling the passengers to remain seated until the aircraft has come completely to a halt. On a stopover between long-haul flights, you might wonder whether you are resting in the course of your duties, or only incidentally.

This is a situation in which the Inland Revenue tends to display a welcome common sense. You won't get taxed for one landing and take-off in a tax year (bad weather at Schiphol; diverted to Stansted), and, as a general observation, you will not be regarded as performing non-incidental duties in the UK unless you make a habit of arriving there.

But try not to get onto a regular route to and from the UK. See below.

Further information, contact the Inland Revenue Foreign Section, HMIT Cardiff 6, Ty-Glas, Llanishen, Cardiff CF4 5TW, tel 01222 753271.

Incidental duties

If you are working abroad, and you have achieved non-resident status for tax purposes, you will still be liable to UK tax on your earnings from duties that you perform in the UK as part of your job. Duties that are taxable are those that the Inland Revenue will regard as being 'of the same kind as, or of similar importance to' the duties that you perform abroad. Duties that are only 'incidental' to your work abroad are not taxable.

Attendance at directors' meetings in the UK will be taxable, for example. The key point here is that the nature of the duties, not their duration, determines the tax liability – except that if you work in the UK for more than 91 days in a tax year, the Inland Revenue will argue that your work cannot be incidental.

Incidental – ie, non-taxable – duties are those which simply 'enable you to do your normal work abroad'. They will include visits to the UK to receive instructions, and going on training courses in the UK as long as you don't do any productive work at the same time. Subject to the 91-day rule, duties performed in the UK will be incidental as long as they're not what you do for a living, or a direct part of it.

Case history: How incidental can you get?

Leo Baxter works in Brussels, for a translation agency. In April, his father fell ill, and Leo, fearing the worst, returned home to Shepton Mallet.

Mr Baxter's recovery was slow, and it was a month before Leo could return to Brussels. He made use of the time by doing some translation work.

The first three days of the visit were at the end of the tax year; Leo was worried because they took him over his allowance of 183 days in the UK. But his accountant told him not to worry. It had been an unavoidable emergency visit, and the Inland Revenue could be persuaded to overlook it. The accountant promised to talk to a contact in the Revenue.

Leo returned to Brussels.

Next day, his accountant called. 'Bad news. Apparently you were working while you were over here.'

'Yes, I was,' said Leo.

'The Revenue are going to argue that it can't have been an emergency visit if you were able to work,' said the accountant. 'That means you're outside the 183-day rule for last year and you'll have to reduce visits this year, to keep within the 91-day average.'

'But you can't mean that the rest of the stay counts as a visit too,' protested Leo. 'Virtually a whole month in this tax year! I'll have to cancel half my holiday visit in the summer!'

'Worse,' said the accountant. 'They're going to argue that you performed incidental duties while you were in the UK. That means a tax liability.'

'But all I did,' protested Leo, 'was translate a couple of documents for the local tax office!'

His accountant just groaned.

Tax allowances and reliefs

If you have non-resident status, you remain entitled to the same UK tax allowances as UK residents. This applies if you are a British citizen. There are a number of other groups listed in IR20 *Residents and non-residents* who may claim UK tax allowances. They are individuals who have a close connection to the UK while not being British citizens, as follows:

- Citizens of the Commonwealth
- Present and past employees of the British Crown
- Widows and widowers of employees of the British Crown
- UK missionary society employees
- Civil servants in British protectorates
- Residents of the Channel Islands and Isle of Man
- Former residents of the UK living abroad for the sake of their health or the health of a member of their family
- Nationals and/or residents of a country with which the UK has a double tax agreement (for which, see page 124) which allows such a claim
- Citizens of the Irish Republic

Note that full UK tax allowances are available for the year of departure from, and return to, the UK.

You will also continue to receive UK tax allowances if you qualify for the foreign-earnings deduction, because in that case you remain UK-resident.

UK tax allowances may be set against your UK-source income. Those applicable to the tax year 1996/7 are:

- A personal allowance of £3,765
- A married couple's allowance of £1,790

Note also that claims for tax allowances must be made within six years from the end of the tax year to which the claim relates. Contact the Claims Branch (International) at St John's House, Merton Road, Bootle, Merseyside L69 9BB, tel 0151 472 6000. If you are a Crown servant, contact Public Departments (Technical Unit) Foreign Section, Ty-Glas, Llanishen, Cardiff CF4 5WN, tel 01222 753271.

In addition to the basic UK tax allowances, you may also be liable to claim

- Mortgage Interest Relief At Source (MIRAS) on your only or main residence in the UK. Briefly, you continue to get tax relief on your mortgage payments on your UK principal residence, by concession, if you are leaving to work abroad and your absence is expected to last no more than four years. MIRAS relief is limited to payments on the first £30,000 of your mortgage.

When things go wrong

The Inland Revenue exists to ensure that you pay what you owe. Tax inspectors no more want you to pay too much tax, than they are prepared to let you get away with too little. But mistakes are made and problems arise, and even though you have professional assistance, you should know how to cope with any disagreements that might arise.

Appealing against a tax bill

You have thirty days in which to appeal. Write to the tax inspector whose address appears on the bill. Set out your reasons for appealing, and, if you are proposing a lower figure, consider enclosing a cheque as it will be held on account.

If you cannot agree a settlement of our appeal, you should write notifying your inspector that you intend to take the matter further. The tax division represented by your inspector will have a body of independent General Commissioners who can hear your appeal, or you can appeal to the Special Commissioners. Details of how to do this are available from The Clerk to the Special Commissioners, 15–19 Bedford Avenue, London WC1B 3AS, telephone 0171 631 4242.

No sensible expatriate appeals without professional assistance, because professionals often have the contacts to reach a settlement without going through the whole procedure. One expatriate's accountant achieved a measure of goodwill for his client, and the immediate withdrawal of an outsized tax demand, by ringing a contact in the relevant tax office, and observing that as far as he could see, the demand could only be explained if somebody had left off a decimal point: the true figure was $48.00; the figure taxed on the demand was £4,800.

Complaining about the Revenue

To make a complaint other than an appeal against a bill, first write to your tax inspector. If that doesn't work, write to the Controller for his division; ask your tax inspector for the address (or see page 226) as a way of giving notice that you are taking the matter further. If that doesn't work, or the address doesn't arrive within a reasonable time, contact the independent Revenue Adjudicator's Office, 3rd Floor, Haymarket House, 28 Haymarket, London SW1Y 4SP, telephone 0171 930 2292.

If you're still not satisfied and the matter is sufficiently serious, write to your MP (see the section on politics on page 88). Any MP is empowered to refer a tax matter to the Parliamentary Ombudsman, or Commissioner for Administration, at The Office of the Parliamentary Commissioner for Administration, Church House, Great Smith Street, London SW1P 3BW, telephone 0171 276 2130/3000. 'This,' as one tax practitioner observed, 'is the nuclear option.'

If you're investigated by the Inland Revenue

The Inland Revenue are unpredictably benevolent with investigations. They can be persuaded not to levy a penalty where a liability has been mistakenly avoided, and sometimes even to write off a debt. But this only happens where a tax accountant in good standing with the Revenue approaches a senior official and demonstrates successfully that the fault has been due to an honest mistake.

Where there is any suspicion of deliberate intent to evade a tax liability, the Inland Revenue will always pursue a claim. They will not stop until the matter is settled either way. Note that there is no effective statute of limitations on a tax liability.

There are two potential danger areas for expatriates. First, their affairs will tend to involve (legitimate) use of offshore investment vehicles; such vehicles are sometimes found in attempts at tax evasion. Secondly, expatriates' financial affairs tend, again quite legitimately, not to be readily accessible to the Revenue. Complexity is a feature of most illegitimate tax structures as well as some legitimate ones.

Your tax affairs should always be potentially an open book. If you're ever in any doubt, better to check it with your accountant now than find out later that it wasn't okay after all, and you're facing a large tax bill.

The Taxpayer's Charter

This sets out your rights as a taxpayer, and the standard of service you may expect from the Inland Revenue. It is set out on page 228.

It is important to you, for the simple reason that the Inland Revenue take it very seriously. This means that they will treat you in the same way that they treat any other taxpayer in a similar situation; fairness and the right to equality are key points. In times of difficulty, when you need a concession, a dispensation or indeed leniency, tax practitioners suggest it is worth asking whether any other taxpayer has ever been granted the concession in question, because if so, surely you're entitled to expect it too?

Self assessment

The Inland Revenue has introduced a new system of tax assessment for the tax year 1996/7 and thereafter. The new system is called self assessment, and the main change is a legal obligation on all those who complete a UK tax return to keep detailed records of all income and capital gains. Once complete, records must be retained by the taxpayers for 22 months after the end of the tax year to which they apply.

Self assessment tax returns are intended to simplify the system for both Inland Revenue and taxpayers. The guidance notes speak of taxpayers having their own 'accounts' with the Revenue, in the banking sense of the term, and receiving 'statements' of their tax position.

But self assessment does not oblige taxpayers to assess their own tax liability to UK tax. Taxpayers will be required to enter on the new-style tax return, figures for income capital gains, relief and deductions. They can then make their own calculation of their tax liability, with the 'step-by-step guide' provided by the Revenue, or they can get their accountant to do it, or they can ask the Revenue to do it for them. As long as the figures are there on the form (and kept on record at home), the taxpayer's legal obligation is complete.

The first tax returns for self assessment will be sent out in April 1997 and annually thereafter. April is when you or you tax adviser should request a return from your UK tax inspector if you are not automatically sent one and you have reason to believe you should complete one. There is an additional new legal requirement that you must request a return within six months after the end of the tax year to which it will apply.

Note that if you have any remaining UK tax liability, you should complete a tax return. Note also that you must complete a return for any income arising out of UK property, whether or not a UK tax liability is incurred by it (see page 170).

The key dates for the self assessment system are

- 30th September, which is the last date by which you should have sent back your return if you want the Inland Revenue to calculate your tax liability for you, or if you pay tax under PAYE and want any over- or under-payments corrected through PAYE, and
- 31st January, which is the last date by which you should have sent back your return if you are including your own calculation of tax liability.

Although the Inland Revenue will not necessarily be calculating your tax liability for you, that does not mean your figures will be accepted without question. The requirement to retain records is partly to avoid the 'can't remember' response to enquiries. The Inland Revenue, being human, can't apply the same amount of attention to every tax return it receives; the best incentive to get it right is to gain a record as a reliable taxpayer, and thus avoid automatic scrutiny, and question-and-answer correspondence every year.

Bear in mind that in keeping records, it is not enough just to be able to show the tax liabilities that fall within a given tax year. It's a good idea to be able to show why other tax liabilities don't need to be included. Keep a photocopy of your tax return when you send it in.

Capital gains tax

Capital gains tax (CGT) is like income tax in that you are liable to it if you are resident for tax purposes in the UK. It is simpler than income tax in that there is no capital gains equivalent to the foreign-earnings deduction. If you're resident for tax purposes in the UK, you're liable for CGT on all your assets, wherever they are in the world.

Note that if you realize gains during the tax year of your return to the UK, even before your actual return, you will incur a CGT liability unless you have been non-resident for a continuous period of three years. (If in doubt, or if the gain is large – see below – and/or your three years do not include three tax years, you should note that the most common piece of advice given by any professional on this subject is that capital gains should be realized in the last full tax year before return to the UK. See page 185 for more on planning your return.)

CGT is chargeable when you dispose of an asset that has increased in value since you acquired it. You don't have to sell it. Giving it away or exchanging it, or indeed receiving an insurance payment for its loss, all count as disposals for CGT purposes. The tax is charged on the difference between the original purchase price and the disposal value, with indexation as below. If the purchase or disposal is not for money, the disposal price is assessed, in the Inland Revenue's words, on 'What the asset might reasonably be expected to fetch had it been sold on the open market at the time of acquisition or disposal'.

Shares and other securities are valued on a mid-price basis, using the lower of

- a figure one-quarter up from the lower of the two prices in the quotation for the relevant day, and
- the figure half-way between the highest and the lowest prices of recorded bargains for that day.

Indexation for inflation is applied to capital gains and losses using the value at 31 March 1982 as the base. This means that assets purchased before then are assessed for CGT, and the gain/loss indexed, using their market price at 31 March 1982 as their cost.

Assets purchased thereafter are indexed from the date of purchase to the date of disposal. Indexation is calculated using the monthly Retail Price Index published by the Department of Employment; the indexation figure to be applied to any particular gain or loss is given in a table recalculated monthly by the Inland Revenue and published, for example, in the Financial Times' Weekend Money section on Saturdays. Multiply the cost of the asset by the indexation figure for the month in which it was acquired, and subtract the result from the gain from disposal (after deductions as in the next section). The indexation figure should be obtained from your tax office at the address given on your most recent tax return, notice of coding or other correspondence with the Inland Revenue. Further information may be obtained from the Capital Taxes Office, Minford House, Rockley Road, London W14 0DF, telephone 0171 603 4622; the Inland Revenue guide CGT14 *Capital gains tax – an introduction* is useful, and there are others. See page 230.

If you dispose of part of an asset, a shareholding for example, the gain/loss is calculated using part of the cost of the asset. Note that there are exceptions to the general rules, and these are detailed below.

CGT planning

If you are about to leave the UK to work abroad, and will thereby achieve non-resident status for tax purposes, you can turn your CGT liability to your advantage, and you should certainly spend some time with a professional adviser deciding the most tax-efficient way to make any capital gains or losses you might wish to realize before or after you go (advice, page 147). Note that getting it right now can have significant benefits when you return to the UK.

This is because of the different treatment under CGT of capital gains and losses, as follows.

- Capital gains. For the purpose of assessing liability to CGT, all capital gains within a tax year are added together. The annual CGT exemption for individuals (£6,300 for the tax year 1996/7) is taken off the figure for the total gain in the year, as are any costs of enhancing the value of the asset (as distinct from maintaining it) and any costs of buying or selling it (ie, commission, advertising, valuation for sale). Also deducted are
- Capital losses (ie, disposals at less than the purchase price). But note that capital losses can be carried forward indefinitely from the tax year in which they are incurred (if they are not used up by being offset against capital gains in that tax year) so that they can be offset against future capital gain.

This is work for a professional, but a frequently quoted CGT opportunity on going to work abroad has to do with the realization of capital losses. Proceed as follows.

First, you should defer realizing any capital gains until you are non-resident for tax purposes and so not liable for CGT. Because your non-resident status is by concession until your first full tax year of non-residence, you should defer any very large capital gain until that first full tax year (not that the Inland Revenue will necessarily seek to deny your concessionary status, but many professionals in this field like to have that extra assurance when protecting large realizations from CGT).

Note that the whole of any large disposal with gains attached, from contract to completion, should occur when you are non-resident in the UK for tax purposes (preliminary negotiations are allowed earlier); there are precedents for regarding a drawn-out transaction which has been carried out in stages as occurring when it began (see the box on Furniss v. Dawson).

Secondly, you should look for any capital losses you may soon wish to make, and make them before you leave the UK. The point is that when you return to the UK, you will probably find yourself making capital gains on the disposal of assets not suited to life back in the UK (foreign currency conversions are subject to CGT, for example), and if you can realize a capital loss while you are still subject to CGT, that loss can be carried forward to offset against any capital gains made after you become resident for tax purposes in the UK again.

Furniss v. Dawson

This is a legal case that was decided in 1984. It is still widely quoted and widely remembered. It has ramifications across the whole of financial and tax planning. Its main point was the determination that where a series of transactions are undertaken together to achieve a particular result, a distinction can be drawn between the 'form' of the series and its 'substance', with its substance (ie, what is actually achieved and whether it can legitimately be achieved) being the deciding factor where the form points in a different direction even if each transaction in the series is in itself legitimately formed. The terms 'letter' and 'spirit' might usefully replace form and substance respectively.

For practical purposes, this means that you may not achieve what you intend to achieve if you

- enter into contractual formalities while resident with the objective of completing a transaction when not resident, or, more widely, if you
- enter into a complex series of manoeuvres which have the sole purpose of shielding you from a tax liability that would legitimately apply in the absence of that series of manoeuvres.

Complexity in financial and tax planning, as has been suggested earlier in this chapter, is not a virtue. When it suits it to do so, the Inland Revenue will act by reference to the spirit of what you have done, rather than the letter.

Furniss v. Dawson does not apply where the rules are simple and their application clear. But taxpayers and their advisers should avoid the temptation to be too clever: complexities in the tax system are not there to be exploited.

How is CGT charged?

Net capital gains (after deduction of the annual CGT exemption and any capital losses in the year and any earlier capital losses still outstanding) are treated as the 'top slice' of income and charged to capital gains tax at income tax rates. Note that unused income tax reliefs and allowances cannot be set against net capital gains. They may be taxed together, but the exemptions/allowances cannot be swapped between them. No-income spouses cannot use their unused income tax allowances to offset capital gains, therefore.

CGT exemptions

You do not pay CGT on transfers of assets between cohabiting husband and wife. Each partner in the marriage has an annual exemption for CGT (the individual's exemption for 1996/7 allows capital gains up to £6,300 to be made without incurring a CGT liability), and no CGT liability occurs until the asset is disposed of outside the marriage.

At this point, the CGT liability is calculated as if the receiving partner had received the asset at the original cost to the transferring partner, plus indexation (from the original date of acquisition by the transferring partner) as in the table. The original cost is multiplied by the indexation figure for the month in which it was bought. More detail in the Inland Revenue guide CGT15 *Capital Gains Tax – a guide for married couples*.

CGT is not normally payable on disposals of

- private motor vehicles
- household good and personal effects (often referred to as 'chattels') up to a value of £6,000 per item
- SAYE contracts and National Savings Certificates and Bonds
- Premium Bonds
- betting winnings
- most life assurance policies
- government securities (gilts) and some corporate bonds
- personal injury compensation
- your principal private residence in the UK. On this one, refer to the Inland Revenue guide CGT14 *Capital gains tax – owner-occupier houses*, and see the section on British property on page 170.

Case history: Bob Ransby's capital gain

When Meredith Ransby was offered the job of running the bank's Frankfurt operation, her husband Bob was delighted. 'I'll sell my business!' he said. 'I'll sell it to Amalgamated Plant. Their MD has been sounding me out for months; I've eaten so much lunch at his expense already that he's practically paid out a reasonable asking price already.'

Meredith was relieved. Bob loved making rivets, and she had been worried that he would be reluctant to leave his beloved factory. But he was clearly delighted.

'And if we handle this right,' he continued, 'I can get the proceeds tax-free. And just the other day I was reading in Rivet Monthly that there's unsatisfied demand for rivets in southern Germany. Maybe I should find out about setting up there . . .'

Bob retired to his study, muttering.

Meredith picked up the phone and called the office. Using her contacts, she could set up the whole deal for him.

It was fortunate that Bob rang his accountant immediately to tell him the good news.

'Things are happening fast,' Meredith told Bob's accountant when he came round that lunchtime to help prepare Bob's accounts for the sale. She explained that a team from the bank was already in negotiation with bankers representing Amalgamated Plant.

'Maybe too fast,' Bob's accountant replied. He asked a series of questions, and then said, 'Meredith, you take up the job in May. That means you'll be leaving the country after the end of this tax year. I want Bob to go on ahead of you.'

'Why?' asked Meredith.

The accountant explained about large capital gains. 'I think we would all feel more comfortable, Bob, if you fly out to Frankfurt before this tax year ends, and stay there. Find a property, learn German, start researching the rivet business. And Meredith, I think it would be a good thing if the negotiations with Amalgamated Plant were to slow down. Certainly, I don't want the other side to make an offer before this tax year ends.'

Meredith was horrified. 'But we can't ask that! I know the bankers on the other side. If we ask for something like that, they'll want a reduction in the eventual price in return. Probably they'll ask for something close to the tax we would otherwise have to pay.'

The accountant was thoughtful. 'We can't enter into a formal agreement to defer the sale until the next tax year,' he said. 'We can't refuse an offer now and then accept it when the next tax year begins.' He paused. 'We must play this one carefully,' he said. He looked at Bob.

After a moment, Bob reached for the phone. 'I'm just going to ring my friend the MD of Amalgamated Plant,' he said. 'I owe him some lunch.'

Today, Meredith and Bob are living happily together in a village just north of Frankfurt, in a house they bought with the CGT-free proceeds of the sale of Bob's business. Meredith is busy doing deals, and Bob is a major player in the southern German rivet industry. He has put on two stone.

Death and CGT

If you die, CGT is not payable on the transfer of your assets to your beneficiaries. Instead, they (or more accurately the executors of your will) pay inheritance tax, which is dealt with next.

If you inherit assets from someone who dies, you acquire those assets at probate value, ie, their value as assessed for inheritance tax.

If there is the slightest possibility of your dying while you are overseas, you should read the section of protecting your assets before you finish your pre-departure planning (page 164). This is doubly important if you are taking dependants such as children overseas and leaving others such as elderly relatives in the UK.

Inheritance tax

This may not be immediately relevant to your situation, but it is a tax liability that will remain with you while you are overseas, and one under which, as detailed below, you can give and be given a tax liability.

A UK inheritance-tax liability may arise in two ways.

1. You are liable to UK inheritance tax (IHT*) on your worldwide assets if you are domiciled in the UK.

2. Any assets you have in the UK when you died are liable to UK inheritance tax, regardless of where you are resident or domiciled.

As the Inland Revenue's guide IHT3 *Inheritance tax – an introduction* puts it, 'here's the good news. More than 96 per cent of estates do not have to pay any inheritance tax. There is a threshold, which changes from time to time, below which you do not have to pay IHT.'

The threshold for 1996/97 is £200,000. Above that, IHT is charged at 40 per cent.

Your estate will include any property you have as well as other assets, and it is conceivable that, even in these days of negative equity, the Inland Revenue is optimistic (or just plain out of date) in its calculation that 96 per cent of estates escape the tax altogether.

The taxable sum is calculated after deduction of funeral expenses and outstanding bills, and there are exemptions. In addition to what the Inland Revenue calls 'lifetime gifts' (interchangeably with the more accurately descriptive term 'potentially exempt transfers'), which are dealt with sepa-rately below, the exemptions are as follows:

- Wedding gifts up to £5,000 to your child; up to £2,500 to your grandchild; up to £1,000 to anyone else
- Payment for the maintenance of your spouse, ex-spouse, dependent relatives and children who are under 18 or in full-time education

---

* *To avoid possible confusion with income tax, inheritance tax is abbreviated to IHT, not IT.*

- Other gifts up to £3,000 in any one tax year, plus any unused balance of the £3,000 from the previous tax year. Note that this exempt sum may be carried forward for one year only, and that any gifts given under this heading are counted as coming first from that tax year's exemption, and secondly from the previous year's. A gift of £4,000 under this heading in a year where no gifts had been given in the previous year would count as £3,000 plus £1,000 carried over; thus, no amount would be outstanding to carry over to the following year.

The above exempt gifts may be given in combinations. For example, you may give a child getting married £5,000 plus £3,000 to give an exempt total of £8,000.

- Also exempt are any number of outright gifts of up to £250 each to anybody who has not received any of the other exempt gifts detailed above. Your child getting married could not receive an exempt £8,250.

Note that husbands and wives are assessed separately for IHT as for other UK taxes, so the child getting married could receive an exempt £16,000. You could both give your child's husband or wife to be, a gift of £250.

Note also that gifts must be gifts; you cannot expect to achieve an exemption from IHT on a gift in which you retain an interest (ie, if you continue to receive income on the invested gift, or if the gift is spent to your benefit).

Minor gifts that are funded out of day-to-day income are generally exempt from IHT if they can be shown to have had no significant effect on your day-to-day standard of living. Such gifts are assessable on a case-by-case basis; tax inspectors prefer not to get bogged down in trivia.

Husbands, wives and charities

Anything you leave to your husband or wife, subject to the condition that both of you are domiciled in the UK, is exempt from IHT. There is an obvious pitfall here. If you leave your whole estate to your spouse, your estate and his/hers become one in the eyes of the Inland Revenue. On the death of the surviving spouse, the whole estate becomes liable to IHT. It is, obviously, bigger than either of your estates separately, so the IHT liability is bigger.

If you have children or other intended beneficiaries, the better alternative is to take measures to transfer portions of your estate to them before your death, by means of lifetime gifts/potentially exempt transfers as discussed below. If your children are minors, the transfers can go into trust for them. Trusts are discussed in the section on protecting your assets, on page 164.

Bequests to UK charities, political parties, museums and the National Trust tend to be exempt from IHT.

Potentially exempt transfers

Outright gifts (or transfers) in addition to the exempt gifts detailed above are exempt from IHT if you survive for seven years after making the gift. To be 'outright', a gift has to cease to be in any way beneficial to you after you have made it. You can make a gift to a trust, see page 164.

An outright gift is, therefore, potentially exempt for the seven years after you make it, and not actually exempt until those seven years have passed.

If you die within seven years of making a gift, the recipient may have to pay IHT on the gift, but only if the total value of all your gifts within the seven years exceeds the IHT threshold.

There is, however, a further complication. The total value of gifts made within seven years of your death, whether or not it is above the IHT threshold, is added to the value of your estate for IHT purposes.

This means that although the recipients of the gifts may not themselves have to pay inheritance tax, the executors of your estate will face a greater IHT burden than if you had not made the gifts at all.

'Taper relief' is applied to the tax on lifetime gifts according to how long you survive after making them. Note that taper relief is only applicable to the tax payable by the recipient, and is not available to your estate's executors; it does not reduce the amount of any gift that has to be added to the estate for IHT purposes.

Taper relief alters the percentage of IHT payable by a recipient of a gift as follows:

If you survive for	The percentage payable is
0–3 years	100 per cent
3–4 years	80 per cent
4–5 years	60 per cent
5–6 years	40 per cent
6–7 years	20 per cent

What should the expatriate do about inheritance tax?

You should make a will before you go overseas, and take steps to secure the orderly transfer of your assets in the event of your death.

This might seem an inordinately gloomy attitude to take towards what might be the job opportunity of your life, but dying with assets in more than one jurisdiction can complicate the process of inheritance considerably, and thereby make life difficult for those you leave behind.

That said, you should approach your IHT planning under two headings:

- Mitigating the liability that your death would incur, and
- Mitigating your liability should you inherit assets from others.

The second of these can be dealt with briefly. Inheriting UK-based assets, particularly if they present you with a UK-source income, can abruptly complicate your tax affairs. Also, if you receive substantial potentially exempt tranfers from living people, for the next seven years you face a possible tax demand that will not be affected by your non-resident status. Note that the total value of gifts given in the seven years will dictate whether you receive a tax demand, not the value of your gift alone.

There are two ways of removing yourself and your estate from liability to UK inheritance tax, either wholly or in part, and not transferring the liability to another domicile. They are not to be undertaken lightly, nor are they easy to achieve. They are:

● Giving up UK domicile. This is only possible if you intend never to return to the UK and to sever all your ties to the UK. If this is the case, you have the additional difficulty that to give up your domicile of origin (ie, the UK), you must establish a domicile choice elsewhere. If your domicile of choice lapses, your domicile of origin is reinstated until another domicile of choice is established.

In practice, this means that you cannot give up UK domicile unless you intend to remain in a particular overseas country for the rest of your life. A track record of successive commitments to domiciles of choice, which are broken when contracts end and job opportunities appear in other countries, will not convince the Inland Revenue. Forget this option unless you reach retirement age overseas, and are sure about where you want to spend the rest of your days.

● Giving assets away to an offshore trust, and surviving for seven years. In addition to straightforward gift-giving to others, you can gift all or part of your estate to a trust that is sited offshore, and, in strictly limited circumstances, continue to benefit from it. This option is included for completeness only. Read page 164, and note that trusts are not to be entered into without extensive and detailed professional advice; this caution, which applies to all tax and financial planning, applies doubly to the use of trusts. They are highly complex, and can have repercussions across the whole of your financial and tax affairs. See also the box on look-through legislation on page 103.

To answer the question at the head of this section, you are probably better off limiting your IHT planning for yourself and your own estate to the following.

● Make a will (see page 164).
● Make sure that your partner has sufficient assets independent of your own to provide for living expenses while your estate is frozen in probate, as it will

be on your death. Probate, in brief, is the process of establishing what's yours, what it's worth, and who's responsible for disposing of it. Note that probate can take time where there are assets in more than one jurisdiction.

- Do not move significant assets into a jurisdiction where forced heirship provisions apply. See page 130).
- Make exempt and potentially exempt transfers according to taste. Transfers to dependents too young to look after them properly can be made into trusts (not necessarily offshore) set up for their benefit. See page 164.
- Consider taking out a whole-of-life insurance policy that will pay out on your death. If such a policy is placed in a trust for your beneficiaries, the pay-out will not form part of your estate and can be used to pay off any inheritance-tax liability. The premiums payable would be transfers of value, and so would take the form of potentially exempt transfers unless they fell within the categories of exempt transfer detailed earlier. See page 119.

As with all tax planning, remember that the aim here is not to escape a legitimate tax liability, but to avoid paying more than you have to. Being levied according to domicile, inheritance tax is a uniquely unavoidable tax for British expatriates. Organize your affairs tax-efficiently, but bear in mind the remarks already made in this chapter about the virtues of simplicity. Complicated tax-planning structures are often more trouble than they're worth.

Further information on inheritance tax is available from the Capital Taxes Office, Minford House, Rockley Road, London W14 0DF, telephone 0171 603 4622.

Value-added tax

VAT is an indirect tax; that is, a tax levied on goods and services rather than directly on taxpayers. It is administered by Customs & Excise, not the Inland Revenue. For VAT purposes, the Channel Islands and the Isle of Man are counted as part of the UK.

The main relevance of VAT to the situation of a person going to work abroad is where goods in the destination country are likely to be more expensive than in the home country. This makes it cost-effective to buy such goods before going overseas and export them.

Deciding what to buy before you go is discussed on page 45. The opportunity that arises is that, depending on where you're going, goods bought for export can be free of liability for VAT in the UK if they are exported in compliance with set procedures. However, you should bear in mind that import duties and VAT (or equivalent taxes) may be payable on the import of new goods into your destination country. Not paying UK VAT may be a significant saving (the full rate is currently 17.5 per cent), but the overall cost of the goods here and there should determine where you buy.

Your VAT-planning opportunity varies according to whether you are buying a motor vehicle or other goods, as follows:

- If you are buying a new motor vehicle for export to a destination within the EU, you have the opportunity to pay VAT in your destination country. Jointly complete VAT form 411 with the supplier of the vehicle (who will supply the form), and export the vehicle within two months of receiving it and with less than 3,000km/1,864 miles on the clock. You should retain a carbon copy of VAT form 411. You must declare the car when you import it to your destination country.
- If you are buying a new motor vehicle for export outside the EU, you must take delivery of the car in the UK and export it from the EU within six months (or within twelve months if you have already lived outside the EU for 365 days in the last two years , or 1,095 days in the last six years). Jointly complete VAT form 410 with the supplier of the vehicle (who will supply the form), and keep a carbon copy.

Note that your exemption from VAT depends on your actually exporting the vehicle in both of the above cases; you will have to pay the VAT if you do not export it, even if this is for reasons beyond your control such as theft. You should therefore insure the vehicle for a sum inclusive of VAT while it is still in the UK.

Full VAT will be payable on the vehicle if it is reimported into the UK (or into the EU if it has been exported outside) within six months of export; thereafter, the VAT payable will generally be calculated on the value of the vehicle at reimportation. After twelve months there are exemptions for Crown servants and others, and if VAT can be shown to have been paid elsewhere. Further information from HM Customs & Excise Information Office, New Kings Beam House, 22 Upper Ground, London SE1 9PJ, telephone 0171 620 1313, or from the supplier of your motor vehicle.

Customs & Excise warn that 'it can be very difficult to import motor vehicles into some countries. You are advised to check with the relevant Embassy or High Commission in the UK before placing an order for a vehicle [that is to be exported as above].' Another problem is that Customs authorization for export can take six weeks to come through. If your timing is tight, raise delivery with your supplier at the outset; direct delivery to your destination country can generally be arranged. Also discuss 'type approval' with your supplier at the outset because different countries require different specifications for cars.

For goods other than motor vehicles, VAT-free export can be achieved by means of

The Retail Export Scheme

This is a scheme operated by some retailers that allows them to refund VAT on goods that are exported from the EU within three months of purchase. It is a voluntary scheme, so not all retailers participate; check before you buy.

If you are leaving for a destination outside the EU, you should obtain a copy of VAT form 435 from the retailer at the time you buy the goods. You will buy them at a price inclusive of VAT. The VAT will be refunded when or after you export the goods.

At the time of purchase, you should also establish the procedure whereby you should apply for your VAT refund. This will be subject to your providing proof of export, which involves your getting VAT form 435 certified by Customs at your point of exit from the EU. Your refund will come from the retailer, not from Customs & Excise.

The procedure for applying for your VAT refund will be one of the following:

- Returning your certified form to the retailer, and waiting for a cheque.
- Returning your certified form to a refund company (working for the retailer) and waiting for a cheque.
- Returning your certified form to a refund company (working for the retailer) which has an outlet at your point of departure, and receiving money on the spot less an administrative charge.

You do not get to choose which of the above happens to you; retailers make their own arrangements. You should get a copy of VAT form 435 from each retailer where you make a purchase (note that retailers and refund companies design their own versions of VAT form 435).

You cannot get a VAT refund for a purchase at a retailer who does not operate the Retail Export Scheme.

You cannot get a VAT refund if you are going to a destination within the EU.

Further information on the Retail Export Scheme is available from HM Customs & Excise Information Office at the address given in the previous section, but a better source would be a retailer operating the scheme.

Unless you are making large purchases at few retailers, you may conclude that the Retail Export Scheme is more trouble than it's worth. Many expatriates do.

Seizure

When importing and exporting items of value, remember that customs authorities have the right of seizure where they believe their rules have been contravened. This is to enable them to confiscate contraband, but can be used more widely. If possible carry with you proof of purchase for such items as cameras, jewellery, etc. If challenged, stay calm. There is a true story of an expatriate who arrived for a UK holiday from a cold climate wearing a fur coat. On the way out again, he was challenged: the coat looked new, where had he bought it, and had duty been paid? He couldn't prove anything, lost his cool, and went home without his coat.

Don't get stuck in the local tax system

If you leave the UK to work abroad, and by doing so achieve UK non-resident status for tax purposes, the possibility is that you will become resident, and thus liable to pay tax, in your destination country.

Many overseas tax regimes use residence* to determine tax liability, and many of these use tests including the 183-day rule to determine residence. Just as the British tax system has evolved over centuries (page 90), so has tax practice in other countries taken time to reach its present form. Also, tax systems do not develop in isolation from each other, and even where a jurisdiction is relatively new, one can detect a process whereby the best points of other systems have been acknowledged, adapted or indeed sometimes directly incorporated. The British tax system is one of the oldest – or at least, one of the first to reach a recognizably modern form – and so is one of the most frequently imitated. Wherever you go to work overseas, you will find echoes of the British tax system.

Because you do not necessarily escape all UK tax liability when you leave to work abroad, but you do become liable to tax elsewhere, you could in theory find yourself liable to pay both overseas and UK tax on the same 'chargeable event' (the term applied to any event, such as receipt of salary, which potentially gives rise to a tax liability).

You do not pay tax twice because of

Double tax agreements

Double tax agreements (DTAs; also sometimes referred to as double tax treaties) are bilateral agreements whereby tax authorities agree that only one tax payment shall be made on any double liability, to the authority, which, by the terms of the agreement, has the stronger claim to the payment. The UK currently has 98 double tax agreements in force, of which a full list appears on page 235.

The Inland Revenue issues guidebook IR146 *Double taxation relief – admissible and inadmissible taxes* (this title to be explained in a moment); there is further information in IR6 *Double taxation relief for companies*, but in fact a summary sufficient for most purposes is given at the end of IR20 *Residents and non-residents*.

---

* *Some countries use the term 'fiscal domicile' in place of 'residence'. More confusingly, others simply use 'domicile'. Such terminological confusions often mask the fact that the underlying concepts are similar to the UK's.*

In addition to the taxes relieved bilaterally under the terms of the 98 DTAs, there are foreign taxes not covered by DTAs, in relation to which the Inland Revenue will grant relief unilaterally. Guidebook IR146 lists foreign taxes that are *admissible* for unilateral relief and those that are *inadmissible*. For completeness, it also lists all the taxes that are admissible for bilateral relief under DTAs. Relief is granted as a tax credit; that is, your liability is not removed, but treated as paid off.

In practice, there are very few foreign tax liabilities that you are likely to pay in full, where you will simultaneously pay an identically rising UK tax liability in full (see below for an explanation of 'in full'). The first and most important thing to know about double tax agreements therefore, is that if you are paying tax twice in full on the same chargeable event, you are almost certainly paying more tax than you are obliged to pay.

You are not protected by a DTA from a liability that only occurs in one jurisdiction. You will not be relieved of a UK tax liability under a DTA where you do not incur an overseas tax liability, and vice-versa. (Note: this whole section only applies where you may become liable to tax in two jurisdictions simultaneously on the same chargeable event; you do not need to be tax-resident elsewhere before you can become not resident for tax purposes in the UK. It is possible to be not resident anywhere for tax purposes, although that status is rarely compatible with full-time employment.)

A further point is that if one of two simultaneously occurring tax liabilities is significantly smaller than the other, you may be required to make a top-up payment to the tax authority granting the relief, so that your total payment is equal to the greater of the two tax liabilities, although it is split between the two tax authorities.

Double tax agreements do not prevent you from paying two tax authorities, only from paying the same tax liability twice, in full.

It follows from this that, although you may have completed a tax return in one jurisdiction and paid tax there, you are not thereby relieved of the obligation to make any necessary tax return in another jurisdiction. Complying with the requirements of non-UK tax authorities is discussed further in the next section; the important point to bear in mind is that your obligation to make returns to the Inland Revenue does not necessarily cease when your obligation to pay UK tax ceases.

A final point about the relief of double tax liabilities is that where a foreign tax liability does not qualify for relief either bilaterally or unilaterally, the Inland Revenue may be persuaded to regard the overseas tax payment as reducing the amount of income or gain that is to be assessed in the UK. If you get to this point, you should be communicating with the Inland Revenue through a professional adviser.

If you encounter a tax that is neither bilaterally nor unilaterally relieved, nor capable of reducing the corresponding UK liability, your adviser should put your case for special treatment, or a review of the rules (or both), to the

Inland Revenue International Division (Double Taxation), Room 319, Strand Bridge House, 138–142 The Strand, London WC2R 1HH. This address may be useful if you are going to a less developed country where the tax system is not stable.

General enquiries about the taxes covered by DTAs should be sent to the Inland Revenue Foreign Intelligence Section, Room 7, New Wing, Somerset House, The Strand, London WC2R 1LB.

When you have established your position with regard to UK tax, and identified not only any outstanding UK tax liability but also any outstanding obligation to complete a UK tax return, your next concern is

Your liability to tax in your destination country

As far as possible, this should be established before you arrive. As will become clear in this section, for some countries the form of your employment contract can have an influence on your overseas tax liability.

As a new taxpayer, you have an obligation to comply with the requirements of the tax system wherein you are arriving as a new taxpayer. Compliance tends to mean informing the tax authorities that you are becoming tax-resident, although this is not necessary in all countries, and completing a tax return, which is also not necessary everywhere.

A source of information that has proved useful in compiling this section is the KPMG International Tax Centre's handbook *Taxation of International Executives*, which provides brief but comprehensive guidance on the tax system of 56 countries and is intended for personnel managers and professional advisers of expatriates (see page 147). Another useful book is Price Water-house's *Individual taxes – a worldwide summary*, and also *Transactions: The International Taxation of Employment Manual* edited by David Frost of J Warwick Hardy and published by FT Law & Tax. This last is slanted towards employers, but gives useful guidance.

But your approach to your destination country's tax regime should not be based on books alone. It will normally be the case that your bank or other adviser will either be able to offer advice on your overseas tax liability, or refer you to a firm that can. If all else fails, you can obtain a list of international accountants with the appropriate expertise from the Institute of Chartered Accountants in England & Wales, Chartered Accountants Hall, Moorgate Place, Moorgate, London EC2 2BJ, telephone 0171 920 8100, fax 0171 920 0547. More on the finding of advice in the section that begins on page 147.

It is of limited use to know the rates of tax in your destination country (see the table). You can work out what you will have to pay if you are liable, and your salary package might contain some element of tax equalization. But information from your employer on currently applicable rates of tax is less use than knowing the following:

1. Whether or not you qualify as tax-resident;

2. Whether your resident (or non-resident) status means that you will be taxed on your worldwide income and capital gains;

3. Whether you will be entitled to tax concessions by virtue of your expatriate status;

4. What is the tax year;

5. Whether your destination country imposes restrictions on the export of capital assets;

6. Whether you will require a tax clearance certificate from your destination country's tax authority before you will be allowed to leave.

7. Whether you may expect to be notified of all taxes, including local taxes, that will be levied against you.

Clearly, the last three of these are the most important. The UK no longer has exchange controls, so you may move money in and out freely. Some other countries impose restrictions (and yet others may introduce them unexpectedly, while you are there). These restrictions may not necessarily be found under the heading 'exchange controls'. Spain, for example, lifted its exchange controls in February 1992, but sums in excess of one million pesetas moving across the border must be reported and tax-cleared. France and the USA are other examples of countries that require you to obtain tax-clearance certificates before you may leave the country after a stay longer than a few months. Tax clearance is a process that can take six weeks or more.

Residence for tax purposes is dealt with briefly in the table. As said earlier, it tends to be modelled on the UK example, but in some countries it may be simpler, and in a few it may not be the basis of tax liability. Note that if you face a regime in which residence (and consequent tax liability) depend on your 'de facto residence' or 'effective centre of economic life' or some other such phrase, you may find that your tax liability is determined according to such factors as:

- The jurisdiction in which the company employing you is resident
- The place where your contract of employment was negotiated and is enforceable
- The place where your salary is paid

These take us back to the negotiation of your contract (page 21); but they also suggest the conclusion that you will probably reach in your assessment of the options vis-a-vis your overseas tax liability. We come to this in a moment; there are other points to take into account first.

Overseas tax regimes fall into three groups as follows:

1. Those in which, if you are resident for tax purposes, you will be taxed on your worldwide income and capital gains. These tend to be what one tax practitioner described as 'the more sophisticated jurisdictions', although note that Hong Kong, Singapore and Japan do not fall into this category (see the table).

2. Those in which your liability to tax is not immediate upon your becoming resident, or in which your status as a resident for tax purposes may be deferred.

3. Those in which you will not be liable for tax on your worldwide income and capital gains.

It would be glib to suggest a parallel between the pace of economic activity in a jurisdiction and the individual tax burden, just as it is an oversimplification to point to any link between the level of state social-security provision and tax rates. But the Scandinavian countries impose a relatively heavy tax burden on the individual, while the Pacific Rim 'emerging market' economies tend to be lightweight in tax terms in that a single contract term will not be sufficient to qualify you for full residence, and thus for liability to tax on anything more than locally occurring income. The countries of the Middle East generally do not impose tax on individuals.

You should find out the tax year in your destination country. This may be 6 April to 5 April, but there are many jurisdictions where it runs from 1 January to 31 December (and exceptions to both of these). If this is the case, there may be a three-month period towards the end of your time overseas during which you will be past the end of your last full tax year overseas, but still in the UK tax year before the UK tax year of your return to the UK. You should also establish dates by which tax returns have to be made. Also find out as soon as possible your reference number(s) as a taxpayer to quote when making enquiries.

And the last point: you can't always count on being told what you owe. This applies mainly to local taxes, but an undischarged liability, however small, however old, can hold up tax clearance. You should know the official and other sources of information on liabilities.

The advice you will get on foreign tax liabilities

This will tend to take the form of a four-point plan, as follows:

1. Make contact with the overseas tax authorities, through your adviser;

2. Make your first overseas tax return with the help of your adviser, and thus become connected to the system (in most jurisdictions, tax returns are sent automatically to every taxpayer who completed one last year);

3. Negotiate your employment contract so that you are paid the bulk of your salary outside your destination country, with a remittance to cover living costs paid into a bank account in your destination country;

4. do not move all your assets into your destination country.

This advice should be considered in the context of all the other tax and financial advice you will be receiving at this stage.

Note that tax clearance to leave, as discussed above, does not relate only to tax liabilities on assets sited in your destination country. A jurisdiction that taxes individuals on worldwide income/capital gains will seek to clarify that liabilities have been discharged on worldwide 'chargeable events'.

Your destination country's tax regime

This table gives an impression of how personal income tax is administered in a number of countries. It is compiled by reference to the books mentioned in the text and with information supplied by consulates in London. Rates given are for the tax year ending in 1995. In the second column, 'df' means that in certain circumstances residence status may be deferred or avoided or is not necessarily immediate upon arrival. Note that the information given in this brief table cannot be comprehensive and should not be taken as a basis for any tax planning. 'Clearance' in this table describes any requirement to notify tax authorities before departure.

Country Basis of l'bility	Defined as	Taxed on	Expat. conc.	Tax year	Rtn by	Rate	Clearance
Australia: Res df	183 days	Worldwide	Limited	End 30/6	31 Oct	Up to 47%	No
Austria: Residence	183 days	Worldwide	None	Calendar	31 March	Up to 50%	Yes
Bahrain: No income tax on individuals							
Belgium: Res df	Econ base	Worldwide	Yes on applic.	Calendar	1 mnth of rcpt	Up to 58%	No
Brazil: Residence	Perm. visa	Worldwide	No	Calendar	30 April	Up to 35%	Yes
Canada: Res df	Home/intent	Worldwide	Limited	Calendar	30 April	Up to 29%	No
Cayman Islands No tax							
China: Res df	'Plce of Abode'	Worldwide	Yeson applic.	Calendar	Monthly	Up to 45%	Yes
Cyprus: Res df	Habit. Pres	Worldwide	Yes	Calendar	30 April	Up to 40%	Yes
Denmark: Res df	183 days	Worldwide	Yes	Calendar	11 June	Up to 67%	Yes
Egypt: Salary earned for work done in Egypt			Limited	Calendar	31 December	Up to 48%	No
Finland: Residence	183 days	Worldwide	No	Calendar	31 January	Up to 39%	Yes
France: 'tax domicile'	183 days	Worldwide	Yes	Calendar	28 February	Complex	Yes
Germany: Residence	183 days	Worldwide	No	Calendar	31 May	Up to 53%	No
Greece: Res df	Intent/home	Worldwide	Yes	Calendar	2 March	Up to 30%	Yes
Hong Kong: Tax l'bility on HK-source employment income			No	To 31 March	31 May	Up to 20%	Yes
India: Taxed on Indian-source rcvd inc.		for 1st 9 years	Yes	To 31 March	30 June	Up to 40%	No
Indon.: Residence	183 days	Worldwide	Yes	Calendar	31 March	Up to 30%	Yes
Ireland: Res/dom	183 days	Remitted inc.	Yes	To 5 April	31 January	Up to 48%	No
Italy: Residence	183 days	Worldwide	No	Calendar	30 June	Up to 51%	Yes
Japan: Taxed on Japan-source inc. for 1st 60 months			Yes	Calendar	15 March	Up to 50%	No
Lux.: Residence	183 days	Worldwide	Yes	Calendar	31 March	Up to 50%	Yes
Malaysian: Res df	183 days	Worldwide	No	Calendar	End-April	Up to 32%	Yes
Mexico: Residence	183 days	Worldwide	No	Calendar	30 April	Up to 35%	No
Neths: Residence	Durable ties	Worldwide	Yes	Calendar	1 April	Up to 60%	Yes
NZ: Residence	Abode	Worldwide	No	To 31 March	7 June	Up to 33%	No
Norway: Residence	183 days	Worldwide	Yes	Calendar	End-Jan	Up to 42%	Yes
Portugal: Residence	183 days	Worldwide	No	Calendar	15 March	Up to 40%	Yes
Saudi: No tax on expatriates							
S'pore: Residence	183 days	Local inc.	No	Calendar	15 April	Up to 30%	Yes
S. Africa: Taxed on local-source income			No	end-February	May/June	Up to 43%	Yes
Spain: Residence	183 days	Worldwide	No	Calendar	20 June	Up to 56%	Yes
Sweden: Residence	183 days	Worldwide	Yes	Calendar	2 May	Up to 55%	No
Switz.: Residence	Home/work	Worldwide	Yes	Bi-annual calendar; varies by Canton			Yes
Taiwan: Taxed on local-source income			Yes	Calendar	31 March	Up to 40%	Yes
USA: Residence	Subst. Pres	Worldwide	Yes	Calendar	Quarterly	Up to 40%	Yes

The third and fourth pieces of advice above are partly precautionary. Tax clearance can be a lengthy process, and the amount withheld in the event of an unpaid local-tax liability (or parking fine) is unlikely to be limited to the amount of the liability alone (and a lot of time can be taken in rechecking the whole of a case where one discrepancy has been discovered).

In jurisdictions where assets crossing the border have to be reported, it can be difficult to export a large sum built up from salary and the investment of salary, because a corresponding previous import of a large sum cannot be demonstrated. (This is also a pitfall of buying property overseas: you must declare assets remitted into a country to buy property, or you may not be able to get them out again, see page 170.)

Exchange controls have been mentioned already.

Exchange rates are another factor to consider here. You would be fortunate indeed to find yourself moving back to the UK and Sterling from your destination country's currency at a time when the currency conversion worked in your favour. More on this on page 146.

Other compelling reasons for not being paid and having all your assets in your destination country go beyond the upheaval of your affairs that will be required to get them out again at the other end of your contract. They point to two other considerations:

- The basis of the legal system in your destination country. If you are going to a Roman Law jurisdiction, as distinct from a Common Law jurisdiction such as the UK, you may find that some of the legal concepts, notably trusts, that you may use in organizing your affairs are simply not recognized. Linked to this is the possible problem of
- Forced heirship. This is where the legal system lays down who are the beneficiaries of your estate, and in what proportions, and in doing so, takes precedence over your will. A remote prospect, perhaps, but it can be uncomfortable to be living in a faraway country with your dependants, and know that if you die, the state is going to decide who inherits what.

Combining the advice on UK and overseas tax liabilities

Move your financial affairs outside the UK tax net. Do not move them into your destination country's tax net. That is the advice you will receive as you prepare to go overseas.

But do not think that this means you should therefore move your financial affairs into a third country, with all the tax consequences that would entail.

There is another alternative which combines the advantage that the bulk of your affairs are outside both the UK and your destination country for tax purposes, with the degree of continuity that you would lose by carrying everything with you to your destination country, and taking it away again when you leave to return to the UK. It doesn't give you an additional tax burden, either.

The answer is to put your money offshore

This is not a complicated thing to do, nor is it necessarily any riskier to park your financial affairs in an offshore financial centre, than it would be to leave them with your high-street bank in the UK. But the offshore financial world offers more than just a safe harbour for assets. It offers a wider range of financial and investment opportunities than you would find at home, and greater potential dangers. Sooner or later you will come across both.

So you should know what you're doing. Before you find out anything else about managing your affairs as an expatriate, you should know about the environment in which most of your assets will be based. This means that you should know about offshore centres. You should know how they work and how they control the activities of the offshore financial institutions based in them. More than that, you should recognize that the controls on financial activity vary from centre to centre, so that where an institution is based has a big influence on how cautious you should be before you invest with it.

Then you can start thinking about what to do with your money.

How do offshore financial centres work?

Offshore financial centres (OFCs) tend to be small (most of them are islands) and all of them are, for taxation purposes (though not necessarily others), independent. OFC's provide a low-tax and liberal environment in which financial institutions can manage assets free of onshore restrictions.

They are 'offshore' in that they tend to be adjacent to countries whose capitals are major international financial centres, and they have tended in the past to draw their business from those onshore centres. The Channel Islands and the Isle of Man, for example, have London, while the Caribbean islands have Wall Street and Luxembourg has Germany. Offshore centres began by offering an unrestricted version of home financial life, just across the water (or, in Luxembourg's case, the border).

But offshore centres are no longer so dependent on their neighbours. Money is increasingly international, and modern communications technology means that financial companies can offer a worldwide service from any location. Local conditions – taxes, costs, etc. – dictate the terms of that service, but not its geographical range.

OFCs, therefore, compete for business across the financial world. Neither you, nor a financial institution persuaded to set up in an OFC because people like you represent a worthwhile source of business, have to stay close to home.

How to use OFCs

A new British expatriate will typically choose one of the Channel Islands or the Isle of Man as the base for his finances. The choice will be dictated by the presence of a branch or subsidiary company* of his home bank or building society. The newcomer to expatriate life will move his bank account to the offshore branch of his bank, his savings account to the offshore subsidiary of his buildings society, and he will buy his financial advice as part of the package offered to expatriate clients by the bank or the building society.

As already suggested in Chapter One (page 26), you should do the same. But you should know that offshore centres compete with each other. They do this by introducing new rules (and relaxing old ones) to enable their financial communities to offer more attractive investments than are available from rival institutions in other centres. Such competitive advantages rarely last long, but sooner or later, as your savings accumulate and you reach a position (if you're not there already) where you want to diversify beyond deposits, you will find yourself attracted by opportunities beyond the British offshore islands.

When this happens, you have reached

A time to be careful

Offshore financial centres differ from each other in significant ways. They would not stay in business for long if they didn't provide regulation to guard against out-and-out criminals, because the big financial institutions have onshore as well as offshore reputations to protect and would depart from an OCF rather than be tarnished by association with a resident villain, but different centres target different 'market segments'.

Some go for beginners; others try to attract what the regulator on one Caribbean island described as 'sophisticated high-net-worth international guys who really know what they're doing'. At the time, he was explaining his island's lack of a depositor-compensation scheme (see below). His point was, if you go to that island, you're expected to know enough about what you're doing never to get into a situation where you might want to claim compensation.

There are familiar British high-street names across the offshore world. Indeed, it is an established precautionary measure to stick with familiar names wherever you go. The thing to remember is that in different places, the financial institutions are working to different rules. And they assume you know that.

---

* *Building societies establish subsidiary companies rather than branches offshore, because otherwise, the terms of the UK's Building Societies Act would oblige them to keep their confidential records onshore, as part of their parent society's records, and there would be a theoretical risk that the Inland Revenue could gain unauthorized access to confidential information about offshore account-holders. There is also the consideration that subsidiary companies have more freedom to complete, with a wider range of products, than building-society branches.*

Balancing respectability and risk

Offshore financial centres used to be known as tax havens. This changed in the early eighties. 'Tax haven' began to have unfortunate connotations (for good reasons), and the accelerating internationalization of money made it clear to the OFCs that the real revenue was to be made from attracting the big names of finance.

So the OFCs bought in technology, and embarked upon the process of upgrading their various public images.

A lot of lessons were learned. The foremost was that technology and marketing mean nothing without the effective rule of law. So the OFCs introduced rules and regulations, and, with varying degrees of support from onshore (see below), their own official bodies to enforce them. Their principal selling points remained that they were havens from 'onshore' tax and restriction, but now they could also point to regulatory protection from investors. They had, as it were, gone respectable.

The somewhat paradoxical consequences of all this is that in an offshore centre, you are in a regulated environment where the players are free to behave as they please. One offshore regulator spoke of 'ring-fencing the playground; letting in good people and letting them do what they liked once they're here'.

OFCs face a constant balancing act between maintaining sufficiently tight regulation to ensure respectability, and taking the risk of allowing the freedom to innovate and compete that is, for financial institutions, most of the point of going offshore. Whatever you might hear to the contrary, the balance isn't always successfully maintained. In an offshore centre, whether you're a financial institution with business to attract, or an individual expatriate with assets to protect, risk and freedom go together.

You are correct to move your assets offshore. But you need to pick your centre, and the institutions who will handle your money, very carefully.

Choosing an OFC

If you do go beyond the 'starting position' of having your money with a familiar name in the Channel Islands or the Isle of Man, the process of investing will tend to be that you find yourself attracted to a particular product. Then you decide that the institution offering the product has a good track record and may be trusted to deliver the performance, income, capital growth, etc. (see later under 'Setting clear objectives') that the product is designed to achieve. Then, lastly, you think about where the institution is based. (A variant of this is, of course, that you are attracted to some variety of money-management service. Read on for investment and portfolio-management services, and see the section on 'Discretion' on page 151; otherwise, refer to the section on 'Finding an adviser' on page 147.)

It is as well to think this process through in reverse. The OFC where the institution is based provides the set of regulations under which the product is offered for sale. It is, therefore, the OFC which ensures that you are not defrauded.

- First point: anybody with whom you do business offshore should be able to tell you the regulatory authority by which he is regulated. This information should appear on his headed paper. If significant sums of money are involved (any sum is significant if it's big enough to be investable), you should check with the regulatory authority. You won't get a reference, but you will know that the person (or rather, his company) has complied with basic requirements and may be expected to continue to do so. A list of the regulators in all the OFCs you are likely to encounter may be found on page 212.
- Second point: different OFCs allow different activities, and what is meant by 'regulated' may differ from place to place. Note also that not all activities are regulated, even in the most tightly regulated centres.
- Third point: the regulation of a product or product provider does not necessarily extend to the salesman selling it. A good product from a reputable company can be offered for sale by a criminal who has obtained brochures under false pretences, and who will cash your cheque rather than passing it on. Check the credentials of the person you are dealing with.
- Fourth point: some countries have no regulatory system whatsoever. You may be safer investing offshore than where you are living.

Licences issued by regulators

There's more than one term for everything. Regulatory authorities ('regulators') are also licensing authorities; they regulate by forbidding activity by anybody to whom they have not issued a licence to practise. Thus, you might find yourself asking a professional who is his regulator, and being told about his licensing authority. Don't be confused, it's just words.

Advice from the UK

Because you are overseas doesn't necessarily mean you are not entitled to UK regulatory protection. A company based in the UK, or a product sold to you from the UK, or advice given to you from the UK, is covered by the UK's Financial Services Act. The deciding factor is where the product/service/advice came from, not where you are.

Differences between OFCs

Under the heading 'A time to be careful' above, an offshore regulator was quoted talking about his centre's target market of 'sophisticated high-net-worth international guys' who knew what they were doing. Some OFCs are to be avoided by the non-professional because their regulatory arrangements are predicated on the assumption that investors will be able to look after themselves, and don't need protecting.

The OFC regulating the product, service or salesman you're looking at may boast one or more of the following.

- Designated-territory status. This means that the UK regards the OFCs regulation as up to UK standards, and has 'designated' the centre as a territory from which products may be sold into the UK.
- Investments that are listed as 'SIB recognized' in the *Financial Times* (or wherever else their prices appear). This means that the investments are run in accordance with UK regulatory standards, as above, and may be sold in the UK. The SIB is the UK's senior regulatory body, the Securities and Investments Board. The alternative category, 'Regulated', means that funds are regulated locally and may not be sold into the UK (although this does not necessarily mean that they are to be avoided; reputable companies can run both SIB-recognized and regulated funds).
- British dependent-territory status. The British dependent territories are to be found in the Caribbean; their regulation is funded by the British Overseas Development Administration (ODA). This status has no explicit link with the suitability of the centre for the risk-averse, but the regulatory apparatus was inserted by the UK and may be assumed to run to UK standards.
- Investor protection. The catch-all term for the protection you receive when you invest with a regulated institution. As said earlier, it varies from place to place, does not exist everywhere, and is worth asking questions about because it does not necessarily amount to
- Compensation. Some centres regulate the activities of institutions but offer nothing to investors when those activities lead to bankruptcy. Other centres will offer limited compensation to the victims of collapse. The existence of a compensation scheme does not remove the obligation on investors to exercise caution.

Questions to ask

Partly to understand the situation, but also partly because salesmen can tend to hurry things when they're trying to get your signature on a dotted line, it is good to have questions ready.

'I'm not quite clear on where this product is going to be managed from . . .'

'Does that mean that the managers are regulated by the authorities in . . .'

'So the authorities in . . . do regulate [banks, fund managers, trust companies, whatever]?'

'What about you? Are you also regulated by the authorities in . . .'

'Is the regulator mentioned on your business card/headed paper?' [If it isn't, don't sign: all regulators require that it has to be.]

'I see, and where is the regulator mentioned on the product brochure?'

'Do you have a licence?'

'What's your registration [or licence] number? And where is the product provider's number on the brochure?'

'I see, so if I wanted to check up on you, how do I do it?'

'What did you have to do to get regulated?'

You need satisfactory answers to your questions, but equally important is the attitude with which they are given. A properly regulated person will sit through this part of the sale process patiently, because your asking such questions is a sign that you're getting ready to buy. A crook will be impatient, or try to get round giving simple answers. End the conversation with:

'That's very interesting, thanks for your time. Leave the paperwork with me, and I'll get back to you if I decide to invest.'

A simple rule of offshore investment, which will be repeated further on, is that there is never any hurry to do anything. Sleep on it.

A cautionary but comforting tale

Barings Bank collapsed, in February 1995, because loss-making activities in Singapore were successfully concealed from both the London and Singapore authorities. London regulated the London head-quarters of the bank, but failed to prevent the collapse; Singapore regulated the Singapore end, but also failed to save Barings.

Some remembered the BCCI collapse a few years earlier, when a debate had followed about whether London or Luxembourg had been the 'lead regulator' of BCCI and so should have taken action. Those with longer memories remembered the Barlow Clowes affair, when regulatory ambiguities between London and Gibraltar had led to many British expatriate investors in southern Spain being defrauded of large sums of money.

Now, regulators are responsible for what happens on their own patch. Information is exchanged, but for every company coming into an OFC, the buck stops with the OFC's regulatory authority.

A little-publicized footnote to the Barings story is what happened to its subsidiary Barings Fund Managers, based in Guernsey. Barings Fund Managers had to close while the catastrophe was sorted out, and its clients could not get at their money.

But Barings Fund Managers was a well-run, properly regulated, solvent and perfectly respectable operation in its own right. It was regulated by Guernsey, and but for problems with its parent, could have continued in business without interruption. Guernsey-watchers were struck by the way other financial institutions on the island offered facilities to Barings Fund Managers clients on the security of their frozen assets, and became aware that Barings Fund Managers staff, on enforced holiday, were receiving calls from recruitment consultants acting for those other institutions.

Proper regulation can stand you in good stead, even in the worst of situations.

Choosing an offshore financial institution

As suggested earlier, you will tend to encounter an unfamiliar offshore financial institution because you have been attracted to a product that fits with your objectives and the balance of investments within your portfolio (these are discussed beginning on page 144). You will not so much choose a financial institution, therefore, as choose a product and then evaluate its provider. (That said, you may identify a class of products in which to invest, and then choose between different providers.)

Many financial institutions in the UK have offshore operations. Among these are banks, building societies, investment managers, life assurance companies, accountants, financial advisers and others. They have come offshore to tap a market to which they do not have access from the UK. Their UK-source products may give rise to UK-source income, for example, which will deter many offshore investors because it will give rise to a UK tax liability. So they launch offshore equivalents of their UK product range.

There is a convincing case to be made for restricting your investment activity to companies that have names familiar from the UK. This is because a company with an onshore reputation to protect will have an added incentive to 'self-regulate' the activities of its offshore arm. In some cases, this has a legal basis: the UK building societies, for example, are obliged to underwrite the activities of their offshore subsidiaries. Most UK banks and many other financial institutions explicitly underwrite their offshire subsidiaries.

But the familiarity of the name is not necessarily a guarantee of anything. There are examples of big-name companies that have gone bust, and if your money is going to be with the offshore arm, it follows that your assessment of whether or not to invest should concentrate on the offshore arm.

Judge an offshore company according to two criteria:

- Whether it is properly constituted, properly regulated and well run in its own right.
- Whether the performance of the products it offers is competitive.

The first of these is the more important. Remembering what has been said about checking the credentials of both the provider of the product and the person or company selling it,* you should establish the regulatory authority to which the company is answerable, and confirm what you are told with the regulator (see page 212 for the necessary address). With the offshore arm of an onshore name, clarify the relationship between the two. Confirm what you are told with the onshore company, having established what office onshore is responsible for the offshore operation. Request a copy of the latest report and accounts.

Note that such references as you receive will not give any indication as to whether or not you should invest your money with the company; they will simply state the present position vis-a-vis the referee's awareness of the company. This is because any negative reference given prior to an actual legal judgement in court is potentially libellous. You will never persuade a financial professional to say that you should not invest your money with a company; if what you are told is potentially ambiguous, you will never persuade a financial professional to admit that he intended what he said to be ambiguous (even if he did). There are those who suggest that the precise phrasing of a comment on a company or individual can be significant, but this is to place too much reliance on the sayings of people who

1. might not be choosing their words carefully after all, or
2. might not know any more than you do. Professionals aren't necessarily well informed.

Ultimately you are on your own.

A final point: small signs of inefficiency are inauspicious. If a company cannot reply to your letter, or cannot provide the information you asked for, this is evidence, albeit small, of maladministration. It cannot be positive, and may be negative. Think how tedious it will be if what goes astray is a cheque payable to you.

As to performance, there are simple rules.

- Prices can go down as well as up;
- Historical performance is not a promise of similar results in future;
- Simulated performance is meaningless.

Find out where the company lists the prices of its investments. These will tend to be in the *Financial Times* daily, and more detailed commentary and performance figures may be found in the specialist expatriate magazines such

---

* *You should establish the degree to which an intermediary is independent of the product provider whose products he sells. Some salesmen are 'tied agents' in that they are contractually committed to offering the products of one company, while others are completely independent. Another point to establish: a salesman paid on commission should not be influenced by the amount of commission he is offered by different companies, although he might be. If you are buying products through an adviser who will receive a fee from you for his advice, you may assume that he is not being influenced by the product providers. See also page 212.*

as *Resident Abroad, The International* and *Investment International* (addresses, page 232). The expatriate magazines all provide regular surveys concentrated on particular product types or on particular offshore financial centres and the products and services available from them.

When judging the performance of an offshore financial institution, concentrate on consistency rather than headline-grabbing short-term excellence. This, and the complicated business of putting together a portfolio of investments that will maximize the benefits of your time overseas, are discussed in the next section.

The expatriate approach to personal finance, savings and investment

This section covers the general principles, and many of the specifics, according to which you should order your financial affairs.

Although the first thing to do when you face working abroad is to find and take professional advice (see page 147), it is equally important to recognize that you do not delegate responsibility for your financial wellbeing to an adviser when you decide to follow his advice – or indeed, when you decide to hand over full or partial responsibility for managing your affairs to any intermediary.

Just as you must take all possible care when choosing your adviser, so you must develop the knowledge and understanding to judge the quality of his advice on a continuing basis. As your situation changes, so your objectives will change, and your needs, and your attitudes. Unless you can keep track of what is being done on your behalf, you will not know whether those changes are being taken into account – or indeed, whether any success achieved is as much as you might reasonably expect.

Any relationship with an adviser will be more likely to prosper on a basis of mutual understanding. It is for this reason that, as is discussed in the section on choosing an adviser on page 147, a competent adviser will begin by asking you questions.

This is partly because he needs to know what you want him to do, but also partly because he needs to get at those of your attitudes that you may not yet have thought through completely. He also wants you to know what he can realistically do for you.

This section begins with the main questions you should be asking yourself, and your adviser will ask you, plus the main factors that will govern your financial strategy during your time abroad. Think things through now so that in future you can operate from a position of strength.

And then of course you can rely on others to take the decisions and do the work for you. But always remember that if you lose money, it's no comfort that it was somebody else's fault.

Is investment really necessary?

Yes. In the expatriate world, personal finance requires a more active approach to investment matters than would be necessary in the UK. To take one example, you cannot operate with more than one currency without taking what a professional would call a 'view' on exchange rates. The role of currencies in your life, and how to deal with them, are discussed on page 146.

As an expatriate, you may be receiving more money than before you went overseas and paying less tax on it, and being offshore, you are freer to do what you like with it than you were in the UK. But freedom brings responsibility: doing nothing, in a world of opportunity, is an option that you should consider carefully before – probably – rejecting it. The 'opportunity cost' of not at least considering ways of maximizing the benefits of your situation is potentially as great as that of keeping your money in a box rather than in an interest-bearing bank account.

Risk, in every sense, including the risks involved in trying not to take any risks, is discussed on page 143.

But there is a third reason why you should develop at least a working knowledge of investment. It is negative. It is, simply, that as an expatriate you do not have to look for investment opportunities; they will seek you out. They will be persuasive, and you will need the know-how to decide whether to fall for them.

This aspect of expatriate life is discussed on page 147.

Your financial affairs on departure from the UK

Refer to the checklist on page 26. You should have your bank accounts at a branch offshore;* these should include an instant-access ('call') account with a cheque book as well as any savings accounts. You should establish standing-order payments to cover continuing UK liabilities, and transfer direct-debit arrangements offshore.

You should have a bank account already open at your overseas location, with a balance equivalent to at least one month's salary and preferably more (see below). If your employer is not paying your salary divided between living costs to your destination country, and the bulk offshore, you should arrange a standing transfer of funds from offshore to this account; expect to vary the amount transferred.

---

* *By concession, the Inland Revenue will not seek to recover tax due on interest accruing to a UK bank or building society deposit account if the account holder declares that he or she is not resident in the UK for tax purposes; this declaration should be made to the bank/building society and will allow interest to be paid gross. However, this concession is subject to a number of conditions, and can complicate an individual's tax position. This tax relief is not available for the years of departure from and return to the UK. It is probably better to transfer all your accounts offshore. Note that UK joint-account interest is taxable if only one holder is not resident.*

Your expenditure will be high at first, as you furnish and equip your accommodation, and then it will reduce as you settle in and, for example, begin to discover the less expensive shops and the markets.

You may have

Investments that were tax-efficient in the UK

You may have a Tax-Exempt Special Savings Account (TESSA) and one or more Personal Equity Plans (PEPs). Additionally, you might have one or more UK life-assurance policies, taken out for one or more reasons.

TESSAs may be held by non-residents. If you have one already, you will already have deposited up to £3,000 in the first year and one or more subsequent-year deposits of up to £1,800. You must hold your TESSA for five years to receive the interest tax-free. If the five-year term ends while you are overseas, there is little point in making further deposits as you can get interest tax-free elsewhere. If, however, the five years will end after you return to the UK, your TESSA represents a method of deferring receipt of a tax-free sum until after you become liable once again to UK tax.

PEPs may not be held by non-residents. If you have a PEP already, it will be frozen from the date of your departure from the UK and you may not make payments into it while you are non-resident.

If you have one or more UK life-assurance policies, check that your life cover will continue after you have left the UK.

Some UK life-assurance policies pay their benefits tax-free to the policy-holder; this is not as attractive to the non-resident as to the resident, because in such cases, the UK life company itself remains taxable on the gains it receives from the life policy's underlying investments. This indirectly reduces the total return to the policyholder.

The tax-efficient alternative for expatriates is to invest in offshore policies with offshore life companies which are free of tax. However, surrender values on 'young' UK life policies are not high, and the proceeds of offshore policies that come to term after return to the UK are generally taxable according to the proportion of their term during which the policyholder was resident in the UK.

This means that there may be a case for allowing UK policies to continue during the non-resident years, because the cost of cancelling them may cancel the gain of replacing them with offshore policies.

Life assurance is discussed further on pages 157 and 181, and in the context of returning to the UK on page 188.

Other UK investments

You may have a portfolio of investments that pay you interest or a dividend income on which UK tax is deducted at source. You are entitled to tax allowances on your UK-source income in the UK tax year 1996/97 up to £3,765 (plus £1,790 married person's allowance) – see page 108.

If your UK-source income falls within your allowance, you will generally be able to have interest paid to you gross by declaring your non-resident status to the organization paying the interest, and to reclaim tax deducted at source on dividends. Beyond this, there are provisions in most double-tax agreements (see page 124) whereby tax is relieved in the UK because it is payable in the country of residence.

There is one important exception to this.

● Gilts (government stocks). For tax purposes, these may be divided into two groups: those which have UK tax on interest deducted at source irrespective of the residence status of the holder, and those on which interest may be paid gross to non-residents. If you have the latter, consider holding onto them; they represent a secure investment vehicle albeit one that has been distinctly sober in performance terms.

It is a general rule of investment that equities and unit trusts and other vehicles that offer the prospect of captial growth should be held in the long term. It follows from this that the treatment of dividend income is not necessarily the primary concern in deciding on a course of action for such investments. However, if you have UK-invested capital that has grown, and on which you experience a tax complication via the dividend income, it may be appropriate to sell once you are not resident and thus not liable for CGT, and then return to the UK market via an offshore fund that invests in UK equities (see page 131 for more on offshore funds).

A financial strategy to make the most of life overseas

The first thing you need when you go overseas is a warning.

There is a great deal of financial advertising targeted at expatriates, pressing this, that or the other investment opportunity. In the next few months, you will receive many mailshots, frequent invitations to investment seminars at local hotels (good social events, but sleep on it before signing anything), and probably a fair number of cold calls from salesmen. This is because the financial world sees new expatriates as people with plans to make and money to invest.

Rule one of expatriate finance: once your money is safely offshore, do nothing for three months at least. You need time to settle in and concentrate on the job, and you need to think about your objectives (see below). You also need time to let some money accumulate in your bank account (which will undoubtedly take longer than three months).

Rule two: your approach to the whole range of investments facing you throughout your time overseas, should never be that you must do something.

Not investing is neutral. Invest because an opportunity fits your objectives, never for any other reason.

It is, therefore, essential to spend your first months overseas.

Setting clear objectives

If you don't know what you want, you can't go out and get it. But you need to establish what's worth wanting, in terms of your being able to achieve it, and it being achievable.

Your first objective is to maintain and improve your standard of living, both now and for the future. Expand on that. Draw up a forward plan under two headings.

1. How your circumstances, financial and otherwise, will be likely to change in the foreseeable future, and

2. What you will need to pay for in the short, medium and long term.

Under the first heading, you might note, for example, that you can rely on your relatively high overseas income for three years, but then face the probability that you will be back in the UK on a lower income.

Under the second, you might list, for example, that you will have school fees to pay in certain years, and that you hope to be able to retire at a particular date. You could equally well write down that you want to spend as long as possible living life to the full and spending every penny you earn.

Whatever you write down, it should be realistic. It should be sufficiently fixed that you can commit yourself to a strategy of achieving it, but you should be able to vary it if your circumstances change. Objectives are never fixed, they constantly evolve. But without them, you can't get anywhere.

Your objectives will begin to indicate whether your portfolio of investments should be structured to achieve income, capital growth, a combination of the two, or one and subsequently the other. Thus, you can start to see the broad shape of a portfolio that will be suitable for you.

Once you know what you want, you should consider how far you are prepared to go to get it. That is, you should weigh up

Risk versus return

When you invest in something that offers a high return, you take a high risk. There are no exceptions to this rule.

All financial intermediaries will be concerned to establish your 'risk'. However, they will tend to go a roundabout way towards establishing it. This is because risk tolerance is more than just a matter of choice.

If you have serious and unavoidable commitments, you cannot be risk-tolerant. If, for example, you have children just entering UK private education and dependent parents just entering private nursing homes, you cannot take big risks on the off-chance that they will pay off. You need to keep your money secure in order to protect your ability to pay the bills. (Note that if you are in such a situation but without sufficient money to pay the bills, taking big risks is not a reliable way to improve matters.)

The more immediate difficulty with establishing risk tolerance is that the promised return on a risky investment is often far more visible than the risk. It is easy to like the headline figures, but overlook the probability that it will not be achieved. The point about risky investments is that they are less likely to deliver what they promise.

There is, however, another consideration under the general heading of risk. It is that some investments do better than others, and that money itself as a medium of exchange loses value. If you do nothing, your assets will gradually dwindle as a result of inflation. If you commit yourself entirely to one form of investment, you risk that your assets diminish relatively because other investments increase in relative terms. Therefore, you should not leave a substantial portfolio in a single form of investment, even if that form is notionally safe: investing in another ultra-safe deposit account when you already have several is to increase your risk of not being in the best-performing investment.

This means that whatever your objectives, your strategy should be to achieve them by means of

A balanced portfolio

At its simplest, this means that you should combine different investments in your portfolio. Their different characteristics will give you a better chance of sustaining a positive return on your money, whatever market conditions. If you hold interest-bearing deposits, for example, you will prosper when interest rates are high but the economic situation in general is not good. At such a time, however, you might devote some of your money to buying equities because these will be low-priced. When the economy begins to recover, your equities will increase in value, but the interest rates on your deposits will go down. You have, therefore, replaced income with capital growth.

But this is a simplistic example. At first, you should concentrate on building up money on deposit so that you will have enough to invest when you are settled. The construction of your portfolio is discussed later (page 151). First, you have more practical matters to consider.

Income, outgoings and the currency factor

Currencies fluctuate. That's the problem and the opportunity. If you are a 'Sterling thinker', in that you are paid in Sterling, and transfer money to and from Sterling-denominated bank accounts, you face a currency transaction every time you pay or receive money in another currency.

Perhaps the answer is to transfer all your assets into the currency of the country where you are working? But if you do this, you face one single massive currency transaction when you return to the UK. The same is true if you are paid in US dollars and operate to and from dollars. [Note that large currency conversions are chargeable events for UK CGT purposes; convert as much as possible back to Sterling in the tax year before you return to the UK.]

The prudent answer is to maintain a substantial balance in each of your primary currencies of operation. The balance should be sufficient that you will not need to make substantial transfers at times other than of your own choosing.

With assests in more than one currency, if you can choose when to transfer assets from one currency to another, you have the ability to make substantial gains in the course of simple day-to-day money management. The key is to avoid forced transfers: budget currency assets to cover that currency's liabilities.

Currency targets

Your starting position will include a balance of Sterling-denominated, UK-oriented investments. With regard to currencies, your approach should be simultaneously cautious and opportunistic: you should have banking facilities (see below) and cash balances in all the currencies in which you may incur liabilities. These will include Sterling, your destination country's currency, the currency in which you are paid if it is not Sterling, any other currency to which you might be exposed (you might find a dollar-denominated credit card useful, for example), and any currency in which you might think of investing (but forget about this one until you find yourself noticing investment opportunities in other currencies). Be aware of shifts in exchange rates, and build up your balances at opportune moments. Don't be tempted to go beyond the amount you think you might need in each currency, and don't imagine that a small gain on an exchange make you a currency speculator. Do this for practical reasons.

Your ultimate target will be a return to Sterling. Dollar thinkers, paid in dollars, should be working towards a portfolio of Sterling investments. Remember that you have a 'finish currency' as well as a start currency, and that having time in hand is crucial. Converting back to Sterling at a bad moment can lose you a lot of money. The end of the tax year before the tax year of your return is a firm deadline to have your most substantial assets in Sterling.

Other-currency banking

Many expatriates run a multi-currency bank account alongside their offshore account. Such accounts are offered by all the main offshore banks, and can provide cheque books, etc. as well as free or cheap switching between currencies. While a local account where you live is necessary, a multi-currency offshore account will stand you in good stead. Make a realistic appraisal of costs, and remember that an account offering facilities in twenty-seven currencies is no more useful than one offering ten, if you don't think you're ever going to need more than five.

Currencies in investment

You can't get away from currencies in investment, unless you do everything in your start currency, which is not a practical limitation to set upon yourself.

The point is that just as a badly timed conversion can lose you money, so can a badly timed realization of even the most high-performing investment, if you do this when the exchange rate is against you.

The answer is, just as above, to back up other-currency investments with banking facilities in their currency, so if you want to 'lock in' a gain by selling the investment, you can do so without having to make a conversion at the same time. There are two transactions here; separate them.

Currencies as investments in their own right

Properly, this section belongs later, in the section on the components of a balanced portfolio (page 152), but it is in the nature of expatriate life that one encounters currencies long before one is thinking about other investments, and to encounter currencies is to become aware of the gains (and losses) that they can be used to make.

It is wrong to think of currencies as a means of making money until you are familiar with all the alternatives. Currencies are volatile and unpredictable. It is a basic principle that investment should be for the long term, and currencies by their nature are difficult to reconcile with long-term planning.

Beyond one's own speculation, there are two main methods of investment in currencies.

Single-currency funds (for more on funds generally, see under 'Collective investments' on page 155) are a method of having your money invested by a professional in a particular currency. Their advantage is that other currencies might be offering better interest rates than Sterling (the Bank of England sets the base rate for Sterling, while the Bundesbank does for the Deutschemark and the Federal Reserve does for the US dollar) and the fund manager will try to maximize the fund's return on the currency.

Managed currency funds move from currency to currency, and seek to benefit from changes in their relative values as well as from each currency's return.

The important thing about currencies and currency traders is that they are sensitive to political and other non-economic shifts. This makes them moveable by 'market sentiment', which is the term for traders' herd instinct.

Remember that currencies are unpredictable. This means that they are not only volatile, but also capable of sustaining a trend for an uncomfortably long time. Don't overextend yourself in a currency you don't want for the long term.

Currencies, credit cards and other liabilities

Investment is not a separate and distinct activity from the rest of your life. Remember to balance your likely liabilities with assets; remember that wherever there is a transfer from one currency to another, there is a potential loss or gain. Credit cards in particular are dangerous; have enough cards to be able to spend and settle in the same currency.

Finding and making the best use of professional advice

It is easy (and explained below) to find the names of tax, financial and other advisers. What is less easy is to get guidance on who is good and who is bad, and equally important, on who specializes in expatriate matters. Long periods can be wasted ringing names on lists of, say, tax advisers, to be told that they don't specialize in matters of residence and non-residence.

This section deals with finding advisers, assessing them, forming relationships with them, and using them. The first rule of advice is that you need it. This is because expatriate tax, finance and life generally is so full of complications and technicalities that do not affect UK residents, that you are in danger of not knowing the questions to ask, let alone the answers.

As was pointed out at the beginning of this section, even something so superficially clear-cut as tax law is a matter of interpretation. The rates, allowances, etc., are not there simply to be applied; they have to be balanced with other factors, and interpreted. On anything where there might be a disagreement, such as the terms of your contract, your position will be a lot stronger if you have professional advice on your side.

How to find a good adviser? Best to approach the answer to that question by taking advice on it.

The professional view on finding advice

To turn the question on its head, when you ask advisers how they come by their clients, they say:

- by personal recommendation
- because their employers refer them
- because they find our name in specialist publications like *Resident Abroad*, *The International* or *Investment International*, or in books like this one.

They tend to agree that there is no single source of advisers, and that it would help if there was one. Some of them suggest that a possible source of a tax adviser would be an estate agent or property manager, because people have properties, and properties lead to tax questions (of which, more on page 00).

As a first rule of advice, it is a good idea to have, or at least be aware of, sources of advice independent of your employer. This is because your needs will not necessarily continue to coincide with your employer's. If you are dismissed, for example, you will not approach the company's solicitor for advice on sueing for wrongful dismissal.

Many advisers mention the Centre for International Briefing (CIB; page 31). This is a source of information, but also a source of sources of further information. The library at the CIB is extensive; use it if you are there for noting down useful addresses as well as reading.

Many advisers mention the *Expatriate Survival Kit* published by FT Magazines; others refer to Employment Conditions Abroad, Going Places and Coronoa Worldwide, who are covered in the section on briefing on page 30. Godwins International (page 20) is an adviser frequently mentioned by advisers because it will advise on the legality of contracts, and on the subject of tax advice and financial planning, it is common to find advisers referring to such organizations as The Fry Group, Wilkins Kennedy, Ambrose Associates and Lomond Asset Management (addresses on page 214).

What advice you will need, and where to get it

Do not go overseas without the names and addresses of lawyers in your destination country, and of lawyers in the UK who have offices in your destination country. The Law Society can supply you with lists of such lawyers (all addresses for this section are given on page 218).

You will also need tax advice, mainly UK-oriented but also on your potential overseas liabilities.

The large accountants such as KPMG and Price Waterhouse have offices in many locations overseas, although they tend to be expensive. The Institute of Chartered Accountants can supply you with lists of chartered accountants, although these lists will not tell you which firms specialize in expatriate tax affairs.

The expatriate magazines cannot recommend tax advisers, but they can provide names of specialists in the expatriate field. *Resident Abroad* in particular issues a list of such advisers.

You will need financial and investment advice. Lists of advisers may be obtained from the Personal Investment Authority (PLA) in London, and from the equivalent bodies in such centres as Jersey, Guernsey and the Isle of Man. Note that the big banks' offshore operations offer various facilities to intending expatriates, and that among these is often reduced-rate access to financial and other advice from designated specialists.

Advice priorities

When you ask advisers for the subjects on which they are most frequently asked for advice, and on which they most frequently need to give advice, they mention UK tax ('Typically, we would end up submitting a 6-page report on what they should do, and why') and methods of investing prudently, with overseas tax coming a distant third. This is because 'all expatriates need to worry about UK tax and how to look after their money; but overseas tax is often hardly a problem. Countries in the Gulf, for example, don't tax expatriates; others, like Singapore, Hong Kong and Malaysia, tax only locally arising income unless you're going there forever.'

Assessing and using an adviser

Advice is as good as the information on which it is based. For this reason, a good adviser will ask questions before he offers any advice. For this reason also, you should provide full answers. This process is worthwhile for the additional reason that it will enable you to formulate more clearly your own objectives, and to establish whether or not they are achievable.

All advisers should be subject to a regulatory authority, as on page 216. There is a further, subjective, consideration.

Advice is for the long term, and an adviser will tend to get more useful to you as time goes by, because he will develop a greater understanding of your circumstances and you as a person. For this reason, go by your instincts. You and your adviser are, ideally, going to be working together for a long time, so there is practical value in choosing an adviser whom you like (and who enjoys his work: the better tax adviser is the one who wants to tell you about his conversation with the Inspector on CGT, not the one who's always keen to get out of the office and buy a round of drinks).

There is a further consideration.

Paying for it

Advice is a commodity. Pay for it. There are various types of adviser, and in the field of financial advice particularly, an important distinction is to be made between those whom you pay, and those who get their income from commission on the investments they recommend that you should buy. A principle is that only if you pay for advice can you be sure that the adviser is acting in your best interests alone. Only if you pay for advice do you have redress against the adviser if it turns out not to have been good advice in the circumstances.

This is not to say that you should never accept anything said by a person who is not going to invoice you for saying it, but you should remember that in any commercial relationship, human nature dictates that the first loyalty is towards the source of remuneration.

Tied agents, independent advisers and disclosure

In the UK and to a limited extent elsewhere, a broker or other intermediary whose work involves recommending investments is obliged to tell you how much commission or other return he gains from selling you one investment rather than another. This applies to insurance products particularly, and the trend is for it to be applied across all investment classes. You should ask for this information, and establish that the broker's judgement is not potentially clouded by the fact that one investment will net him a bigger return than another.

You should also establish whether an intermediary selling you an investment is a 'tied agent', in that he only recommends one financial institution's products and services, or an independent adviser, in that he can look across the whole range of investments in a particular class to find those that will suit you. The distinction here is akin to that between pubs tied to a particular brewery, and free houses.

The limits of advice

When you act on a piece of advice that turns out to be wrong, you're the one who loses money. Note that regulation is as much concerned with competence as with fraud.

There is a saying that fools are more dangerous than criminals, because fools are doing it all the time. An incompetent adviser can cost you dearly in lost opportunities as well as lost money, and for this reason you must not only take great care over the process of choosing somebody whose advice you will follow, but also remember that whoever is advising you, you can't completely divorce yourself from responsibility for ensuring that you are doing the right thing, and that your affairs are in a proper order. Even where an accountant completes a tax return for you, for example, you're the one who has to sign it, and you're the one responsible for any wrong figures.

It's your money and your future. You can and should get advice on just about everything to do with working abroad, but the rule is: if it doesn't feel right, don't do it until you've got a second opinion. Trust advisers, but trust yourself more.

Portfolio management services

Beyond straightforward financial advice is portfolio management. You can hand over some or all of your money to a professional manager who will invest it for you. There are two types of portfolio management, and these are

Discretionary management

in which the manager is free to do as he thinks fit with your money, without consulting you first, and

Advisory management

in which the manager has to seek your approval before he does anything.

There are degrees of discretion, in the sense that one can set a limit on the amount that can be invested or liquidated without approval, and one can set limitations such as 'nothing in tobacco companies'. The argument for professional management is akin to that for collective investments (page 155), and the argument for granting discretion is that you might miss the price that persuaded the manager to buy, by being unobtainable to give your approval in time. There is also the additional administrative burden for an advisory manager of having to record different buying and selling prices for each client, and some companies will not accept advisory portofolios.

However, there are other considerations.

- Are you sufficiently expert to handle your investments to your own satisfaction, and
- Will you have the time?
- If it all goes wrong, would you be happier if you had made your own mistakes? Losing money feels a lot worse if somebody lost it for you – and you paid him to do it.

The argument for granting discretion is that without an eye on the market, you will miss out on important opportunities that won't recur. You won't sell in time, either.

The common pattern is for expatriates to start out more or less completely discretionary, using the bank but not being active enough for the time factor to matter. Then they get advisory, as they become more informed, and clearer on their own attitude to risk, objectives, etc. Finally, they're so successful, and so in demand as clients because of the amount of money they now have, that they go back to discretionary, but on their own terms.

Constructing your portfolio of investments

The single most important thing to know about any single investment opportunity is that it isn't necessary. You don't have to do any of it.

Nor does anybody know better than you do. Even the most closely reasoned analysis of a market, replete with figures and percentages and trends, doesn't turn a forecast into a safe bet.

Take advice on where to invest and what investments to choose, but make your own final decisions based on your objectives (page 141), and invest defensively. The primary purpose of spreading your assets across a balance of the investment vehicles described below is not to make yourself rich, but to defend yourself against the damaging effects of inflation and fluctuating economic conditions.

Investments for your portfolio

At times of uncertainty or recession, investors keep a substantial proportion of their assets liquid – ie, in instant-access interest-bearing deposits – for two reasons. When an economy is in recession, interest rates are higher to stimulate investment; and when companies and their shares are doing badly, the most clearly visible possibility is that they will do worse. So money is kept close to home, where at least it will be safe (even if it will not appreciate) and where it will be readily available if needed (in case of, for example, redundancy).

Overlooking the truism that the best time to invest is when prices are at their lowest (overlooking it because in practice this is potentially risky and very difficult to do), the clear sign that the 'bear' (pessimistic) market has given way to a 'bull' (optimistic) market is that retail investors (you and I) start to migrate across to the 'next-safest' investment class, which combines a better potential reward with slightly greater risk.

This tends to happen well after the lines on the various graphs measuring the economy's performance have passed their low points; indeed, when much of the gain to be had from buying low is already in the past. Note that a bear or bull market is defined by investors' perception of what is happening, rather than necessarily what is actually happening. Note also that professionals take into account what they think we're thinking: if we're all buying, prices will be going up and they'll be looking for a moment to sell.

In compiling a balanced portfolio, you move across the spectrum of possible investments, buying when market conditions make it advantageous to do so. What you buy depends on the objectives you want to achieve by investing, and thus on whether the characteristics of the particular classes of investment match those objectives.

But you should also spread yourself across the whole range of possible investments, so that at least some part of your portfolio will perform well whatever the market's doing. Don't move out of something to move into something else; have both in proportions that vary according to market conditions.

When professionals talk about a 'migration from deposits', they are referring to a progression from the least towards the most potentially rewarding investment vehicles (remember that riskiness increases in line with potential reward). The following is a list of possible components of your balanced portfolio, in approximate order of their distance from 'safety' as represented by deposits. Remember that a mix is safer than putting all your assets in one investment class.*

Banks and building societies

The liquid end of the spectrum. Building societies tend to offer marginally higher rates, and to be more enthusiastic proponents of products they call 'bonds' (see next) which are in fact fixed-term deposits offering a higher rate for locking in your money for one or more years.

Both banks and building societies do more than just hold money and pay interest on it, but in purely investment terms, their role is to offer

* call accounts: instant access, generally interest-bearing in a small way, with chequeing facilities. Potentially denominated in more than one currency for settling liabilities in more than one currency (see page 146). A call account is as useful, and offers as much investment potential, as a roll of banknotes in the back pocket. But some of them qualify as
* high-interest cheque accounts, which are high interest in relation to prevailing rates and are more 'investable' than call accounts. These shade into
* short-term deposits of a week, month or more; the term is defined as a notice period for withdrawals, with higher rates to compensate for this greater inflexibility. These would be the liquid place to keep money in the short-to-medium term.

All of the above offer rates of interest which vary according to the prevailing base rate set by the Bank of England in the case of Sterling accounts, the US Federal Reserve in the case of US dollar accounts, and the appropriate central bank for other currencies.

In addition to variable-rate instruments, there are

* fixed-term deposits (and building-society 'bonds'), which offer a fixed rate of interest for a fixed term of one or more months or one or more years. Larger sums of money qualify for
* money-market rates, which are the (higher) rates your bank itself can get for lending money in the money markets. Such rates are quoted at the time of deposit, to be fixed for a term of a week, a month or longer, and reflect the money market's view of the future for rates generally. You might be quoted,

---

* At the bottom of most 'rules' of investment is a simple proverb: don't put all your eggs in one basket. The 'science' of investment is a lot simpler than many people think it is, although the practice remains difficult.

for example, the choice of 7% for a week or 6.75% for a month, which would indicate a bearish view; higher rates for longer commitments would suggest optimism.

The choice between fixed and variable rate deposits depends on your view of the likely direction of interest rates during the term of your deposit. Remember that nobody can be confident on this point, and that quoted rates will be calculated according to the consensus professional view. If you make the correct choice, but this is in line with what everybody expected to happen, you will not gain in a big way. Only if you are correct against the widely held view will you benefit significantly from your choice. But you lose out if you are wrong.

There is another consideration arising out of the fact that the commitment of money for a fixed term generally also fixes the interest rate for the term. Whereas variable-rate fixed-term deposits generally impose a time penalty for early withdrawal (ie, unless you give the required notice, cessation of interest is backdated for a given period), fixed-rate deposits often do not permit withdrawals except at specified times (ie, after one year) or up to specified amounts. Bear this in mind if you are depositing money which you will require at some time in the future.

The advantage of deposit-based investments is that they provide an income while – to a greater or lesser extent – keeping your money liquid. The disadvantage is that your capital does not increase, so that it is vulnerable to the effects of inflation.

Bonds

Literally, bonds are promises to pay (in the sense, 'my word is my bond'). They are instruments whereby governments and other bodies seek to raise money from investors by promising a given return. Thus, they are in effect contracts between issuer and investor (or 'subscriber' to a new bond issue).

Bonds come in a variety of forms and offer a variety of promises. In the most common use of the term, they are a flexible vehicle around which can be constructed a medium- or long-term planning package – you pay now for the promise of a larger sum of money later – or which can be bought and sold in the way that equities (see below) can be bought and sold.

When the word 'bond' is used on its own, the investment vehicle being described is most likely to offer a fixed rate of interest over a fixed term at the end of which your investment will be redeemed 'at par' (which will be explained in a moment). The investment will tend to be buyable and sellable during its term, and the best-known example is the British government bond, or 'gilt'. (Life assurance 'bonds' vary significantly from this description in that they are a contract involving an obligation to commit money for a given term – or pay regular premiums for that term – in return for the promise; they are, therefore, not buyable and sellable. See under 'Life assurance' below).

For expatriate purposes, those gilts on which the interest is payable free of UK tax (they are marked as such in the gilt listings in the *FT* and elsewhere) represent a secure if not particularly high-performing investment. They are grouped by the time remaining before they are redeemed.

They are traded at a discount or premium to the capital value at which they will be redeemed. Thus, 8% Treasury 2013, which pays interest tax-free to non-residents, might be buyable at a quoted price of, say, 85p. This means that for every 85p you invest, you will receive 100p in 2013, if you hold it that long. You have bought at a discount, and the price will fluctuate between now and 2013 (towards 100p near the end). The interest payable on your investment of 85p will be 8% per annum on a notional 100p. You have, in effect, bought the right to 100p for 85p.

The security of a bond depends on the security of the issuer. With conventional bonds such as gilts, the advantages are security, so that such bonds become particularly attractive in the face of turbulent markets, with a fixed income and some prospect of capital gain. Gilts, like deposits, are a 'bedrock' component of a portfolio, and in most circumstances, not one of the sources of performance.

Note that not all bonds offer the security and stability of gilts. Just because something is described as a bond does not mean that it has the characteristics described. Bonds are promises, no more, and not all promises are reliable.

Collective investments

Most expatriates arrive at a portfolio consisting mainly of these. There are various different types of collective investment. The one thing they have in common is that they collect (sometimes the term 'pool' is used) the assets of more than one investor, and invest them together. By this means, they achieve a broader spread of investments than would be achievable by an individual acting alone. A single investor with, say, £1,000 could not invest in 1,000 different investments, but he could if he combined with 1,000 other investors. The resulting £1,000,000 would be enough to buy a significant stake in each of them.

Collective investments are professionally managed according to a set of objectives which may be anything from achieving a reliable income by investing in gilts, to taking risks for high returns in emerging markets (see later). Those objectives should match your own; more precisely, they should complement what is achieved by other parts of your portfolio. Note that although a collective investment offers a spread, it does not, in itself, offer sufficient balance to constitute the whole of a balanced portfolio. This is because its single objective is not necessarily grounded on security, nor is it your objective. Treat it as one investment in your portfolio.

When considering an investment in a collective, you are effectively considering taking on a manager for your money. Look at the performance figures, which appear in the *FT* every weekday but in more detail in the *FT*'s Weekend Money on Saturdays and in the expatriate magazines (page 232) for consistency of performace over time. This is important: a single good performance might be the result of luck, but a manager who does well consistently in changing market conditions has got something extra to offer.

There are several types of collective investment, but the main distinction is that between those that are closed-ended, and those that are open-ended.

Closed-ended collective investments are those that are launched as companies by the issue of a fixed number of shares which are then traded on a stock exchange. The shares fluctuate in value, but the number of shares is not influenced by the trade in them – this is why the company is regarded as closed-ended. Investment trusts are closed-ended; they are companies and their share prices are quoted alongside other companies.

Open-ended collective investments are created by the issue of units; they expand and contract as those units are bought and sold by investors because the number of units can be increased or decreased according to demand. Unit trusts are open-ended: their units are traded by their respective management companies, who are responsible for investing the proceeds of unit sales.

Whether a collective investment is closed-ended or open-ended makes a significant difference to its potential performance and its potential risk. If in doubt the way to distinguish between the two is by how it is priced. If it is closed-ended it will have a share price. If it is open-ended it will generally be quoted as having an offer and a bid price (but see below). These are, respectively, the price you will have to pay for your units and the price you will be paid if you want to sell them back to the managers – ie, they offer to sell, and bid to buy the units back. The higher price you pay, the lower you receive.

The structures of collective investments can vary from the above generalizations, and are presently under review in the UK. When looking at any collective investments, you should find out which of the above it is (or most resembles), so that you can determine its characteristics as an investment vehicle, as follows.

- Closed-ended. Investment trusts buy shares in companies. Because they are companies themselves, their own share price might represent a discount (or indeed a premium) on the share prices of their investments. As companies, they can borrow money ('gear') to fund investment or pay liabilities where otherwise they might be forced to sell holdings at a disadvantageous time. As companies they are freer in what they can do. All this makes them riskier but potentially more rewarding than open-ended collectives.
- Open-ended. Unit trusts, mutual funds and offshore funds are generally sums of money held in trust by a trustee and managed by a separate management company. The trust deed dictates the investment policy according to which the management company must act. They are priced

on their underlying investments and there is no discount/premium. Open-ended investments cannot borrow and their managers generally have less freedom of action. They are less risky but slower performers than equivalent closed-ended collectives. You will come across 'UCITs' and 'SICAVs' among other acronyms; these are forms of open-ended collective. You will find that many offshore funds have single prices; what distinguishes them is that they are sold in units.

You may hear talk of

- Open-ended investment companies (OEICs, pronounced 'oicks'; this name is under review). These are effectively single-priced unit trusts.

Collective investments are a way to achieve diversification at a lower cost, and are therefore a safer way into any given market than direct investment. They offer capital growth and income and professional management. Their risk and reward potential should be assessed in the light of the market in which they invest, they are a safer way into it than direct investment, but they do not make the market itself any safer.

Life assurance

In investment terms, life assurance products are mainly, though not exclusively associated with medium- and long-term planning for such contingencies as school fees and pensions (see later). They are contractual agreements between life assurance companies and their clients.

There are three types of life assurance policy as follows.

- Endowment policies. These are the type mainly used for investing. Benefits are payable at the end of a predetermined period, or on death.
- Whole of life policies. With these in their conventional form, benefits are payable on death, whenever it happens. As benefits are generally paid without a tax liability in the UK (see below), conventional whole of life policies are commonly used in estate planning to offset inheritance tax, etc. Other forms are offered as 'bonds', see below, with which the end of the term is specified, but does not have to be death.
- Term policies. Benefit payable on death within a specified term. These are not relevant here.

More than any other investment product, life assurance policies should only be entered into on the basis of clearly thought out objectives. This is because they are long-term commitments, and in many cases involve a commitment to paying regular premiums for longer periods than you are overseas (longer periods, therefore, than you can count on your present salary).

Note that although both endowment and whole of life policies have a 'surrender' value if you seek to cash them in before the end of their term, these are generally low in terms of the premiums you have paid. This is because the early premiums go to paying set-up costs and other charges, so that value only begins to build up after the policy has been in existence for some time. There is a market in second-hand endowments, which offers a better price for a policy than its surrender value, and a way of buying a long-term policy at a point where it has existed for long enough to be a medium-term investment. More on this from The Association of Policy Market Makers, The Holywell Centre, 2 Phipp Street, London EC2A 4PS, telephone 0171 739 3949, fax 0171 729 5143.

The value of life assurance products is that they offer the assurance of a minimum sum at a set date. Whole of life policies for investment are offered as 'bonds' with a particular investment objective, ie property bonds, equity bonds, etc. Endowment policies for investment are similarly aimed at particular objectives. Both types fall into three broad categories as follows.

- With profits policies. A minimum sum is assured, to which bonuses are added at regular intervals and at maturity. The bonuses, once added, cannot be taken away. With profits policies perform best when their term includes a period of economic prosperity, so that the life assurer does better and the bonuses are bigger.
- Without profits policies. The sum assured is what you get.
- Unit-linked policies. The policy has a minimum sum assured and is divided into units in one or more underlying funds which may be invested in any investment sector. It is, therefore, effectively a collective investment into which the life assurer puts money on behalf of the policyholder. The value of units changes with the performance of the underlying fund, and if at the end of the term their value is greater than the minimum sum assured, there is an effective 'bonus'.

A variant combining aspects of the first and third of these is the 'unitized with-profits policy', where the underlying fund performance dictates the regular bonus that is added to the policy.

Where there is more than one underlying fund in which a policy is invested, the policyholder can generally dictate switches between funds at low or no cost.

Policies are either single-premium, in that a single lump sum is paid at the beginning of the term, or regular premium, where monthly payments are made. In the UK, policies regarded as 'qualifying' by the Inland Revenue, in that they run for ten years or more and have an approximately constant level and frequency of premiums (these rules vary from policy to policy) are able to pay proceeds tax-free to the policyholder at the end of their term. Note that even in these circumstances, tax is generally paid by the life company on the proceeds of the underlying investment, so that an expatriate would choose to invest in policies offered by an untaxed offshore life company rather than a taxed onshore one.

Life policies are planning vehicles for long-term capital growth. Some single-premium policies allow withdrawals during their term, so there is effectively an income, but all policies are a long-term contractual commitment with the constraints that this implies.

In circumstances where a series of capital sums are required over a period of years, an option is to invest in a series of life policies with staggered maturity dates. Another is the use of annuities, deferred or not, with which a capital sum purchases an income.

Equities

When you buy shares in a company, you bet on the prospects for the company itself, and for the business in which it is engaged. Direct investment in equities is considered a better long-term investment than deposits or bonds, both for historical reasons – equities have historically outperformed most other investment media in the long term – and because equities manufacture value out of wider economic prosperity. But you have to get the right equity within the right sector, and for this reason most expatriates go into equities via offshore funds.

Property

If you have a house, you have an investment. It's not doing very well at the moment, and it's about as illiquid as you can get. But it is a store of value, and it can be made to give you an income. See page 170.

Note that the present is not necessarily a reliable guide to the future, and just because everybody thinks property is no longer good for capital growth, doesn't mean they're right. Before you take steps to cash in this particular component of your portfolio, reflect that there will probably be a time when you need to reinvest in property. The only thing you can rely on, between now and then, is change.

Derivatives and commodities

These are risky. They are investment opportunities that derive from other investment opportunities. They are risky because they are dependent on factors outside themselves – they derive risk factors as well as their very existence from other investments – and for other reasons as discussed below.

The derivatives market derives from the commodities market and has a clear historical foundation. Commodities – wheat, orange juice, coffee – are necessarily ordered in advance of delivery. Their producers – the wheat farmers, etc. – need capital to fund production. Their customers – breadmakers, say – need certainty of supply.

It suits both sides of a commodity transaction to buy and sell ahead of physical delivery. So a deal is struck giving a right to a given amount of a commodity at a given price.

But the price of the commodity itself continues to fluctuate right up to the date of delivery, due to, say, the weather influencing the harvest in the case of 'soft' (generally, planted) commodities, and general supply and demand with 'hard' commodities – ie, metals. (Money itself is also a commodity, as below.) So the right to buy (or sell) at a given price is more or less valuable according to how the commodity's price is fluctuating.

The contract to buy or sell is the entity traded as a derivative – it is the 'future' derived from the actual trade in the commodity. One can also buy the right to buy or sell a future – this is an 'option' on a future. Futures have to be traded before the date of delivery, and options, of course, expire at that date. The cost of the future or option is a fraction of the underlying buying price of the commodity at the time the deal is struck – typically 10 per cent – but increases in value nearer delivery date if it is a right to buy at a price below market price (and vice-versa – see below).

Money is a commodity and there are, therefore, financial futures for investment, and options on financial futures. Their underlying commodity is currencies, from which derive interest-rate, bond and index futures.

Derivatives trading came into mainstream investment as a method of 'hedging' a portfolio; that is, providing against a downturn in the markets underlying the main investments in a portfolio by buying a future and/or an option on an investment that would go the other way in such a situation (one might buy a lot of dollars and the option to buy a lot of Sterling, for example).

But these days, futures and options are traded for themselves. Part of the risk with futures arises out of the fact that, although one pays only around 10 per cent, one's exposure is to the full commodity contract price – ie, the underlying 100 per cent. If the commodity price goes your way by 10 per cent, you make 100 per cent of your intitial investment – and more in the same ratio if the trend continues. If it goes against you by 10 per cent, you lose everything. If it goes further against you, you face a 'margin call' from your futures broker to cover his further exposure on your behalf.

The defence against this is to set a 'stop loss' if the trend goes against this beyond a certain point. Options are less risky than futures because they grant a right but not an obligation to buy a future, and no further commitment. One's exposure is, therefore, limited to one's initial outlay.

Futures are risky because on a brief explanation they can sound simple in a way they are not. Their prospects are governed by extraneous factors such as the weather, or, in the case of a financial future, an economy or a currency's performance. They are further governed by market sentiment – a bet on something as abstract as an index is a bet that you will not be alone in feeling good or bad about its prospects.

You will probably encounter them via funds with or without guarantees (see page 163). Unless you have the time to go into derivatives trading virtually full time, do not do it other than via a fund, and then only with a small proportion of your portfolio.

Alternative investments

This is the term for that part of your investment portfolio which should be fun. If it is true that a portfolio comprising entirely bank deposits is risky because something else might do better than bank deposits, it follows that an entirely sensible portfolio might lose out if an eccentric investment pays off for once. With this is mind, keep a little back for enjoyable but not necessarily sensible investments such as prints, pictures, books, laid-down cases of port, porcelain dolls, toy cars, memorabilia. Any expatriate who has put possessions in storage has a potential trove of appreciating alternative investments.

Note that 'investing alternatively' is not supposed to be an excuse for a shopping spree.

Factors to consider when you invest your money

You will do this with advice, and it may be done for you (see below), but that does not remove the obligation upon you to know what is going on. What follows is a brief resume of points you should remember when investing in, or being sold, an investment.

Security comes first
Nothing is worth the risk if you're going to lose sleep over it. Do not invest in something because it might make you a million, but because it fits with your objectives, and your personal 'risk profile'.

Invest for your own reasons
If you want to buy a clock-alarm-radio, or a set of executive luggage or a gold-plated pen, you don't prefer one that comes with an investment plan attached. Yet somehow the other way round it's still worth the while of mailshotters to attach such irrelevant 'freebies' to investment offers. If you want the product, accept the gift. If you want the gift, it'll be cheaper in a shop.

Understand what you're doing
Nothing in investment is so complicated that it cannot be explained to you. If you do not understand what you are being asked to buy, don't buy it.

Ask stupid questions
Salesmen know they've got you when you start asking the questions you were embarrassed to ask when you were just thinking about it, but need to know now that you've committed yourself to buying. Give yourself an advantage by asking stupid questions before you're committed.

Sleep on it

Buy it tomorrow. There's only a hurry if the salesman doesn't want to give you time to think about it and realize it's not for you.

Think about the opportunity cost

This is what you lose by not doing something else with the money. It's a thought worth keeping in mind if you are having the beginner's difficulty with selling a non-performing investment. It is only too easy to convince yourself that if markets in the long term tend to move upwards, so your investment will, in due course, recover. But what if, over that long, drawn-out recovery period, you had had the money for another use? Might it not have moved upwards more quickly?

Invest for the long term

You're not building up prosperity for next week; you're building it up for the rest of your life.

You don't have to do it at all, and it may be the wrong move anyway

If you don't do it, you won't necessarily be worse off, and you'll probably sleep easier. There isn't ever one single 'right thing to do'; there are only ever sets of alternatives, some of which will turn out to have been more right than others.

Nobody knows better than you do

There might be people who are better informed than you are, and their information might make them sound convincing. But that doesn't make them infallible; it just makes you unhappier if you believe them and they turn out to have been wrong.

Doing nothing is not necessarily wrong

In crashes and other hostile market situations, you are more likely to be right if you do nothing, than if you sell out. Everybody's favourite crash is still the '87; hardly more than a year later, market indices were higher than they had been pre-crash. And yet the uproar in the immediate aftermath was that people hadn't been able to contact their brokers to sell out quick enough.

If everybody's doing it, it probably is wrong

Once a consensus develops that an upward trend is set fair to continue indefinitely, the professionals will start to look for opportunities to sell. Their thinking will be that uninformed money is raising prices beyond a level thought sustainable by informed money, which will itself seek to get out before the bubble bursts. A counter-trend will develop.

One can extrapolate from this a further rule: look for the counter-argument. There should be two sides to an investment; cons to weigh against the pros. If there aren't, be suspicious. Some investments are risky. The dangerous ones are those where the risk isn't obvious. Ask yourself where you will stand if it goes wrong.

Be careful of the word 'guaranteed'

Sometimes it doesn't mean what you might think. Usually, it is used in the context of an ostensibly risky investment, and what is guaranteed is the return of your capital after a fixed term plus a percentage gain. There might be a 'rolling guarantee' in which you get your money plus a return over, say, six months, and then the combined total is your guaranteed capital for the next six months. The return is thus rolled over from guarantee period to guarantee period.

Futures funds, for example, are often packaged with a guarantee. They're risky, you can lose everything, but if there is a guarantee that you won't, everything looks different. But note that what is not guaranteed is that the fund will invest as if it was investing solely in futures and the investment went well. What is guaranteed is your capital and a small return.

By making an investment apparently safe, a guarantee reduces its potential return. This is because of the way the guarantee is structured. Some of your money is invested in futures, or whatever is the headline investment, and the rest goes into something safe that will, at the end of the term of the guarantee, have appreciated sufficiently to return the guaranteed amount.

Thus, £100 in a guaranteed futures fund might actually be £90 in the rock-solid, low-performance, blue-chip safe investment, and £10 in futures. Fine, but think about the opportunity cost (above) of that £90.

Apply the 'opposites test'

If you find yourself on the receiving end of a hard sell, apply the opposites test to what you're being told. This works on the basis that a claim has value only if the opposite claim could equally well be made. Thus, 'We will use sophisticated methods of analysis and draw on the expertise of our highly trained team of professionals to identify opportunities in the US bond market,' cancels down to 'We will invest in the US bond market,' because that's the only part of the statement with a possible opposite (ie, we will invest in something other than US bonds). The salesman could not say, 'We will stick a pin in a price list and ask a passer-by to suggest a good investment,' which is roughly the opposite of what he said, so the claim is valueless.

When being sold to, you want to get at what the investment actually does, rather than anything about the manager's attitude to his work. Then you can decide whether it suits your needs, and if it does, start to check out the salesman and his product.

Safeguarding your assets

If you are going to a country which is politically unstable, or where there are limits on the amounts of money which may be taken out at the end of your stay, a simple safeguard is not to take your assets into the country. But in such a situation, you may find that administering your assets becomes problematical. The first priority is, therefore, to find a means whereby your assets can continue to be administered according to your wishes, but in your absence.

Asset administration

You can leave your money in an offshore bank, but bank managers do not tend to be active administrators of their clients' assets. You can hand everything over to a discretionary portfolio manager, but such an individual will tend not to administer standing-order payments and other ongoing administrative necessities..

One option is to grant either limited or complete

Power of attorney

to a relative or professional adviser whom you trust to administer your affairs as you would wish them to be administered. This option allows for flexibility on what needs to be done and how it should be done, and having a trusted individual in the UK who can act for you is a useful precaution if you are far away and under pressure and need something done fast.

But having somebody empowered to act for you does not remove one set of potential problems. In some circumstances, and if you are working in some countries, the simple fact of your owning your own assets can give rise to tax liabilities or administrative problems, or both, that would otherwise not be there. Such problems can be overcome by the use of

Offshore trusts and offshore companies

A trust, and particularly in this context an offshore trust located in an offshore financial centre, is a legal entity capable of owning assets. It is set up by a settlor, who places assets in the trust by effectively gifting those assets to the trusts and ceasing to be their owner (as you might expect, this transaction potentially gives rise to an inheritance-tax liability). The trust then owns those assets and is administered by trustees who act according to the terms of the deed whereby the trust was created, and by reference to a 'letter of wishes' supplied by the settlor. The trust will have one or more 'beneficiaries' for whose benefit it is administered.

Trusts are used, for example, to overcome the potential problem of 'forced heirship' whereby, in some jurisdictions, if you die, the authorities will put aside your will and pass on your assets according to local rules on who inherits what. Trusts are also used to pass on money to children who are too young to used it responsibly – the trust deed dictates that they will inherit when they reach, say, twenty-one – and they are a means of avoiding probate: trusts do not die when their settlor dies, so their assests can go on being available to surviving dependants while probate is established and the estate is valued for tax, etc.

There are many varieties of trust, and they can be used to reduce or avoid tax and other liabilities. Partners are among those who can be beneficiaries. But the most important two things to know about trusts, particularly offshore trusts, are:

- that they can complicate your whole financial and tax position and should only be considered as part of an overall, thought-out strategy, and that
- the tax and other authorities who have oversight of your affairs will be interested to know why you are using trusts, and they will be empowered to 'look through' them (see page 103) if, for example, a tax liability would exist but for the single fact of the existence of the trust.

Trusts should be regarded as administrative vehicles rather than tax-planning vehicles. They are often used in conjunction with offshore companies in the ownership of such assets as properties overseas, and, for example, yachts.

With an offshore company, you do not cut the link of ownership, but divert it. Thus, you own the shares of the company rather than directly the property it owns. Many countries will use their look-through powers to tax and otherwise deal with a company according to where it is owned and controlled rather than where it is established. Hence the joint use of company and trust: if the company is owned and controlled by a trust which is also offshore, the look-through approach is confounded.

Some countries, like Spain, will levy additional tax on company-owned properties. It is, as a general principle, a good idea to regard trusts and companies as administrative vehicles. They can enhance your tax-efficiency, but only where they are used as part of an overall tax-planning strategy.

Under the heading of safeguarding your assets, there is a more overt danger that you must avoid.

Fraud

People can lose most or all of their money when they are successfully defrauded. They can end up living in flats not houses, they can be forced to take their children out of fee-paying schools, and they can cease to be able to afford to pay the premiums on their pension plans and health insurance.

Even when you are defrauded in a small way, it can leave a bitter memory, and in a subliminal way, reduce your opinion of yourself: you were gullible.

But the worst thing about fraud is that it always happens to people who don't think it can happen to them. And it always happens again. No matter how tight regulation becomes, no matter how many warnings are issued to investors to avoid 'get-rich-quick' schemes, no matter how many horror stories are repeated, it always happens again.

Assume that you are not proof against a fraudster. Assume that your natural common sense will not protect you. Expatriates, who are widely believed to be paid more than stay-at-homes and taxed less, are popular targets. Fraud only works because it is convincing.

Frauds have a number of characteristics in common. First, they are convincing, but in a particular way. They make you look for reassurance that this time, it's okay, even though you know that the claims made for the possible return on the investment are above – not necessarily much above – what common sense tells you is achievable. Frauds often claim to get their returns on the basis of safe-sounding investments such as gilts, and the explanations of how they work are often mostly simple. They always play on your natural inclination not to disappoint – in that, for example, the fraudster will be sufficiently friendly that you begin to have personal reasons for not wanting to disappoint him by turning over your money. You begin to tell yourself that it must be okay. You begin to look for reassurance – which is readily available from the fraudster.

You might be utterly convinced by an investment opportunity. If so, sleep on it. Very few legitimate investments will become unavailable overnight, once they have been offered to you and however the unavailability is expressed. If it's not there tomorrow, you have been dealing with a crook who decided overnight that he might have been rumbled.

Another characteristic of frauds is that they often require secrecy. No deal is so good you can't tell your accountant. No legitimate salesman will target you out of a whole community of British expatriates; he will want you to tell your friends. Note that criminals are aware of the advice you will receive to ask who regulates their activities, and will be able to answer that one. Check their answers; a phonecall will suffice (don't ask if this person is a criminal but if the name appears on the list of members). Remember that just because a fraudster says he represents a well-known financial institution, doesn't mean he's telling the truth. And remember that a company name, however impressive it may sound, is nothing more than a name.

Remember also that criminals read advice like this, and adapt their approaches accordingly.

Case history: An opportunity to be missed
Denzil Holbert was delighted to receive an invitation to an investment seminar at the Hotel Americaine. He was bored with his financial adviser's endless preaching about caution, and felt that he was ready for some action.

He was a senior man after all, and after only six months in the posting, he had built up £20,000 in a high-interest deposit account.

He asked around at the International Club.

'Oh, sure, we're all going. It'll be a laugh. And drinks afterwards, did you see? Eats too, with any luck.'

The seminar was fascinating. The idea was to make a high return from a leveraged investment in British gilt-edged stock, hedging the downside with a managed exposure to a countercyclical combination of emerging-market funds and some direct currency investment across a basket of . . .

Denzil didn't really understand the detail, but he liked the idea of hedging the risk. That was sensible. And gilts were safe. He spoke to the man afterwards, and made an appointment to see him the next day, in his hotel suite. They couldn't really talk over the drinks; in fact, Denzil had to apologize for his fellow expatriates.

'They've been here a lot longer than I have; they never seem to treat these occasions seriously, just as an excuse for a party.'

Next day, Denzil was cautious. Boy, did he know all about caution. He told the man he had no more than £5,000 to invest.

The man asked him a lot of questions about his job and his plans and his investment objectives. Denzil felt reassured. This was how it should be.

But then the man said, 'Don't tell me you've only got £5,000. Come on, that job, that salary; you've been here six months. I bet you've got a lot more than that. I mean, I respect your caution. But if I had, say, £20,000 to invest in this scheme, I could achieve your objectives for you, all in one go. You don't trust me; that's fine, I understand. But think about it.'

Denzil was horribly embarrassed to be caught out not trusting the man. So embarrassed that he immediately wrote out a cheque for £20,000. The man suggested that in view of the state of the markets, which represented a rare buying opportunity, maybe an accelerated transfer would be in order? Denzil, in a combination of euphoria and embarrassment, agreed. The man helped him draw up a faxed author-ization, and looked away as Denzil added his password.

It wasn't until the following afternoon that Denzil finally admitted to himself that he might have made a mistake.

But he was a senior man, after all, and he ought to be able to trust his own judgement. And hadn't the man sounded awfully plausible?

And – wait a minute – hadn't the man said there was a forty-eight-hour cooling-off period during which the investment could be cancelled? Denzil had until tomorrow to think about it. Then, if he wanted to, he could phone the man and say that he had changed his mind. He poured a drink and told himself not to be such a wimp.

Denzil had a bad night. He woke in a cold sweat at 6am and phoned the hotel.

He wasn't really surprised to be told that the man had checked out immediately after his meeting with Denzil.

He phoned his bank. The accelerated transfer had gone through, as authorized.

Denzil never saw his money again.

But he joined in the laughter at the International Club, at what an obvious con that had been.

'But we had a good party out of it, didn't we? Denzil, you talked to him, what did you make of him?'

'Obvious crook,' replied Denzil.

And later on, he fired his financial adviser. He couldn't bear the thought that he might find out what he had done.

How to complain

If you think you are the victim of serious fraud, you should act immediately, calmly, by contacting the regulatory authority responsible for the company in question (page 216). It may be appropriate also to contact the police, but if there is a possibility that you might be mistaken, remember that airing your complaint too widely might lead to time-wasting inconvenience, the issuing of apologies, and at worst, the possibility of slander and/or libel actions against you.

Now read on.

If things go wrong, for whatever reason, you are too far away to waste valuable time getting cross about it. Sit back and think it through. Is this more likely to be delay, incompetence or fraud? Will there be more to be gained from waiting a few more days, than complaining?

If you decide to complain, think about how to do it before putting pen to paper. However justified they might be, some complaints are more successful than others; the difference is in how they are made.

The most common cause of complaint is human error. The most common form of reaction is over-reaction. What tends to be concealed in glossy marketing brochures and enthusiastic sales talk, is that the job itself will be done by real human beings. The shortfall between what seems to be promised and what you get is thus widened by the methods used to obtain you as a customer.

This has a practical implication. Your complaint will initially be handled by somebody who is not responsible for the fault in the first place, and who does not have the authority to do anything about it. This person's function will be limited to deciding whether to send you a holding letter, or pass your complaint on straight away to be resolved. The best result you can achieve at this stage, by telephone or by letter, is to persuade this person to act on your behalf within your company.

You will find that complaints are superficially well handled by any company with any claims to a reputation. This is because, in the minds of the people who sell to them, expatriates live in tight-knit communities where word of mouth has a disproportionate effect. They think that if they upset you, you'll tell everybody about it.

There are, therefore, training courses in dealing with the public. The downside of the training and the belief in word of mouth is that companies' attention is focused on providing a smiling face, sometimes to the exclusion of dealing with the complaint itself. They'll be nice about it whether or not they're taking you seriously. So don't settle for charm; aim to explain your problem and get it understood. Remember that if you get heated, you force the other party to think more about calming you down, than about sorting things out for you. Remember also that many companies instruct staff who have contact with the public not to admit liability in any situation, so it is a 'no-win' approach to try to get the first voice on the phone to say sorry.

If you take the opposite approach, and write directly to the chairman with copies of all your relevant financial records, copying the whole bundle to the editors of national papers and expatriate magazines, you will get a response (copied upstairs) from somebody at the company. But if the original fault was minor, you will lose goodwill and there will probably not be any friendly gesture such as waiving the annual charge, etc., to re-establish good relations. A further consideration is that by going to the top, you give yourself only one chance; you can't go back down to all those middle-rankers who might have decided in your favour. Unless you are genuinely as outraged as this approach suggests, it is probably not the best strategy.

When you complain, do so with a clear objective in mind. Spell this out in your letter (it is as well to write to confirm anything verbal, even if it is in the form of a thank you for being so sympathetic over the phone, so as to have a record). You might, for example, explain that you want the amount credited back to your account, or whatever, and you would suggest that a sum of, say, £100 would compensate you for the cost and inconvenience of dealing with the matter. There is, usually, a budget that can be applied to restoring good relations, and front-line managers generally have authority to spend it. You might add that you would be grateful for a response within, say, two weeks. If you phone, get the name, but don't criticize the individual by name in subsequent correspondence.

If your first approach doesn't work, go up the ladder of responsibility. Take the complaint to the departmental manager, then to his manager, and finally to head office (asking for the next name in each case, and making it clear that you are still not satisfied; this sometimes gets results). Do not send more copied correspondence than is strictly necessary, and put the substance of your complaint in your covering letter. This should ideally be two typed sheets at most, double-spaced, and more concerned with the specifics of your situation than with abstract appeals to the addressee's sense of fair play. All companies get letters of complaint, and the idea is not to look like one of the aberrant ones.

If you don't get satisfaction from the company, write to the regulator (page 216). You will have found out the responsible regulator when you invested with the company. If you are complaining to an offshore-regulated subsidiary of a UK company, write to the offshore regulator, but advise the UK company that you are copying the letter to its UK regulator (and do so). Complain about building societies, offshore as well as onshore, to the Building Societies Commission as well as any other regulator.

If you have got this far without satisfaction, at least one of the following statements is true.

● Your complaint is not justified;
● If you want to go any further, you are going to have to take legal action;
● You should cut your losses before this gets seriously expensive.

Before you do anything else, read through the collected correspondence, and get a friend to do the same. If your friend says that although he agrees with you, strictly speaking, by the letter of the law, the other side is in the right, give up. No amount of pressure will persuade a company to act according to your wrong interpretation of the terms of a contract, for example, and if you haven't got a goodwill gesture out of them by now, you won't get one by hitting them with lawyers. They have the judgement of the regulator on their side by now.

If you're going to go on, there are precedents for success by tenacity. But lawyers are expensive in any country.

What to do with your British property

If you own your home in the UK, you have three options when you go away.

1. You can sell it. This may take time. You need somebody to open the windows and keep it fresh for when potential buyers arrive, and if it's a house with a garden, to do the mowing. Meanwhile, you will still be paying the bills. Generally speaking, your insurer will accept the 'moral responsibility' to continue your cover while the property is on the market, but cover might be reduced because you have varied from the conditions of the policy by leaving it unoccupied, or failing that, renewal might not be offered with reduced cover.

2. You can rent it to tenants, perhaps even to foreign expatriates coming to the UK. This will bring you an income, but you need to find somebody who will collect the rent and liaise with the tenants. Your property may not appeal to tenants prepared to pay high rentals.

3. You can leave it empty. This is the simplest option. But the house may deteriorate. You will need to find insurance.

Selling and buying

A popular variant on the first and second options is that you can sell the house you're leaving behind to work overseas, and use the proceeds to buy a more 'tenant-friendly' property to rent out while you're away. This is sensible. Being an absentee landlord is lucrative but competitive, and incoming tenants with company money to back them will go for exactly what they want. And face it – you're probably not leaving your home in immaculate decorative order. Selling your home and then buying an investment property and then selling that to buy a property to come home to is a way of gaining an income and simultaneously remaining in property if prices do start to rise again. Note that buying a UK property from overseas, as a home for when you return to the UK rather than as an investment, is dealt with in Chapter Four (page 188).

Whichever of the above options you choose, you will sooner or later decide that you need to find a manager to handle the administration. You can get a list of property managers from the Association of Residential Letting Agents (ARLA) at Maple House, 53–55 Woodside Road, Amersham, Bucks HP6 6AA, telephone 01494 431 680, fax 01494 431 530. The larger estate agents will have their own property management departments, and with them, what you lose in personal service, you may gain if your intention is ultimately to sell the property.

If you choose to rent, and you go for the sell-and-buy option, you should certainly use a manager. Not because you can't do it yourself, although it would be difficult to devote the time and the effort, but because the best tenants, company people with housing allowances, will work through the managers their companies have used before and recommend.

Get the manager to do the buying and the decorating. This is an established business for companies such as London Central Portfolio (LCP), 32 Bryanston Square, London W1H 7LS, telephone 0171 723 1733, fax 0171 724 1744, and many expatriate owners never see the investment properties that they buy for income while they are away. National characteristics are a factor here – Americans like flats with power showers and large kitchens; the Japanese like to be in St John's Wood; the French all want to be within child-delivering range of the French School in West London – and whatever the truth of all this is, the agent will know that your taste in furnishings is not likely to be competitive for a short- to medium-term professional executive tenant (the highest-paying kind) who wants something efficient and sees the property as one of the more status-related factors in the salary package. If you're looking for rented property in your location overseas, are you looking for a comfortable, lived-in version of the local look, with local plumbing and amenities, or (to put it at its worst) something blandly international which has been freshly painted and decorated and everything works?

Declaring your income from UK property

One of the quirks of the British tax system is that you should always declare to the Inland Revenue income you receive from renting out British property. The obligation to declare income received from British property applies whether or not you are liable to pay any tax on that income. Note that any overseas landlord who agrees to comply with the UK's self-assessment tax regime will now be entitled to receive his rent gross. For this, the landlord must provide his property manager (or tenant) with a tax-clearance certificate issued by the Inland Revenue.

Mortgage interest relief

If you have a mortgage on your home in the UK, and you receive UK tax relief on your mortgage payments, this will generally continue to be granted to you (under the Inland Revenue's extra-statutory concession A27) if you are going overseas by reason of employment and if you expect to return to your home within four years. Mortgage interest relief for the UK tax year 1996/97 is 15 per cent on the first £30,000 of your mortgage loan. Note that mortgage payments are allowable as an expense when calculating the profit made on renting a UK property for UK tax purposes, but that the rules are complex and advice should be taken from a specialist tax adviser (page 147).

Insuring your rental income

Brokers like Winter Richmund, 40–46 Chapel Street, Marlow, Buckinghamshire SL7 1DD, telephone 01628 470470, fax 01628 470444 offer policies insuring that once the tenancy agreement is signed, you receive your rental income for the term of the agreement. Part of their service is to vet prospective tenants, and they will provide names of property managers who offer their policies as part of their service.

Leaving your property empty

There are insurance policies explicitly designed for empty properties. They require that you appoint a 'responsible person' (or professional; confirm your choice of person with the insurance company) to make regular visits to the property and act as a keyholder (notify the local police that the property is empty, and tell them who has the key); and that you leave the property showing 'signs of normal habitation'. Tables and chairs should be set out, beds should have pillows under their covers, etc. An example of such a policy is the Weaver Homeowner's Policy from Europea IMG, Provender Mill, Mill Bay Lane, Horsham, West Sussex RH12 1TQ, telephone 01403 230000, fax 01403 251884.

If you are going to leave your property empty, it is best not to advertise this fact too widely. But plan to stay at it when you visit the UK, and expect to spend at least some of your time on maintenance when you are back home. Note that all your arrangements should be confirmed with your insurance company; claims can be repudiated if, in their judgement, a problem that has caused expense can be traced back to your not having made satisfactory provision.

Owning overseas property

It would be surprising if you chose to buy a property to live in while you were working abroad. Unless you know the country well already, you should take a considerable amount of time living there and getting a feel for the way of life before you commit yourself to buying. Then you should think about the prospect of your wanting to sell the property again if you do not stay in the country beyond your present contract.

Some expatriates decide to buy holiday properties abroad. They think of holidays, and rental income, and possibly even early retirement if their finances have done particularly well, and they contact such companies as The Overseas Homes Group, Kea House, 71 Yockley Close, Camberley, Surrey GU15 1QQ, telephone 01276 676281, fax 01276 692374, who specialize in Spanish properties along and inland of the Mediterranean coast. They may also contact the many international developers who advertise in the expatriate magazines, such as Taylor Woodrow, Taywood House, 354 Ruislip Road, Southall, Middlesex UB1 2QX, telephone 0181 578 2366, fax 0181 575 4553, or a British estate agent with an international presence such as Knight Frank & Rutley, 20 Hanover Squae, London W1R 0AH, telephone 0171 629 8171, fax 0171 753 0638.

If you are thinking of buying property abroad, you should consider the following points:

- The legal process of buying a property aboard is different from that in the UK, and you will need local representation. Contact The Law Society in the first instance (page 218).
- Exchange rates may move against you and make maintenance, etc., more expensive. Have a bank account denominated in the currency of your property costs (page 27).
- When you come to sell a property abroad, particularly a development

property, you may be in competition with the people who sold you the property. Find out whether the selling agent handles resales.

- When you come to sell, you may find that you have bought a type of property that does not appeal to the locals, so you have only expatriates like yourselves as possible buyers.
- In some countries, it is difficult to move large sums of money out, unless you can produce the documentation showing that it came in through proper channels.
- Owning a property via an offshore company (page 131) is not necessarily an effective way of reducing tax liabilities on the property.
- If you are buying a property in the hope that it will be 'self-financing' through rental income, you should consider buying through an agent who will handle the rental and, eventually, the resale, and you should not have to count on a regular stream of rental income to finance the property.
- There is a strong argument for testing the market for such a large investment by renting from another owner in the same place before buying. Don't let on at first that you're thinking of buying, and when you do reveal your intention, think about how long it takes the owner to name a price for his property.
- All property, however much you are pleased to own it, consumes time and worry. Don't buy if you're likely to lie awake wondering whether you left the tap on, with three months to go before your next visit.

Health insurance

It would be surprising if your contract of employment failed to include health-insurance cover. This is a standard part of the package for a job, both in the UK and overseas. The problem is that different parts of the world present different health risks, so that a British company's home scheme, designed for employees in the UK, will not necessarily cover you for what you may encounter elsewhere.

Many companies now recognize this, and buy sets of tailor-made insurance schemes for their expatriate employees. These come from specialist providers in the expatriate market, who design their policies to meet the needs of individuals in different locations overseas. There are many such providers, including BUPA International, IPH, ExpaCare, PPP and Medicare (a list of names and addresses for health-insurance providers appears on page 219).

But it is not cost-effective for a large company to buy as many health-insurance policies as it has expatriate employees, and even company schemes designed specifically for groups of expatriates will only cover the broad range of risks. If you are one of fifty or more expatriates in the same place, doing the same thing, you will generally find that the company expatriate scheme covers you. If you're on your own, or one of only a few expatriates in your location, read the terms of the company policy carefully. You may be better advised to buy your own personal health insurance (and in that case, to ask the company to contribute to it, rather than incorporate you in the redundant-for-you company plan).

First point to check: your contact may state that medical expenses will be paid. But check the benefits schedule of the company policy to find out what medical expenses are included. No insurance contract is open-ended, and even in the most generous, you will find exclusions.

There is a wide range of personal schemes on the market, from specialist providers including those mentioned above (see page 219 for addresses). You may cover yourself entirely, or use a personal plan to plug the gaps in a company plan (but if you prefer the latter option, think through the possible administrative hitches in claiming from two insurers simultaneously – and confirm that one policy does not invalidate the other).

Personal schemes cover a wide variety of possible adversities, and offer different levels of cover. This no more than reflects the wide variety of circumstances in which expatriates find themselves, but it makes it difficult to choose a policy to suit you. Here's a checklist of inclusions that you might want to find specifically included in your own insurance policy.

- In-patient treatment
- Hospital room & board (for how long?)
- Out-patient treatment
- Local ambulance
- Provision for a parent accompanying a sick child (which parent? both?)
- Emergency evacuation (where to? how covered are you when you get there? see below)
- Home nursing
- Childbirth (what about complications? is the newborn covered, and for how long after birth?) Note that cover for pregnancy doesn't generally begin until more than nine months after you've taken out your policy; see below for pre-existing conditions, but bear in mind that the moratorium on cover for this one will also last nine months.
- GP services (meaning what, in local terms?)
- Emergency dental treatment
- Routine dental treatment (how regularly?)
- Dread disease
- Long-term incapacitation. Permanent disability cover is offered by a variety of insurers including William Russell and Goodhealth (for contact details, see page 219), and can offer 75 per cent of your current salary up to a maximum just below six figures, for the rest of your working life.

Further points to consider are as follows.

Costs and payments

In what currency are your premiums payable? If you are paid in dollars, look for a policy for which you will pay in dollars, rather than facing a currency conversion.

The premium for a policy including most or all of the provisions listed above, for a couple between 35 and 40 with two children under 10 and living (for the sake of the example) in the Middle East, would be in the region of £1,500 to £2,500, although this is not a useful guideline figure because your premium will depend on a wide variety of factors and will vary according to which combination of provisions you choose to include. Note that cheapest is not necessarily best in health insurance.

Does the policy you're considering include the facility to pay the hospital directly, and in the right currency, rather than just reimburse you afterwards? Most insurers will require you to pay small claims yourself, and then seek reimbursement, but you should check that above a certain limit (say the local equivalent of £1,000), the insurer will pay up now rather than later, and pay the hospital. What is the arrangement for confirming to you that payments have been made?

Linked to the above, some insurers can provide lists of hospitals with which they have direct-payment arrangements. If you have any choice in the matter, it may be preferable to arrive at a hospital which already has dealings with your insurer.

Check the level of cover. If the worst happens, and you need emergency evacuation because of a dread disease that will lead to long-term incapacitation, are you covered, and for how much for how long? Travelling by air ambulance can cost upwards of £15,000. If you're covered for long-term care, ask what they mean by long term. Your upper limit for cover should be well into six figures, if not seven.

Will your premiums increase as you get older? Will they be increased if you make a claim? It is as well to plan health insurance without reference to the fact that you're coming home in a few years. Plan for a change of mind.

Exclusions

These fall into a number of categories.

1. Pre-existing conditions. If you have any, declare them at the outset. Otherwise, not only will they not be covered if they come to light later, but they may invalidate your policy. Pre-existing conditions can be covered in a policy, subject to a possible upward adjustment in premiums or an initial moratorium (of, say, two years) after which they may come into cover, but only if they are explicitly mentioned.

2. Exclusions that don't fit in with your lifestyle. If you are a mountaineer, say, in your spare time, or if you enjoy waterskiing or other (relatively)

dangerous sports, read the policy carefully for any hint that cover does not extend to self-inflicted conditions, and declare your dangerous sport. Remember that 'dangerous' is as understood by the claims-handling department of your insurer. If your lifestyle includes such 'bad' habits as drinking amounts that your insurer might consider too much – think about it.

Also, watch for exclusions that might remove cover from certain of your work activities such as operating heavy machinery (or being in the presence of heavy machinery).

3. Accidents. A properly comprehensive health-insurance policy should cover you against accidental damage to your health as well as illness.

4. Travel. Most policies base their premiums on the area where the insured person is based as well as on the cover extended. If you go on holiday to the US from Asia, say, are you moving out of the area of your cover? If you are evacuated to a hospital in, say, the US, does your cover go with you?

Also check that your cover is inclusive of return visits to the UK.

5. War and civil disorder. What if you travel into a war zone? More likely, what if the country where you're working turns into a war zone? What about disturbances that do not amount to war, but are still dangerous? Most policies will continue to cover you for the damages of war but subject to the condition that you do nothing to expose yourself to danger. Note that this might be expanded so that you must act according to any directive from the Foreign Office via the local embassy/consulate (see page 49 for registering your presence in your destination country). A situation might arise, for example, in which your continued cover depended on your staying at home for the duration of the emergency.

The 3am questions

Whatever insurance you take overseas with you, company or personal or both, there are a couple of questions that will occur to you suddenly, probably in the middle of the night, probably at the low point of your post-arrival depression. You should have answered them to your own satisfaction before you leave the UK if possible, and certainly before you need to make a claim. The first:

'If I am unconscious in a country where they will want an imprint of my credit card before giving me any treatment, how will they know I'm insured for all costs?'

The answer is that you should receive from your insurer a plastic card with the details of your cover. You should carry it at all times, preferably not with your credit cards in the wallet that will be the first thing to be removed from your pockets when you are found slumped at the side of the road. Some such 'cover cards' have a hole for a string round your neck (as do the discs carrying the information that you are allergic to certain drugs).

The card will give the hospital admission desk a number to ring to confirm that your insurer will pay for your treatment. It should be in the local language as well as English, and, like a credit card, should carry symbols recognizable locally.

Second question:

'If I am brought into hospital, and whatever time it is here, it's 2am UK time, and they ring the number on my card, who's going to pick up the phone?'

Whether the number rings in the UK or elsewhere, your insurer will probably advise you not to ring it to make sure it works, because you will be using a line on which an emergency call might want to come in. Insurers hook up with international emergency-response organizations who will have you on their database; the insurer is only as good as the organization at the end of the phone.

Third question:

'Who decides what treatment I need? What discretion does the local doctor have to spend my insurer's money?'

Sort this one out now. You will find that, as a general rule, if the hospital to which you are brought is either unacceptable or incapable of making an informed decision in your terms as to its suitability (standards vary, and your idea of acceptable standards might be higher than what the locals think will be adequate for you), there will be a doctor within visit or telephone range of you, whose judgement your insurers will accept. Give some thought to the amount of information you should routinely carry, in addition to your cover card, and know that doctor's number.

Fourth question:

'If I'm carted off to the local boneyard, rather than the expatriate hospital, and there isn't even a phone, what do I do?'

It is as well to have some procedure, at home and at work, for finding you if you don't turn up when and where you are expected. This is not one that can be covered by insurance, and it's up to you to know

1. where the local hospitals are that an ambulance might take you to, and

2. where people will be, if you need them in an emergency.

In some parts of the world, your personal security requires you to vary your route to work (page 62). Don't take this to such an extreme that you're beyond the reach even of the people who can help you.

Hospitality and hotels

If you can possibly not eat suspect food at a social event, don't eat it. Otherwise, be prepared for the physical consequences of not offending your host. Also, bear in mind that just because food is prepared in an international hotel, it is not necessarily safe. The same rules apply to hotel food as to food anywhere else. You can spot the serious international businessman by his habit of asking for his Coca-cola or gin and tonic without ice.

Emergency evacuation

This is a separate heading because you need to clarify

- What it will cost, and thus how much total cover you will need to be still safe if this chunk is taken out
- Who decides you need evacuation. You, the local doctor, the insurer?
- Who decides where you go
- Who comes with you, if anybody
- Who gets told that you've been evacuated. It would be difficult to reach this situation without your partner and colleagues knowing what was up, but it is as well to be clear on this
- Whether you're covered where the air ambulance takes you, after your course of treatment is completed
- Who pays for the return flight once you're well again

Planning for the future

One sales technique is to invite you to draw a line representing your life from today to the end. On that line, you mark the points at which you will need access to substantial amounts of money.

This is a useful thing to do. Two heavily marked stretches of your line will be the school-fee-paying stage of your children's lives, and your own retirement. The line, and the marks on it, are a clear indication of the investment objectives according to which your portfolio should be structured.

There are two general approaches to financial planning for the future. The first is to commit money now to a spread of investment vehicles that will appreciate in the long term, and the second is to invest in vehicles such as life assurance policies (page 157) with a set maturity date coinciding with an expected liability. Both of these approaches should be used in your own future planning.

In the offshore world particularly, you should note that plans structured to a set objective, ie 'school-fee-plans' and 'pension plans', are managed portfolios of investment vehicles that suit the particular objective. They are not the only way to achieve that objective, nor are they necessarily all you need to do to achieve that objective. As with all investment, remember that you are the one who loses if the strategy doesn't work, so that you are the one with final responsibility for getting it right.

Note also that long-term planning vehicles are generally structured so that they are adaptable to a variety of long-term objectives.

Working back from the far end of the line, your future-planning priorities are as follows.

Pensions

The questions are: how, and to what extent, can you maintain the provision that you already have; and how can you compensate for any part of your provision that may not continue after you go overseas?

Your pension at the moment consists of state pension and company pension.

The UK state pension and National Insurance

To maintain your entitlement to a full UK state pension on retirement, you must keep up your UK National Insurance contributions. If you are going overseas for a UK-based employer, and if you are going to a European Union country or one with which the UK has a reciprocal agreement on this subject (such countries are listed in leaflet NI38 from the DSS, see below and page 236), you will continue to pay UK Class 1 (ie, full-time employed) contributions for a specified period varying from one year in the EU to five years under some reciprocal agreements. If your stay overseas will last longer than the specified period, you will cease to be liable to pay UK Class 1 contributions and will tend to become liable to pay into your destination country's social security system.

After you have ceased to pay UK Class 1 contributions, you have the option to continue making Class 3 (ie, voluntary) UK National Insurance contributions. If you want to do this, you will find application form CF83 at the back of leaflet N138.

Opinions differ on whether it is worth maintaining UK National Insurance contributions after you have ceased to be liable to do so. The UK state pension is a small income for the outlay, and yet on the other hand, the outlay is small. Note that your Class 1 contributions after you go overseas maintain your right to unemployment benefit if you have to come home unexpectedly early, and a full contribution record will entitle you to the same benefits after your scheduled return to the UK.

Guidance and leaflets on UK National Insurance, reciprocal agreements and benefits generally are available from the Overseas Branch of the Department of Social Security, Longbenton, Benton Park Road, Newcastle-upon-Tyne NE98 1YX, telephone 0191 213 5000.

Your company pension

Take independent advice (page 147) on this subject as the rules are complex and have been going through a process of change implemented by the Inland Revenue. The changes are likely to continue.

It used to be the case that expatriates were only able to stay in their UK employer's company pension scheme in very narrowly defined circumstances. These restrictions have been eased, and may be eased further.

It is likely (this statement is not in itself a piece of advice) that you will be advised that you can stay in your company scheme, and that you will find yourself able to do so for a period of three years after you leave the UK (after which you will have to seek the Inland Revenue's permission to stay in the plan any longer). It is also likely that you will have the option of transferring into a UK personal pension plan as an alternative to your company scheme. Note that UK company and personal pension plans receive favourable UK tax treatment that is not meted out to those offshore plans that are structured to work as pension plans (below); this is a consideration if a factor in your long-term planning is a return to the UK in the medium term.

Offshore personal pension planning

Whether to augment a UK company/personal pension or to compensate for its absence, you may consider taking out one of the many offshore 'pension plans' on the market. These are life assurance contracts of various kinds (page 157) structured to pay our benefits either as capital or effectively as income (ie, a series of contracts with successive expiry dates will give you an 'income'). Their great merit is flexibility, in that they can be adapted to suit a range of future-planning requirements, but it is potentially misleading to describe them as 'pension plans' because they are not given the same tax treatment as UK pension plans, or indeed as 'retirement plans' because their flexibility allows them to be instruments for planning for a wider variety of capital requirements.

Such plans require either a capital payment at the outset, or a long-term commitment to regular premium payments. You should not commit yourself to any regular-payment plan unless you are confident that you can keep up the payments over the term of the plan rather than just the term of your present contract of employment. Some plans allow for variation or deferment of premiums, but it is a general principle that you can't just stop paying premiums and expect the same benefits as you originally took out the plan to achieve.

Note that the tax treatment of offshore plans varies. Some plans receive favourable treatment by the Inland Revenue, in that you are not taxed after your return and on the plan's maturity, on that part of the benefit that may be attributable to your period of non-residence. Some plans may be transferred into equivalent UK personal pension plans that do receive favourable UK tax treatment. There are subjects on which to ask questions before you sign the contract. (Be clear on whether you are committing yourself to a single-premium – ie, capital payment in advance – or regular premium plan. If you inadvertently sign to pay a regular premium that represents your whole available capital, you may have difficulty extricating yourself.)

The use of such plans is best considered not just in the context of pension planning, but also with regard to

School fees

Whatever the age of your children now, school-fee planning is like retirement planning in that it breaks down into a process of investing current income and capital so as to ensure a flow of capital repayments and income at given dates in the future.

The Independent Schools Information Service (ISIS) produces a free booklet entitled simply 'School fees', and advisers such as Gabbitas Educational Consultants will offer guidance (more on educational advice on page 80). There are specialist school-fee planners such as C Howard & Partners and the School Fee Insurance Agency who will offer tailored plans, and many schools themselves offer school-fee 'composition schemes' whereby lump sums now provide partial school-fee payments in future (these offer uncompetitive surrender values, and you should check the terms on which you can obtain the benefits, you have paid for if you do not, in the end, send your children to that school).

If you have capital, a popular option is to buy an 'educational trust plan' which works as a tax-efficient annuity providing a guaranteed sum three times a year to meet each term's fees. A similar effect can be achieved by investing in a series of with-profits endowment policies with maturity dates coinciding with school-fee payment dates.

Remember that all long-term financial planning, whether for school fees or financial security in retirement or anything else, is a form of investment, and the rules of investment apply. You should invest your assets in a balanced portfolio, as on page 144, and you should remember that taking bigger risks is not a reliable way to secure bigger returns. You don't have to provide for the whole of a long-term liability in advance, remember.

The cost of further education in the UK

Read this section if your children are half-way through their schooling, and likely to think of going on to UK further education afterwards. If, as seems likely, they live with you abroad (boarding school doesn't count as where they live), they may have difficulty qualifying as 'home students' rather than 'overseas students' when the time comes to establish who's going to pay for their post-school education.

This matters. For a first full-time further-education course, the state will pay to a home student a mandatory award, consisting of tuition fees and a means-tested grant (your means, if you're supporting the student) towards living costs, and it will make available a student loan repayable (after the course finishes) in instalments at an index-linked rate without interest.

The overseas student doesn't get an award, so has to pay the tuition fees plus all living costs, and doesn't get the offer of a loan. Not just that, but the tuition fees charge to an overseas student are very much higher than those payable by a home student.

To use illustrative figures for the academic year 1995/96*, a home student would pay fees of around £2,000 for an arts course, while an overseas student would pay around £7,000. On top of that, an overseas student would pay individual college fees at a collegiate university – Oxford or Cambridge – of around £3,000.

How does a British expatriate child qualify as a home student?

First point: the decision on whether or not to grant home-student status, and then whether or not to pay a mandatory award, rests with the Local Education Authority (LEA), not with the Department of Education. Your first task is to get an LEA to accept that you fall within its catchment area.

Generally, the LEA to which you apply should be the one for the area in which you were resident before you left the UK (if you are in the Channel Islands or the Isle of Man, for education purposes you haven't left; see below). If you have retained property there, and can state that you intend to return, your case will be easier.

If you don't know the address of your LEA, your children's school will be able to help, if it's in the UK, or you can contact the Department for Education at Sanctuary Buildings, Great Smith Street, London SW1P 3BT, telephone 0171 925 5555, fax 0171 925 6971. The school may also be able to supply the application form of an award.

If you have problems getting your LEA to consider your case, argue. Point out the many reasons why you may be considered ordinarily resident for education purposes in its catchment area. There is a good reason not to take no for an answer at this stage, which is explained in the next section. If arguing doesn't work, your last resort will be to try the LEA for the college offering the course to which you will apply.

You must apply at least four months ahead of the start of your course. That early, you may not even know whether you have a place on it. But consider the following:

- If you don't get your first choice, you will still want an award for your second, third, fourth or fifth choice; and
- Resources are finite, and there will be many other prospective students applying for awards. If you're a borderline case and you've left it so late that there's no money left . . .

Trouble is, there isn't a rulebook. Eligibility for financial help is at the discretion of the LEA who will have to provide it, and there are no directives from on high to influence the decision, only guidelines.

* *For awards purposes, the academic year is assumed to being on 1st September, 1st January, 1st April or 1st July, according to the term in which the course begins. Student loans are payable on the first day of the course.*

The main one says that whether your children get state financial help with the cost of a degree or other course depends on their 'ordinary residence' in the three years before the academic year in which their course starts. But even this isn't as simple as you might think.

Ordinary residence for education purposes

This is not ordinary residence in the tax sense as detailed on page 92. It is ordinary residence in what the Department for Education (DfE), calls the 'British Islands', which include the Channel Islands and the Isle of Man as well as England, Scotland, Wales and Northern Ireland.

Crucially, a further-education student will not qualify for an award and loan as a home student if ordinary residence in the UK was achieved by virtue of residence at a boarding school during term-time. As the DfE's booklet *Student grants and loans* explains it to the student, 'if you were living here mainly to receive full-time education and would normally have lived elsewhere, you will not usually be regarded as having been "ordinarily resident" in the British Islands.'

Note the words 'normally' and 'usually'. The sentence before that one says, 'If you were away from this country because you or your family were temporarily employed abroad, you may be treated as if your "ordinary residence" in the British Islands had not been interrupted.' Note 'may'. Note also that 'temporarily' here refers to a break in the three-years qualifying period, not an absence of years. The DfE had indicated that a two-year or three-year absence may be regarded as temporary, subject to other conditions being satisfied; but it is up to the LEA first to take your case, and then to award you money.

CHAPTER FOUR

PLANNING TO RETURN TO THE UK

'Leaving this place is quite a comedown for some people, and despite all the times you were at the end of your tether, you can end up missing the buzz of making do in difficult surroundings – and the social life in particular.'
Expatriate, Asia
'I've employed five returning expatriates in the last year, from Saudi. Boy, do those guys have problems getting back in. All that freedom and responsibility, and now fitting back into the structure of a British company. One of them's still with us, though.'
Personnel Director, London

This has been the great neglected area of briefing for expatriate life. You cannot expect to come home and just pick up where you left off, either personally, socially or professionally. After years away, you must plan your return as if you are going to another foreign country; that is, you must plan for everything that comes under the general heading of 'culture shock' as well as for tax-efficiency and financial wellbeing. Organizations like the Centre for International Briefing. Going Places and Corona Worldwide (page 30) now all provide briefing courses for returning expatriates, and these are well worth considering. Such courses will cover financial questions for returnees as well as more general cultural questions, and should not be left until you come home (see below); they are a worthwhile use of a home leave.

This chapter assumes that your intention is to return to the UK after the expiry of your present contract. That is not necessarily what you will do, and alternatives are discussed below. The first question to settle is timing.

When should you start planning your return?

Moving back to the UK is potentially as stressful and time-consuming as going overseas in the first place. You may not have time to complete all your preparations before you move back, but what matters is that you review your situation thoroughly, with professional input, well in advance. Some things can be safely overlooked, others can't. You should at least know what you can afford to overlook. A financial adviser mentioned in the context of moving back to the UK is Dorian Hannington of Lomond Asset Management, 84 Coombe Road, New Malden, Surrey KT3 4QS, telephone 0181 949 8811, fax 0181 949 6237.

Plan for your return before the UK tax year in which it's going to happen. A UK tax year runs from 6 April to the next 5 April. If you are planning to return to the UK on, say, 4 April 1998, you should either delay your return by forty-eight hours, or get your planning settled before 5 April 1997. Note that planning takes time. You should be thinking about your return from the time you go overseas, and you should be beginning to take action with at least six weeks in hand before the UK tax year of return begins (this not least because instructions to financial institutions can be lost or not acted upon, and you need time to chase them).

Note that although the priority is to act before the UK tax year of return, there can be reasons to act before your overseas-residence tax year of return. This is a point on which to take advice well in advance; see page 147 for finding advice; see the table on page 129 to find out what is your overseas tax year.

Before you start thinking about your return, you should think about

Contract renewal

In a company with experience of employing expatriates, it should be understood that you will need to discuss your future before the tax year of your return to the UK. Although advance guarantees are not given in this kind of conversation, on either side, you should be able to get a better idea than at the beginning of the contract, of whether you are likely to be offered a renewal, and whether you would be likely to accept it.

Of course, you will not be told that they're not intending to renew but they want you to continue working hard anyway, and this is a conversation to handle carefully, without pressing for commitments that can't be given. Do not convey the slightest hint that you might be thinking of leaving even if you are offered renewal, and take the approach that you are keen to go on, and/or (according to your circumstances) that, although there's a fresh challenge with the company back home, you've enjoyed your time here, and are keen to see that the achievements of your time here are built upon. Remember that when you arrived, you were to some extent an unknown quantity, but that now, you have proved yourself.

Before talking to the company, talk to your partner, and consider your family back home. You may judge that even if you do renew, you will need to spend some time in the UK between contracts. How long you can spend in the UK between overseas contracts is discussed below.

You should also be thinking about alternatives. Some expatriates find that after a time overseas, they can work anywhere but in the UK; others just take the precaution of checking the worldwide jobs market before committing themselves to going home. This is a time of upheaval; better to make all the changes at once, than get home and start the whole process all over again a few months later.

If you decide that you would like to stay overseas but not with the same employer, you do not have to make all the arrangements before your contract expires. As explained below, you will have time in hand after you return to the UK. This is, however, a time for careful planning, and you should aim to formulate as clear a set of objectives as possible, at the outset.

Sources of further jobs overseas, and other factors to consider if you decide not to return to the UK for good, are considered later in this chapter.

If you are intending to return to the UK, you should have a clear set of

Planning priorities

This list of priorities according to which you should plan your return to the UK is as follows.

Tax

In the country where you are living overseas, you should establish whether you need to make a tax return or obtain tax certification before you can remove yourself financially (see page 27).

Your bigger priority is your approaching resumption of tax-residence in the UK.

The year of your return is divided in two for tax purposes by the Inland Revenue, and in general, you will pay tax in the UK only on earnings, etc. relating to the period after you have arrived in the UK permanently and thus resumed UK-resident status for tax purposes (which is examined in detail on page 92). However, this split-year approach is by extra-statutory concession, and it is widely considered to be worthwhile to realize substantial capital gains while you are unequivocally non-resident (ie, in the UK tax year before the UK tax year of your return). This is particularly important if you have not been overseas for long enough to achieve not ordinary resident status for tax purposes as well as non-resident status.

Remember that currency gains are chargeable to Capital Gains Tax (CGT), so that ideally, any major transfers from other currencies back to Sterling for your return should also be effected in the last UK tax year of your absence from the UK. As discussed elsewhere (page 112), capital losses while you were liable to CGT (ie, before you left the UK) may be carried forward indefinitely to offset against capital gains; now is the time to use them.

Note that any salary which is payable in respect of terminal leave at the end of your contract will be UK-taxable if you spend that terminal leave in the UK.

Investments, gains and bed-and-breakfasting

With the caveat that substantial gains should be realized in the UK tax year before the UK tax year of your return, the general rule is that you should 'bed-and-breakfast' your investments before the date of your return to the UK. Bed-and-breakfasting means selling to realize capital gains before you become liable for CGT, and then reinvesting immediately afterwards. By doing this, you ensure that any capital gain will be calculated from the recent reinvestment date rather than from the original investment date.

Note that you should reconsider your investment strategy in the light of UK tax-efficiency. This means that you may wish not to reinvest some of your realized gains in the last weeks of your non-resident status, but to hold them until you are once again resident and thus able to take advantage of such investment vehicles as Personal Equity Plans (PEPs), Tax Exempt Special Savings Accounts (TESSAs) and, if you have built up substantial capital and like taking risks, Venture Capital Trusts (VCTs) which are either not available to non-residents or of limited tax efficiency unless you are tax-resident.

Insurances

It is generally not a good idea to invest in insurance 'bonds', sometimes referred to as 'personal portfolio bonds' in the months before you return to the UK as a means of escaping tax on your assets. The tax regime on such 'bonds' is presently favourable but under review by the Inland Revenue.

The general rule on insurance products is that they are investment contracts designed to achieve an objective in capital planning, not tax avoidance. Note that where the proceeds of a UK policy are payable tax-free to a UK resident, tax on that policy has been paid already by the life company.

You should confirm with the life assurer whether there is provision for an offshore 'pension plan', which will not quality for favourable tax treatment in the UK because it does not meet the UK definition of a pension plan, to be transferred into a UK-tax-efficient form.

Property

You will need to give notice to your overseas landlord.

If you are returning to a UK property that has been rented in your absence, you will need to instruct your agent to give notice to your tenants. You may need to set in train the process of selling your rentable property (page 170) to raise funds for the purchase of a suitable property in which to live.

If you have sold your UK property and not bought to rent, you will need to start looking for somewhere to live. A list of 'property search' agents appears on page 222. Such agents can draw up a shortlist of properties that meet your requirements, and can even handle the purchase for you in the unlikely event that you decide to commit yourself before you return to the UK and see the property for yourself. You may consider it sensible to move into a serviced flat (page 79) for a period of weeks or possible months, and do your own house-hunting.

Note that mortgages for UK property are generally more easily obtainable if you are intending to return to live in the property, and if you can show continuity in your employment.

Schools

Do you need to give a term's notice?

Both partners' careers

Both of you should draw up CVs and start networking if you haven't already. This is particularly important for the 'trailing spouse', who will be, to some extent, out of touch with developments in his or her industry. The Dual Career Network, which will be useful at this stage, is mentioned in the box on page 17.

But before either of you makes any firm long-term career commitments, you should also both begin to prepare yourselves for

Culture shock

You will be warned that the UK will have changed during your absence, and you will be told to expect surprises. This is justified. When you return after an absence of years, not only will new buildings have gone up, familiar landmarks been demolished and new roads been built, but the cultural background will have changed.

This means more than a new crop of soap operas and new words and phrases entering the language from unpredictable sources ('Why,' a recently returning expatriate asked, 'is Michael Heseltine called Hezza?'). It means changed assumptions and values at almost a subliminal level. Cultures change quickly, and British culture, being heterogeneous, changes more quickly than most.

But the real change you will find when you come back to the UK is in yourself. One of the reasons for 'repatriation failure' is that, as one personnel manager described it at a recent conference, 'they come back and find they have to cram all that experience back into the same old package, and none of the people around them understand it or can share it.'

Your stay-at-home colleagues and friends haven't just been through the disruption of coming home from another country. They didn't go to work abroad; they haven't had any of the experiences you've had, and as one returned expatriate put it, 'they just don't see the point of the things you try to tell them.'

Coming back to the UK is coming to a country that is, at least for a time, more foreign than it is familiar. Treat is as another posting, and expect the same depression and sense of dislocation as when you went overseas.

It wears off, same as it did before, but you will realize that both professionally and personally, you have gained from what you have experienced. Professionally, your CV is stronger than it was, and personally – you've passed the test.

So what are your prospects? You may be returning to your old job with your UK employer, and you may be happy to do that. But don't expect the welcome to last, and remember that your ways of dealing with people at work have changed while you've been away; in subtle ways, you've changed. But the people who have been here all along are the ones who are right about the way they do things, and you're the one that has to adapt.

There's a powerful argument that an expatriate posting shouldn't count for nothing in a career, and that if you find yourself coming back to do the same thing as before, you're letting yourself be wasted. If you were careful about accepting the overseas job in the first place (page 20), you shouldn't find yourself in this position, but companies change over the years, and the plans for you now may not be the plans that they had for you when you went away.

Turn your unfamiliar attitudes and approaches to advantage. While you're still 'new' in your reclaimed UK job, take the opportunity to discuss the use that the company – and you – will make of your enhanced skills. You have a lot more to offer now, and you should get that across.

Of course, you have a lot more to offer to another employer, if you find the settling-back process difficult, and you should not overlook the 'networking' value for yourself of re-establishing old contacts and making new ones. Don't waste this opportunity to project yourself to other possible employers in the UK.

Some expatriates change their minds about coming to the UK, and decide to go overseas again. This is potentially a very positive career choice, especially if you are not 'fussy' about where you go overseas. If this is the case, you are one of a rare breed, the 'international employee', and you should look for an opportunity to use that term about yourself at any job interview.

If you decide not to say in the UK

By definition, you will reach this decision after you have returned to the UK. You become resident for tax purposes in the UK from the date of your return. It is likely that if you decide to go overseas again, you will not be continuing your current contract of employment to do so. In this situation, you must go overseas again, or find a contract of employment that will take you overseas again, within 183 days of your return (you must also ensure that your time in the UK does not average above 91 days per year over any period of years overseas of which this year will be part up to a maximum of four years) if you are to put a case that your not resident and not ordinarily resident status was not interrupted by your return.

Otherwise, you will be subject to UK tax on the remittance basis (page 99) for the year of your return.

Finding a job overseas

The two main sources of jobs overseas are the fortnightly *Overseas Jobs Express*, Island Publishing, Premier House, Shoreham Airport, Shoreham by Sea, West Sussex BN43 5FF, telephone 01273 440220, fax 01273 440229, and the monthly *Jobs International*, Magmaker Ltd, Cromwell Court, New Road, St Ives, Huntingdon, Cambs PE17 4BG, telephone 01480 496130, fax 01480 495514. They carry a wide range of advertised vacancies, but do not necessarily carry everything that is available at the top end of the overseas jobs market.

The *Financial Times* on Wednesdays and *The Times* on Thursdays are generally held to be good for senior vacancies overseas, while the *Daily Telegraph* on Thursdays is a source for marketing and engineering posts. The *Sunday Times* is widely used by recruitment consultants.

Preparing to go overseas again

No posting is a complete preparation for another posting, except in that most important sense – frame of mind. If you decide to go overseas again, don't fall into the trap of thinking that because you've done it once successfully, you'll find it easy this time.

An expatriate, describing her move from Asia to eastern Europe, said, 'I thought I'd give it a month for the depression stage, but in the end it took three.' The cycle will be the same as last time, easier because you now how it goes, but taking its toll on you nonetheless.

So accept the offers of briefing, gather all the information, and above all, be prepared.

If you have spent three years overseas, a few months in the UK, and now you are going overseas again for another period of years, you should give some thought to whether you intend to continue this pattern in the long term. Some expatriates talk about how 'home' has become the family unit rather than a particular corner of the home country.

They mean this positively, and although there is a downside with many careers that reaching the top is not compatible with a mobile lifestyle, the upside is that if you are suited to the international life, you face a wider range of opportunities both in your career and, ultimately, for retirement. You can also accumulate assets more quickly, and retire earlier.

So turn back to page one, and get reading.

'*The UK becomes, despite sentimental attachment, an uninviting prospect for return. Expatriation sets you on a road that has every likelihood of keeping you offshore for longer than you intended, possibly for good. Accepting a contract over here for the first time is more significant for the consequences on your career than you can realize, especially as regards the likelihood of remaining overseas. You make a lot of international contacts and friendships, and move in a world that is simply bigger, with many more opportunities.*'

Businessman, Middle East

CHAPTER FIVE

USEFUL INFORMATION

The addresses in this chapter are given in the order in which they appear in the book. They are accompanied by further useful addresses in the same field, and are listed under appropriate subject headings. Suggested further reading, including Inland Revenue guides and expatriate magazines, may be found on page 229.

Useful addresses

Note that once you are overseas, the code for telephoning and faxing the UK is 44. This replaces the initial 0, so that 0171, for example, becomes 44171. Dial first the international code from where you are. From Denmark, for example, you would dial 0900 44171 for an inner London number.

When phoning from one country to another, always say that you are phoning from overseas. In some countries, the USA for example, it is established practice to answer calls and put them immediately on hold. This notionally honours such advertised commitments as 'We'll pick up the phone within three rings, guaranteed'.

Introduction

Sources of books

Books etc.
120 Charing Cross Road
London WC2H 0JR
telephone 0171 379 7313, fax 0171 836 0373

Hatchards
187 Piccadilly
London W1V 9DA
telephone 0171 439 9921, fax 0171 494 1313

Lonely Planet Publications
10 Barley Mow Passage
Chiswick
London W4 4PH
telephone 0181 742 3161, fax 0181 742 2772

Telephone directories

For the truly well prepared, overseas phone directories can be obtained from:

BT International Directories
RDC Warehouse
Longridge Road
Preston PR2 5AY
telephone 01772 793390, fax 01772 797797

Chapter One: Before You Go

Employment Conditions Abroad
Anchor House
15 Britten Street
London SW3 3TY
telephone 0171 351 5000, fax 0171 351 9396

Eurocost
1 rue Emile Bian
L-1235 Luxembourg
telephone 352 40 48 06/7/8/9, fax 352 49 57 13

Instant Search
4 George Street
Whalley
near Clitheroe
Lancashire BB7 9TH
telephone 01254 822288, fax 01254 822221

The Foreign Office
Travellers' Advice Line
0171 210 4197

DTI Export Publications
Admail 528
London SW1W 8YT
telephone 0171 510 0171, fax 0171 510 0197

Corona Worldwide (The Women's' Corona Society)
The Commonwealth Institute
Kensington High Street
London W8 6NQ
telephone 0171 610 4407, fax 0171 602 7374

Christians Abroad
1 Stockwell Green
London SW9 9HP
telephone 0171 737 7811

Dual Career Network
Fenham House
Four Elms
Edenbridge
Kent TN8 6NE
telephone 01732 700555, fax 01732 864171

International Translation Resources
1 Dolphin Square
London W4 2ST
telephone 0181 742 7422, fax 0181 742 8080

John Wason Ltd
72 South Street
Reading RG1 4RA
telephone 01734 568800, fax 01734 568094

Overseas Branch
Department of Social Security (DSS)
Longbenton
Benton Park Road
Newcastle-upon-Tyne NE98 1YX
telephone 0191 213 5000

RAC
PO Box 499
South Croydon
Surrey CR2 6WX
telephone 0181 686 0088, fax 0181 667 1041

AA
PO Box 50
Basingstoke, Hants RG21 2EA
telephone 0345 500600, fax 0113 279018

National Savings
Marton
Blackpool
Lancashire FI3 9YP
telephone 01253 766151, fax 01235 693182

The Centre for International Briefing
Farnham Castle
Farnham
Surrey GU9 0AG
telephone 01252 721194, fax 01252 711283

Going Places
84 Coombe Road
New Malden
Surrey KT3 4QS
telephone 0181 949 8811, fax 0181 949 6237

Expatriate Management Limited
St Clement's House
2 Clement's Lane
London EC4N 7AP
telephone 0171 280 7732, fax 0171 280 7733

World Health Organisation
Distribution & Sales
1211 Geneva 27
Switzerland

British Airways Travel Clinics
35 Wimpole Street
London W1
telephone 0171 486 3665

Oxford University Press Distribution Centre
Saxon Way West
Corby
Northants NN18 9ES
telephone 01536 746337, fax 01536 741519

Medical Advisory Services for Travellers Abroad (MASTA)
The London School of Hygiene and Tropical Medicine
Keppel Street
London WC1
telephone 0171 631 4408, fax 0171 323 4547
(MASTA's enquiry line is 0891 24100)

BUPA Health Screening Centre
Battle Bridge House
300 Gray's Inn Road
London WC1X 8DU
telephone 0171 837 6484, fax 0171 837 6797

Family Planning Association
27 Mortimer Street
London W1
telephone 0171 636 7866

International Planned Parenthood Federation
Regent's College
Inner Circle
Regent's Park
London NW1
telephone 0171 486 0741, fax 0171 487 7150

Securicor Network Europe
Unit B
Ponton Road
Vauxhall
London SW8 5BA
telephone 0171 622 2313, fax 0171 498 5357

HM Customs & Excise
Thomas Paine House
Angel Square
Torrens Street
London EC1V 1TA
telephone 0171 865 3000, fax 0171 865 3105

Manor Car Storage
PO Box 28
Clavering
Saffron Walden
Essex CB11 4RA
telephone 01799 550022, fax 01799 550021

The Royal Society for the Prevention of Cruelty to Animals (RSPCA)
Causeway
Horsham
West Sussex RH12 1HG
telephone 01403 264181, fax 01403 241048

Passports for Pets
44 Little Boltons
London SW10 9LL

British Association of Removers (BAR)
3 Churchill Court
58 Station Road
North Harrow
Middlesex HA2 7SA
telephone 0181 861 3331, fax 0181 861 3332

Royal Mail Redirection Service
telephone 0800 444844

Chapter Two: The First Year Abroad

Language Line
18 Victoria Park Square
London E2 9PF
telephone 0181 983 4042 (interpreters on 0181 981 9911), fax 0181 983 3598

The Passport Office
Clive House
70–78 Petty France
London SW1
telephone 0171 799 2290

Language Studies International
Woodstock House
10–12 James Street
London W1M 5HN
telephone 0171 499 9621, fax 0171 491 0992

Linguarama
Queen's House
8 Queen Street
London EC4N 1SP
telephone 0171 236 1992, fax 0171 236 7208

The Linguaphone Institute
St Giles House
50 Poland Street
London W1V 4AX
telephone 0171 287 4050, fax 0171 434 0451

World-Wide Education Service (WES)
35 Belgrave Square
London SW1 8QA
telephone 0181 866 4400, fax 0181 429 4838

Mail order companies

Goodies by Post
PO Box 285
Guernsey GY1 1WR
telephone 01481 722686, fax 01481 714234

Global Presents
Unit 16
Talina Centre
Bagleys Lane
London SW6 2BW
telephone 0171 731 3000, fax 0171 731 1219

Fortnum & Mason
181 Piccadilly
London W1A 1ER
telephone 0171 465 8666, fax 0171 437 3278
Worldwide delivery but some brochure items marked not suitable for export

The Antique Wine Company of Great Britain
The Old Stables
Thorpe Hall
Thorpe Constantine
Staffordshire B79 0LH
telephone 01827 830707
Wine in presentation boxes with original copy of *The Times* of recipient's
date of birth, worldwide delivery subject to local restrictions

Comics By Post
Hamer 20th Century Books
4 Springfield
Woodsetts
Worksop
Notts S81 8QD
telephone 01909 569428
Copy of *Dandy* or *Beano*, etc. for recipient's date of birth

Harrods Mail Order
Admail 1234
London SW1A 2XX

Savoy Group Services
Unit 1
The Willows Centre
17 Willows Lane
Mitchum
Surrey CR4 4NX
telephone 0181 648 7701
Savoy coffee, Savoy bathrobes, even Savoy hand-made beds; worldwide
gifts of the type you would associate with the hotel

Car hire companies

Avis Rent-a-Car
Avis House
Park Road
Bracknell
Berkshire RG12 2EW
telephone 0181 848 8733, fax 01344 710112

Expat Car Rental
Continental Reservation Centre
Crowthorne House
Furzen Lane
Ellens Green
West Sussex RH12 3AR
telephone 01403 823030, fax 01403 823228

Locost Car & Van Hire
South Woodham Garage
Old Wickford Road
South Woodham Ferrers
Chelmsford
Essex
telephone 01245 324101, fax 01245 325529

Regent Car Rental
1B Bath Road
Heathrow
Middlesex TW6 2AA
telephone 0181 759 4180, fax 0181 759 4190

Educational and related information

Gabbitas Educational Consultants
Carrington House
126–130 Regent Street
London W1R 6EE
telephone 0171 734 0161, fax 0171 437 1764

The Independent Schools Information Services (ISIS)
56 Buckingham Gate
London SW1E 6AG
telephone 0171 630 8793, fax 0171 630 5013

Universal Aunts Ltd
PO Box 304
London SW4 0NN
telephone 0171 498 8200, fax 0171 622 1914

State Boarding Information Services (STABIS)
43 Raglan Road
Reigate
Surrey RH2 ODU
telephone 01737 226450, fax 01737 226775

State schools with boarding facilities

Berkshire Reading School 01734 261406
Buckinghamshire Royal Grammar School, High Wycombe 01494 524955
Cambridgeshire King's School, Peterborough 01733 62143
Cornwall Launceston College 01566 772468
Cumbria Dallam School 01539 63224, Keswick School 017687 72173
Derbyshire Lady Manners' School 01629 812671
Devonshire Queen Elizabeth's Community College 01363 775264
Dorset Beaminster School 01308 862633, Shaftesbury School 01747 854498, Woodroffe School 01297 442232
Essex Hockerill Anglo European School 01279 658451, Royal Grammar School, Colchester 01206 577971/2
Hampshire King's School, Winchester 01962 852059, Westgate School 01962 854757, Peter Symond's Sixth Form College 01962 852764
Hertfordshire St George's School 01582 765477
Kent Cranbrook School 01580 712163, Roger Manwood's School 01304 613286
Lancashire Royal Grammar School, Lancaster 01524 32109
Leicestershire Ashby Grammar School 01530 413759, Burleigh Community College 01509 268996, Rutland Sixth Form College 01572 722863

Lincolnshire Cordeaux High School 01507 606555, De Aston School 01673 843415, King Edward VI School, Louth 01507 600456, King's School, Grantham 0146 63180, Skegness Grammar School 01754 61000
Norfolk Wymondham College 01953 605566
North Yorkshire Ripon Grammar School 01765 602647/8
Nottinghamshire Southwell Minster School 01636 814000
Oxfordshire Burford School 01993 823283
Shropshire Adams' School, Wem 01939 232328, Adams' Grammar School, Newport 01952 810698
Somerset Brymore School 01278 652369, Sexey's School 01749 813393
Surrey Gordon's School 01276 858084, Royal Alexandra & Albert School 01737 643052
West Sussex Steyning Grammar School 01903 816346
West Midlands Old Swinford Hospital School 01384 370025

International

Council of European Schools in the European Community (COBISEC)
c/o The British School of Brussels
Chaussée de Louvain 19
Tervuren
Belgium 3080
telephone 32 2 767 47 00, fax 32 2 767 80 70

The European Council of International Schools (ECIS)
21 Lavant Street
Petersfield
Hampshire GU32 3EL
telephone 01730 268244, fax 01730 267914

The International Baccalaureate Office
Route des Morillons 15
CH – 1218 Grand-Saconnex
Geneva
Switzerland
telephone 41 22 791 0274, fax 41 22 791 0277

Universities and Colleges Admisions Service (UCAS)
Fulton House
Jessop Avenue
Cheltenham
Gloucestershire GL50 3SH
telephone 01242 222444

Political information

D Division
The Home Office
50 Queen Anne's Gate
London SW1H 9AT
telephone 0171 273 3347

House of Commons
General information 0171 219 3000
Parliamentary information 0171 219 4272

Conservatives Abroad
Conservative & Unionist Central Office
32 Smith Square
London SW1P 3HH
telephones 0171 222 9000, extension 2728 or 2308

Labour International
The Labour Party
150 Walworth Road
London SE17 1JT
telephone 0171 277 3362

Liberal Democrats Campaigns Department
4 Cowley Street
London SW1P 3NB
telephone 0171 222 7999

Chapter Three: Financial Planning

Inland Revenue Claims Branch (International Section)
St John's House
Merton Road
Bootle
Merseyside L69 9BB
telephone 0151 472 6000

Inland Revenue Public Departments (Technical Unit) Foreign Section
Ty-Glas
Llanishen
Cardiff CF4 5WN
telephone 01222 753271

Inland Revenue Foreign Group
HMIT Centre 1
Queensway House
East Kilbride
Glasgow G79 1AA
telephone 013552 28733

Inland Revenue Marine Section
HMIT Cardiff 6
Ty-Glas
Llanishen
Cardiff CF4 5TW
telephone 01222 753271

The Clerk to the Special Commissioners
15–19 Bedford Avenue
London WC1B 3AS
telephone 0171 631 4242

Revenue Adjudicator's Office
3rd Floor
Haymarket House
28 Haymarket
London SW1Y 4SP
telephone 0171 930 2292

The Parliamentary Ombudsman (Commissioner for Administration)
The Office of the Parliamentary Commissioner for Administration
Church House
Great Smith Street
London SW1P 3BW
telephone 0171 276 2130/3000

Capital Taxes Office
Minford House
Rockley Road
London W14 0DF
telephone 0171 603 4622

HM Customs & Excise Information Office
New Kings Beam House
22 Upper Ground
London SE1 9PJ
telephone 0171 620 1313

Inland Revenue International Division (Double Taxation)
Room 319
Strand Bridge House
138–142 The Strand
London WC2R 1HH

Inland Revenue Foreign Intelligence Section
Room 7
New Wing
Somerset House
The Strand
London WC2R 1LB

Offshore regulators

Here are the names and addresses of the regulatory bodies in the main offshore
financial centres (OFCs). Confirmation of membership and authorization to
practice should be sought before investing any significant sum of money with
an institution based on an OFC.

The Central Bank of the Bahamas
PO Box N-4868
Nassau
Bahamas
telephone (809) 3222130, fax (809) 3224321

Bermuda Monetary Authority
Sofia Building
PO Box HM 2447
48 Church Street
Hamilton
Bermuda HM 12
telephone (809) 2955278, fax (809) 2927471

Financial Services Department
Government of the British Virgin Islands
Road Town
Tortola
BVI
telephone (809) 494 4190/4381, fax (809) 494 5016

Cayman Islands Government Banking Inspectorate
Grand Cayman
telephone (809) 9497900, fax (809) 9497544

Banking Supervision and Regulation Division
Central Bank of Cyprus
80 Kennedy Avenue
Nicosia, 1395
Cyprus
telephone (357) 2 379800, fax (379) 2 378152

Financial Sector Department
Central Bank of Ireland
Dame Street
Dublin 2
telephone (3531) 6716666, fax (3531) 6716561

Financial Services Commission
Suite 943
Europort
PO Box 940
Gibraltar
telephone (350) 40283/4, fax (350) 40282

Financial Services Commission
Valley House
Hirzel Street
St Peter Port
Guernsey
telephone (481) 712706, fax (481) 712010

Securities & Futures Commission
12th Floor
Edinburgh Tower
15 Queen's Road
Central
Hong Kong
telephone (852) 840 9222, fax (852) 521 7836

Financial Supervision Commission
PO Box 58
1–4 Goldie Terrace
Upper Church Street
Douglas
Isle of Man
telephone (624) 624487, fax (624) 629342

Financial Services Department
Cyril Le Marquand House
The Parade
St Helier
Jersey
telephone (534) 603000, fax (534) 70957

The Institut Monetaire Luxembourgeois
L-2983
Luxembourg
telephone (352) 402929221 (banking)/(352) 402929251 (funds), fax (352) 492180

Business Development Department
Malta Financial Services Centre
Attard
Malta
telephone (356) 441155, fax (356) 441188

Secretariat of the Swiss Federal Banking Commission
Marktgasse 37
CH-3001 Bern
Switzerland
telephone (4131) 161911, fax (4131) 696126

Offshore Finance Centre Unit
Post Office Building
Front Street
Grand Turk
Turks & Caicos Islands
telephone (809 94) 62791, fax (809 94) 62821

Some advisers

This is only a small selection of the tax and financial advisers active in the expatriate field.

The Equitable Life
Albert House
South Esplanade
St Peter Port
Guernsey
GY1 1AW
telephone (01481) 716021, fax (01481) 712069

Bacon & Woodrow
Albert House
South Esplanade
St Peter Port
Guernsey GY1 1AW
telephone 01481 728432, fax 01481 724082

Wilfred T Fry (Personal Financial Planning) Limited
Crescent House
Crescent Road
Worthing
West Sussex BN11 1RN
telephone 01903 231545, fax 01903 200868

Information on second-hand endowment policies
The Association of Policy Market Makers
The Holywell Centre
1 Phipp Street
London EC2A 4PS
telephone 0171 739 3949, fax 0171 729 5143

UK regulatory authority
You can obtain lists of members appropriate to your requirements, though not recommendations. Names of financial advisers should be obtained from the Personal Investment Authority. Remember that complaints should be addressed first to the member firm.

Securities and Investments Board (SIB)
Gavrelle House
2–14 Bunhill Row
London EC1Y 8RA
telephone 0171 638 1240

Self-regulatory organizations (SROs)
Investment Management Regulatory Organization (IMRO)
5th Floor
Lloyd's Chambers
Portsoken Street
London E1 8BT
telephone 0171 390 5000

Personal Investment Authority (PIA)
7th Floor
1 Canada Square
Canary Wharf
London E14 5AZ
telephone 0171 538 8860

NB: A complaint about a member firm of one of the SROs should be directed to:

The PIA Ombudsman Bureau
Centre Point
103 New Oxford Street
London WC1A 1QH
telephone 0171 240 3838

The Securities and Futures Authority (SFA)
Cotton Centre
Cotton Lane
London SE1 2QB
telephone 0171 378 9000

Recognized Professional Bodies (RPBs)

Chartered Association of Certified Accountants (ACCA)
29 Lincoln's Inn Fields
London WC2A 3EE   *(tends to be Smaller Practices)*
telephone 0171 242 6855

Institute of Actuaries
Staple Inn Hall
High Holborn
London WC1V 7QJ
telephone 0171 242 0106

Institute of Chartered Accountants in England and Wales (ICAEW)
Chartered Acountants Hall
Moorgate Place
London EC2P 2BJ
telephone 0171 920 8100

Institute of Chartered Accountants in Ireland
Chartered Accountants House
87–89 Pembroke Road
Ballsbridge
Dublin 4
telephone 00 353166 80400
Includes Northern Ireland

Institute of Chartered Accountants of Scotland
27 Queen Street
Edinburgh EH2 1LA
telephone 0131 225 5673

Insurance Brokers' Regulation Council (IBRC)
15 St Helen's Place
London EC3A 6DS
telephone 0171 588 4387

The Law Society
113 Chancery Lane
London WC2A 1PL
telephone 0171 242 1222

The Law Society of Northern Ireland
Law Society House
98 Victoria Street
Belfast BT1 3JZ
telephone 01232 231 614

The Law Society of Scotland
The Law Society's Hall
26 Drumsheugh Gardens
Edinburgh EH3 7YR
telephone 0131 226 7411

Association of Residential Letting Agents (ARLA)
Maple House
53–55 Woodside Road
Amersham
Bucks HP6 6AA
telephone 01494 431 680, fax 01494 431 530

Health insurance providers

BUPA International
Imperial House
40–42 Queens Road
Brighton BN1 3WV
telephone 0273 323563

IHI danmark
64a Athol Street
Douglas
Isle of Man
telephone 0624 677412

IPH
PO Box 488
Boreham Wood
Herts WD6 4AW
telephone 0181 905 2888

OHRA
17 East Links
Tollgate
Chandlers Ford
Hampshire SO5 3TG
telephone 01703 620620

PPP
PPP House
Tunbridge Wells
Kent TN1 2PL
telephone 01892 512345

WPA
Blackbrook Park
Taunton
Somerset TA1 2PE
telephone 01823 623000

Government departments

Department of Social Security, Overseas Branch
Longbenton
Benton Park Road
Newcastle-upon-Tyne NE98 1YX
telephone 0191 213 5000

Department for Education
Sanctuary Buildings
Great Smith Street
London SW1P 3BT
telephone 0171 925 5555, fax 0171 925 6971

Chapter Four: Planning to Return to the UK

UK property-search agents
Association of Relocation Agents (ARA)
Premier House
11 Marlborough Place
Brighton BN1 1UB
telephone 01273 624455
ARA publishes an annual Directory of Members throughout the UK.

The Wilson Group
5 Raphael Street
Knightsbridge Green
London SW7 1DL
telephone 0171 589 4164
Central London and Southern England. Will buy properties from £200,000 to £1.5 million plus in London; from £300,000 to £3 million plus outside. Fees: £500/£1,000 registration for London/country, then 2 per cent of purchase price

Recruitment consultants for jobs overseas
Mercer Gray
2 Conduit Street
London W1R 9TG
telephone 0171 493 4669, fax 0171 499 2508

Financial Recruitment International
Southmead
Long Hey Road
Caldy
Wirral L48 1LY
telephone 0151 625 0565, fax 0151 625 0058

PA Consulting Group
123 Buckingham Palace Road
London SW1W 9SR
telephone 0171 730 9000

Nicholson International
Bracton House
34–36 High Holborn
London WC1V 6AS
fax 0171 404 8128

Selector Europe
16 Connaught Place
London W2 2ED
telephone 0171 493 1238

Recruitment Matters
15 Great Eastern Street
London EC2A 3EJ
telephone 0171 377 1600, fax 0171 377 1801

Devonshire Executive
7 Birchin Lane
London EC3V 9BY
telephone 0171 895 8050, fax 0171 626 2092

MSL International
32 Aybrook Street
London W1M 3JL
telephone 0171 487 5000

HMSO bookshops

49 High Holborn
London WC1V 6HB
telephone 0171 873 0011, fax 0171 831 1326

71 Lothian Road
Edinburgh EH3 9AZ
telephone 0131 228 4181, fax 0131 229 2734

16 Arthur Street
Belfast BT1 4GD
telephone 01232 238451, fax 01232 235401

9/21 Princess Street
Albert Square
Manchester M60 8AS
telephone 0161 834 7201, fax 0161 833 0634

68/69 Bull Street
Birmingham B4 6AD
telephone 0121 236 9696, fax 0121 236 9699

33 Wine Street
Bristol BS1 2BQ
telephone 01179 264306, fax 01179 294515

Orial
The Friary
Cardiff CF1 4AA
telephone 01222 395548, fax 01222 384347

Further Inland Revenue Addresses
Controllers of Executive Offices

If you are not able to settle a complaint to your own satisfaction with your tax office, you should write to the Controller for the area in which it is situated.

(General comments should go to the Customer Services Manager at the same address.)

England and Wales
East
Mr M J Hodgson
Inland Revenue East
Midgate House
Peterborough PE1 1TD

London
Mr J F Carling
Inland Revenue London
New Court
48 Carey Street
London WC2A 2JE

North
Mr R I Ford
Inland Revenue North
100 Russell Street
Middlesbrough
Cleveland TS1 2RZ

North West
Mr I S Gerrie
Inland Revenue North West
The Triad
Stanley Road
Bootle
Merseyside L20 3PD

South East
Mr D L S Bean
Inland Revenue South East
Albion House
Chertsey Road
Woking GU21 1BT

South West
Mrs M E Williams
Inland Revenue South West
Longbrook House
New North Road
Exeter EX4 4UA

South Yorkshire
Mr A C Sleeman
Inland Revenue South Yorkshire
Sovereign House
110 Queen Street
Sheffield S1 2EN

Wales and Midlands
Mr M W Kirk
Inland Revenue Wales and Midlands
Ty Rhodfa
Ty Glas Avenue
Cardiff CF4 5TS

Northern Ireland
Mr R S T Ewing
Inland Revenue Northern Ireland
Level 9
Dorchester House
52–58 Great Victoria Street
Belfast BT2 7QE

Scotland
Mr O J D Clarke
Inland Revenue Scotland
Lauriston House
80 Lauriston Road
Edinburgh EH3 9SL

Accounts Offices
Cumbernauld
Mr A Geddes
Accounts Office Cumbernauld
Cumbernauld
Glasgow G70 5TR

Shipley
Mr P Clarke
Accounts Office Shipley
Bradford
West Yorkshire BD98 8AA

The Taxpayer's Charter

You are entitled to expect the Inland Revenue

To be fair
- By settling your tax affairs impartially
- By expecting you to pay only what is due under the law
- By treating everyone with equal fairness

To help you
- To get your tax affairs right
- To understand your rights and obligations
- By providing clear leaflets and forms
- By giving you information and assistance at our enquiry offices
- By being courteous at all times

To provide an efficient service
- By setting your tax affairs promptly and accurately
- By keeping your private affairs strictly confidential
- By using the information you give us only as allowed by the law
- By keeping to a minimum your costs of complying with the law
- By keeping our costs down

To be accountable for what we do
- By setting standards for ourselves and publishing how well we live up to them

If you are not satisfied
- We will tell you exactly how to complain
- You can ask for your tax affairs to be looked at again
- You can appeal to an independent tribunal
- Your MP can refer your complaint to the Ombudsman

In return, we need you

- To be honest
- To give us accurate information
- To pay your tax on time

Further reading

Inland Revenue guides

These are available free from the addresses that follow. None is bigger than A5; no single guide would be heavier than the basic letter post rate if you are sending an SAE.

Note that the guides are not necessarily up to date. They are revised at intervals, but not for minor adjustments in the tax rules. In each case, the date of the latest revision is given.

Use the Inland Revenue's guides for a basic grounding in the rules as they will apply to you. Note that most expatriates find that even if they are not liable to pay UK tax, they do have an obligation to make a return to the Inland Revenue. Take advice on this and see, for example, page 90. Also note that self-assessment (IR142 and page 90) obliges all *potential* UK taxpayers to maintain financial records for tax purposes.

IR1 Extra-statutory concessions. In the Inland Revenue's words, these are 'relaxations of the tax laws to give taxpayers a reduction in the amount of tax they need to pay'. June 1994

IR6 Double taxation relief for companies. Don't be fooled by the title; this is interesting for individuals as well. March 1994

IR20 Residents and non-residents – liability to tax in the United Kingdom. If you're going to get any of them, get this one. It tells you how to work out whether you are resident in the UK for tax purposes. November 1993

IR28 Starting in business. Something to leaf through before you return to the UK. October 1993

IR37 Appeals against tax. Useful background, but no more than that: take professional advice if you need to make a claim. March 1995

IR45 Income Tax, Capital Gains Tax and Inheritance Tax – what to do about tax if someone dies. Useful to have at hand if you might receive bad news from home during your time overseas. May 1995

IR58 Going to work abroad? Primarily for UK residents for tax purposes who will retain that status while employed abroad. April 1992

IR89 Personal Equity Plans (PEPs). A basic guide to something you can't keep going while you are overseas. June 1992

IR90 Tax allowances and reliefs. Including guidance on how to claim them August 1994

IR114 TESSA – Tax-free interest for taxpayers. The rules on Tax Exempt Special Savings Accounts. November 1990

IR120 You and the Inland Revenue – Tax, Collection and Accounts Offices. Where do you write, who do you call? Frequently reprinted in various languages and formats

IR123 Mortgage interest relief – buying your home. A basic guide to MIRAS. May 1994

IR142 Self assessment. An explanation of the new system that is introduced generally from the tax year 1996/97. Not to be left until just before you return to the UK. September 1994

IR146 Double taxation relief – admissible and inadmissible taxes. A listing by country. Probably more than you need, but worth knowing about just in case. March 1995

CGT14 Capital Gains Tax – an introduction. What's liable for CGT, what isn't, and how to calculate gains and losses. May 1992

CGT15 Capital Gains Tax – a guide for married couples. Exemptions, and how to calculate gains and reliefs. November 1990

IHT1 Inheritance Tax. Detailed. For most purposes, IHT2 and IHT3 (below) are sufficient. January 1991

IHT2 Inheritance tax on lifetime gifts. How much you can give away, and to whom. Whether there will be a tax liability, and if so, how it will be worked out. May 1993

IHT3 Inheritance Tax – an introduction. Basic guidance on the circumstances in which IHT becomes payable. September 1992

There are also three guides to what happens when your UK tax affairs become problematical. They are:

Code of Practice 1 Mistakes by the Inland Revenue. How do you make a claim for redress? February 1993

Code of Practice 2 Investigations. How do local tax offices go about chasing up what they think are discrepancies in your tax affairs, and how do you react? May 1995

Code of Practice 8 Special Compliance Office Investigations – Cases other than suspected serious fraud. You hear from the Special Compliance Office if the discrepancy is too big for the local office, and should read Code of Practice 8 if Inland Revenue thinks you have either blundered or deliberately tried to evade a tax liability short of serious fraud. If you are offered the chance to make a full disclosure of irregularities, that – as you would read in Code of Practice 9 – is the sign that they think you're guilty of serious fraud.

Code of Practice 9 Special Compliance Office Investigations – Cases of suspected serious fraud. Both 8 and 9 were last published in January 1995

In case you need it, there's also

AO1 How to complain about the Inland Revenue. How to approach the Adjudicator's Office in the event of an irretrievable breakdown of your relationship with the Inland Revenue. April 1995

For the complete list of guides and details on where to get them other than local tax offices, you ask for the *Catalogue of Leaflets and Booklets*, also known as the *IR List*. June 1995

Books

Note that books and series of books vary in their strength and weaknesses. If your destination country is not represented in a series of country guides in a bookshop, don't automatically go for another series; check another country to judge whether it would be worth trying to order the one you need.

All-Asia Travel Guide, ed Michael Westlake (Far Eastern Economic Review Publications)

Bed and breakfast in the United States and Canada, Lois Sealey (Home Base Holidays, 7 Park Avenue, London N13 5PG, tel/fax 0181 886 8752)

Business Singapore: An A to Z Guide, ed. Amanda Evans (British Business Association, 41 Duxton Road, Singapore 0208 telephone (65) 227 7861, fax (65) 227 7021)

The Daily Telegraph Guide to Working Abroad, Godfrey Golzen (Kogan Page, London)

The ECIS Higher Education Directory (ECIS, Petersfield, Hampshire)

Employee Benefits in Europe and US, ed. Howard Foster (Longman Law & Tax, London)

The Equitable Schools Book, ed. Klaus Boehm and Jenny Lees-Spalding (Bloomsbury, London)

The Expatriate Survival Kit (*Resident Abroad*, FT Magazines, Greystoke Place, Fetter Lane, London EC4A 1ND, telephone 0171 405 6969, fax 0171 831 9136)

Expatriate Tax and Investment Guide, David Phillips (Longman Law & Tax, London)

French Housing, Law & Taxes, Frank Rutherford (Sprucehurst Ltd, London)

The Hong Kong Leisure Guide, Kim Silver (Silver Press, Silver Head Ltd, GPO Box 4957, Hong Kong)

How to Live & Work in Belgium, Marvina Shilling (One of a series of country and other guides from Northcote House Publishers, Plymouth)

Individual Taxes – A Worldwide Summary (Price Waterhouse, London)

The International Schools Directory (ECIS, Petersfield, Hampshire)

International Travel & Health (World Health Organisation, Geneva)

The Investment and Savings Handbook, ed. Harry Littlefair (Longman Law & Tax, London)

Japan, Richard Lloyd Parry (Cadogan Books, London)

The Knowledge: A Guide to Living in Port Moresby, ed. Bob Williams (IMPS Research Pty Ltd, PO Box 986, Port Moresby, Papua New Guinea, telephone 21 3283, fax 21 7360)

Live & Work in Italy, Victoria Pybus and Rachael Robinson (one of a series of country and other guides from Vacation Work Books, Oxford)

Living in France, Phillip Holland (Robert Hale, London)
Living in Spain (Blackstone Franks, London)
Offshore Investments Simplified, Robert H V Cooke FCIS (Hale, London)
Prices and Earnings Around the Globe (Union Bank of Switzerland)
Setting up in Hong Kong, Fiona Campbell (FDC Services Ltd, GPO Box 2724,
    Central, Hong Kong, telephone (852) 845 5777, fax (852) 845 7555)
Taxation of International Executives (KPMG, Amstelveen, Netherlands)
The Traveller's Handbook, ed. Melissa Shales (WEXAS Ltd)
Transactions: International Taxation of Employment Manual, ed. David Frost (FT
    Law & Tax, Pitman, London)
Travellers' Health, Dr Richard Dawood (Oxford University Press)
Very Simple Arabic/Simple Etiquette in Arabia, James Peters (Stacey International,
    London)
Which School 1995, ed. Derek Bingham (John Catt Educational Ltd)
World Radio TV Handbook, ed. Andrew G Sennitt (Billboard Books, Oxford)
Worldwide Tax Guide (Pannell Kerr Forster, Melbourne, Australia)

Expatriate magazines

Resident Abroad
FT Magazines
Greystoke Place
Fetter Lane
London EC4A 1ND
telephone 0171 405 6969, fax 0171 831 9136

The International
FT Magazines
Greystoke Place
Fetter Lane
London EC4A 1ND

Investment International
Charterhouse Communications Group
4 Tabernacle Street
London EC2A 4LU
telephone 0171 638 1916, fax 0171 638 3128

Expat Investor
Tolley Publishing Ltd
Tolley House
2 Addiscombe Road
Croydon
Surrey CR9 5AF
telephone 0181 686 9141, fax 0181 760 0588

BBC Worldwide
Department P
PO Box 76
Bush House
Strand
London WC2B 4PH
telephone 0171 257 2211, fax 0171 240 4899

French Property News
Wisefile Limited
2a Lambton Road
London SW20 0LR
telephone 0181 944 5500, fax 0181 944 5293

Boletin Informativo
Institute of Foreign Property Owners
Avda. de L'Alt Rei
En Jaume 1, 15,2,9
Apartado de Correos 418
03590 Altea (Alicante)
telephone (96) 584 23 12, fax (96) 584 15 89
(The Boletin carries details of debts registered against properties and listed in the Boletines Oficiales of the ten most popular Spanish provinces for British residents. This is essential information and is not notified to property owners by the authorities.)

Other information

Union Bank of Switzerland's prices around the world

These take Zurich as their base. The first and second columns are taken from Union Bank of Switzerland's Prices and Earnings Around the Globe for 1994 (next update due 1997). The third and fourth columns are this book's own exercise in rebasing the figures to London as 100, rounded off, to make the comparison simpler from a UK perspective. As with all such data, they are useful to the extent that you have 'typical' spending habits as defined by the compilers, and are subject to variations in the prices of – in this case – 111 goods and services. Note that these are local spending patterns; expatriates tend to find life more expensive at first.

City	Prices excl. rent	Prices incl. rent	Rebased excl. rent	Rebased incl. rent
Tokyo	132	142.7	190	193
Lagos	101.4	91.8	146	124
Oslo	101.3	95.8	146	129
Zurich	100	100	144	135
Geneva	95.8	94.9	138	128
Copenhagen	94.7	92	136	124
Singapore	88.2	94.8	127	128
Stockholm	87.2	85.2	125	115
Paris	84.8	87	122	117
New York	83.2	93.8	120	127
Seoul	82.4	87.3	118	118
Helsinki	82.1	79.3	118	107
Buenos Aires	80.4	77	116	104
Frankfurt	78.6	79.8	113	108
Vienna	78	77	112	104
Dusseldorf	77.1	79.4	111	107
Chicago	75.7	81.2	109	110
Brussels	71.8	72	103	97
Adu Dhabi	71.3	78.1	102	105
Luxembourg	70.4	75.2	101	101
London	69.6	74.1	100	100
Amsterdam	68.8	70.3	99	95
Hong Kong	68.4	97.5	98	132
Los Angeles	68.2	75.4	98	102
Taipei	68	74.6	98	101
Houston	67.5	65.8	97	89
Tel Aviv	67.4	65.8	97	89
Bangkok	64.6	70.1	93	95
Milan	64.4	70.4	93	95
Dublin	63.4	62.6	91	84
Manama	62	63.4	89	86
Sydney	61.8	63	89	85
Montreal	60.9	59.2	88	80
Madrid	60.6	63.5	87	86
Toronto	57.5	60.3	83	81
Rio de Janeiro	54.8	60.6	79	82
Athens	54.4	56.7	78	77
Panama	54.2	60.8	78	82
Sao Paulo	54.2	61.1	78	82
Kuala Lumpur	53.5	59.9	77	81
Jakarta	53.2	70.6	76	95
Bogota	52.8	54.4	76	73
Lisbon	51.4	55.9	74	75
Mexico City	50.1	54.6	72	74
Nicosia	49.9	48.5	72	65
Cairo	48.7	59.5	70	80
Johannesburg	47.8	46.1	69	62
Manila	47.6	51	68	69
Budapest	43.3	43.4	62	59
Caracas	40.8	39.9	59	54
Prague	35.9	34.8	52	47
Nairobi	31.3	30.2	45	41
Bombay	30.4	38.8	44	52

Double tax agreements

The UK has comprehensive bilateral double tax agreements with the following countries. These ensure that you do not pay tax twice on one chargeable event. Where a double tax agreement does not cover a potential double tax liability, the UK may allow tax relief unilaterally. Double tax agreements are discussed in more detail on page 124, and in the Inland Revenue's guide IR146 *Double taxation relief – admissible and inadmissible taxes.*

Antigua and Barbuda
Armenia
Australia
Austria*
Azerbaijan
Bangladesh
Barbados
Belarus
Belgium*
Belize
Botswana
Brunei
Bulgaria
Burma (Myanmar)
Canada
China
Croatia
Cyprus
Czech Republic
Denmark
Egypt
Falkland Islands
Faroe Islands*
Fiji*
Finland*
France (inc. Guadeloupe, Guyane, Martinique and Reunion)* **
Gambia
Georgia
Germany*
Ghana
Greece*
Grenada
Guernsey (inc. Alderney, Herm and Lithou)
Guyana
Hungary
Iceland

India**
Indonesia*
Irish Republic* **
Isle of Man
Israel
Italy**
Ivory Coast
Jamaica
Japan
Jersey
Kazakhstan
Kenya*
Kiribati & Tuvalu
Korea (South)
Kyrgystan
Lesotho
Luxembourg*
Malawi
Malaysia
Malta
Mauritius*
Moldova
Montserrat
Morocco
Namibia
Netherlands* **
New Zealand
Nigeria
Norway*
Pakistan**
Papua New Guinea
Philippines
Poland
Portugal*
Romania
Russia Federation
St Kitts & Nevis
Sierra Leone
Singapore
Slovak Republic
Slovenia
Solomon Islands
South Africa* **
Spain

Sri Lanka
Sudan
Swaziland*
Sweden**
Switzerland* **
Tajikistan
Thailand
Trinidad & Tobago
Tunisia
Turkey
Turkmenistan
Uganda
Ukraine
USA**
Uzbekistan
Yugoslavia
Zambia
Zimbabwe

* These agreements give a right to UK tax allowances and reliefs, which are discussed on page 108.
** In these cases, there is a separate agreement covering inheritance tax on estates and gift tax (ie, specific forms of CGT).

Countries with which the UK has reciprocal agreements on National Insurance

In the countries listed, and in the EU countries, British expatriates are able to continue paying UK Class 1 National Insurance. The effect of these agreements is to prevent double payment of NI, and to protect pension rights. Note that the agreements with the countries below do not cover state health care, which is treated separately for reciprocation purposes. Further information may be obtained from the Department of Social Security, Longbenton, Benton Park Road, Newcastle-upon-Tyne NE98 1YX, telephone 0191 213 5000.

Austria
Barbados
Bermuda
Cyprus
Finland
Iceland
Israel
Jamaica
Jersey & Guernsey
Malta

Mauritius
Norway
Philippines
Sweden
Switzerland
Turkey
USA
Ex-Yugoslavia

INDEX

accidents, traffic 55
accommodation 10, 20, 33-4, 36, 188-89
  UK tax implications 95
  visiting UK 78-9, 205-07
accountants
  international 126
  see also advisers
advice, educational 74, 80, 182, 200, 207
advisers
  financial
    addresses 214-16
    investments 139, 147-50, 161-63
    regulation 149-50, 216-17
    return to UK 185-86
    tax 91-2, 99, 103, 109, 113, 120,
      125-26
    tied agents 150
    unofficial experts 103
AIDS 54
aircrew 101n 106
airlines, and unaccompanied minors 81
alcohol
  and Arab countries 60, 74
  and travel 46
aliens, registration as 33
allergies 35
allowances 8, 10-12, 20
  see also salaries; tax, allowances
animals 55
  and children 68-9
anthrax 55
Arab countries
  and alcohol 60, 74
  and passports 32, 60, 68
  see also islamic countries
banks xii, 43
  accounts 22-4, 27, 132, 140, 153-54
    overseas 23, 27, 140

document safe custody 36, 43
  offshore 22-4, 27, 43, 132, 137, 140, 148
    see also offshore institutions
BBC World Service 63-4
blood transfusions 55
body language 53, 59, 61
books 231-32
  HMSO bookshops 225-26
  mail order xii, 193-94
  phrase books 25, 35, 232
    see also language learning
  see also guide books
bribery 66-7
briefing xii, 3, 12, 21, 25, 30-2, 70, 191
  for return to UK 185
bugging devices 68
building societies
  accounts 153-54
  offshore subsidiaries 132n, 137
business cards 44-46, 58-59
career implications 13-15
  spouse ix, 2, 8, 10, 13, 15, 17, 189
cars 12, 40
  hire in UK 77-8, 203-05
  problems when importing 122
  security 63
  storage 40, 198
  taking abroad 29, 40
  and VAT 122
Centre for International Briefing (CIB)
  31, 148, 185, 196
charities, and inheritance tax 118
children 10-11, 18, 30
  and animals 68-9
  family activities 73-4
  and inheritance 117-8, 165
  qualifying as a 'home student' 183-84
  see also education; families

Christians Abroad 17, 195
Christmas presents 74, 200
churches 17
civil unrest/war 49, 177
clothes, for hot climates 38
clothing allowance 11-12
clubs 47-48, 50-51
colleagues
  expatriates 71
  local 71-2
  overseas, making contact before going
    25-6
communications technology 67
commuting home 33
complaints
  fraud 168-70
  tax bills 109-10
computers 38-9
Consul, British 49-50
contraceptives 35
contracts 1, 9, 14-5
  disputes 21-2
  failure to complete 2-3
  insurance 28
  localization 9-10
  negotiation 19-22, 127
  non-UK companies 15
  renewal 186-87
  tax implications 27
  terms and conditions 13, 19-22
  translations 22
Corona Worldwide 16, 22, 31-2, 81,
  148, 185, 195
  see also Women's Corona Society
cost of living 5-6
Council of European Schools in the
  European Community (COBISEC)
  83, 209
cover cards, health insurance 177-79,
  221
credit cards 26-7, 43, 78, 95, 99, 145,
  147, 177
culture shock 3, 16
  and return to UK 185, 189-90
customs
  clearance 41-2
  seizure of goods 123-24

CVs x, 2, 189-90
  for spouses 17
danger 16
  avoidance of 62-6
  see also emergencies
death
  and capital gains tax 117
  and forced heirship 130, 164-65
  and inheritance tax 117-21
  and probate 121, 165
dental checks 29, 35
Department for Education 183-84, 221
Department of Social Security (DSS),
  overseas branch 196, 221
Department of Trade and Industry
  (DTI)
  Country Profiles 16
  export publications 195
dining out 73
documents 44-5, 50
  false 68
  stored in UK 36
dogs, danger from 68
dress
  in Africa 60
  in Asia 58
  in islamic countries 60
drivers 12, 20
Dual Career Network 17, 189, 195
e-mail 67
education xi-xii, 10-11, 74, 79-84, 143
  children resident in UK 184
  further education 84, 182-84
  guardianships xii, 81
  see also schools
elections 84-9
electrical goods 38-9
emergencies
  civil unrest/war 49
  crisis management 64
  domestic 47
  telephone numbers 51-2, 63
  see also danger
Employment Conditions Abroad (ECA)
  5-7, 31, 73, 148, 194
  Country Profiles 6, 17, 24-5, 33-4
espionage 66, 68

Eurocost, *Cost of living comparison indices* 6, 17, 194
European Council of International Schools (ECIS) 83-4, 209
European Union 32
  national insurance 29, 236
Expatriate Survival Kit 25, 32, 148
export, of bought goods 121-24
families
  and contract renewal 186
  emergency precautions 63
  implications for 17-18
  and inheritance tax 117-18
  life abroad 72-4
  see also children; relatives, elderly; spouse
Family Planning Association 35, 197
feng shui 57
finance
  advice *see* advisers
  assets 164-70
  exchange rates 130, 173
  fraud 165-70
  investments xii, 140-7
    alternative 161
    bed-and-breakfasting 99, 188
    bonds 154-55
    collective 155-57
    commodities 159-61
    currency 144-47
    derivatives 159-61
    equities 142, 159
    futures 160, 163
    gilts 142, 154-55
    investment trusts 156
    offshore funds 156-57, 159
    portfolios 141-44, 151-61, 182
    property 159, 170-73
    shares 156
    unit trusts 142, 156-57
  offshore financial centres (OFCs) 15, 131-39
  PEPs 141, 188
  planning xii-12, 26-7, 90-184
  school fees 182
  strategy 142-47
  TESSAs 141, 188
  VCTs 188

first-aid kit 45
flights
  children's assisted 11
  home 11
  unaccompanied minors 81
food, dangers 55, 178
Foreign Office, guidance on foreign countries 16, 195
fraud 165-70
furniture, buying overseas 37-8
Going Places 31, 148, 185, 196
guide books xiii, 16, 25, 48, 231-32
  see also books
hazards, cultural 53, 56-62
  Africa 60-1
  Arab lands 59-60
  Asia 57-9
  with colleagues 71-2
  Europe 61-2
  gender related 65
head office, relations with 26-8, 72
health and fitness 28-9, 34-5, 53-6
  see also injections
hepatitis B 55
hiv 54-5
HM Customs & Excise 40, 121, 198, 211
holidays in UK 77
  see also leave
Home Office, D Division 86, 209
Hong Kong, and dragons 57
hotels
  on arrival 30, 47
  and social life 30, 50, 65
  suspect food 178
  in UK 78-9, 205-07
House of Commons 209
immunization *see* injections
income tax *see* tax
Independent Schools Information Service 80, 182, 207
injections 25, 29, 34, 54
Inland Revenue 90-1
  addresses 210-11, 226-28
  change of tax status, intended 97-8
  investigations 110
  revenue adjudicator 109

telephoning 98

form P45 26, 98

form P85 26, 98

guides

    extended list 229-31

    CGT14 *Capital Gains Tax - owner-occupier houses* 115

    CGT15 *Capital Gains Tax - a guide for married couples* 115

    IHT3 *Inheritance tax - an introduction* 117

    IR1 *extra-statutory concessions* 100

    IR6 *Double taxation relief for companies* 124

    IR20 *Residents and non-residents* 91, 95, 108, 124

    IR58 *Going to work abroad* 91, 101

    IR146 *Double taxation relief...* 124-25

see also tax

insurance

all-risks personal 28-9, 42

contact lenses 35

general 28

health 20, 174-79, 219-21

    emergency evacuation 179

    exclusions 176-77

    premiums 176

hire cars 78

house 24, 172-73

house contents 36

life assurance 11, 121, 141, 157-59, 181-82

    bonds 154, 188

    offshore life policies 141, 158

    second-hand endowments 158, 216

medical 11, 28

removals 42

rental income 172

International Baccalaureate (IB) 84, 209

International Planned Parenthood Federation 35, 197

International, The (magazine) 139, 147

interpreters 51, 69

Investment International (magazine) 139, 147

investments *see* finance, investments

invitations 59

islamic countries

    Living in a Muslim Country 16

    see also Arab countries; dress; hazards, cultural

Israel, and passports 32, 60, 68

jet lag 46

job-seeking, work overseas 191, 224-25

KPMG 148

KPMG handbook *Taxation of international executives* 126

language learning 3, 12, 30, 69-71, 199-200

    see also books, phrase books

law

jurisdictions 130

lawyers 43, 148

power of attorney 25, 36, 164

probate 121, 165

representation if arrested 49

leave 11

terminal 187

see also holidays

magazines

addresses 232-33

see also individual titles

mains voltages 39-40

malaria 34

marmite 46, 75

Medical Advisory Services for Travellers Abroad (MASTA) 34, 197

medical checks 29, 34-5

medical records 29

medical treatment 55

medications, drugs 29, 35

merchant seafarers 101n 105-06

MIRAS 108, 172

moneybelts 46, 63

National Insurance 11, 20, 29, 180, 236

National Savings 30

National Trust, accommodation 79, 206

offshore financial centres 15, 131-39

    regulation 132-35, 212-14

offshore institutions 137-39, 164-65

    see also banks, offshore; building societies

offshore pension plans 181, 188

ombudsman *see* parliamentary ombudsman
optical prescriptions 29, 35
outfitters 38, 198
overseas vacancies 191
parliamentary ombudsman 109-10, 211
parties, farewell 19
partners
  provisional UK non-resident status 96-7
  UK tax allowances 96
  see also spouse
passports 32, 49, 60, 68, 199
  lost 49
pensions 11, 20, 180-81, 188
pets 40-1, 198-99
  overseas 69
political parties (UK) 85, 88-9, 209-10
politics, discussing 60, 62, 66
preparations ix-xi, 23-32, 43
presents 74-5, 200
Price Waterhouse 148
  Individual taxes - a worldwide summary 126
professional institutions, addresses 217-19
property
  overseas 28, 173-74, 188
  in UK xi, 24, 28, 159, 170-73
    buying 188-89, 222-24
    leaving empty 24, 37, 44, 172-73
    renting 170-72, 188
    selling 170-71
quarantine, pets 40
registration, at embassies and consulates 47, 49
relatives, elderly xii, 18-19, 25, 74, 143
  see also families
removals 10, 25, 35-42
  firms 41-2, 199
residence permits 32-3
Resident Abroad (magazine) 25, 32, 75, 139, 147-48
retail export scheme 38
retirement 191
  see also pensions
return to UK
  emergencies 100
  incidental duties 106-07

and not staying 190-92
planning xi, 185-92
tax arrangements 23, 27, 186-87
working visits 76-7
salaries ix, 5-12, 22-3
  and terminal leave 187
  see also allowances
schools 48, 50, 74, 189
  assisted places 82
  boarding, in UK 80-83, 182, 184, 208
  British, overseas 81-3
  bursaries 82
  international 81-3
  notice of departure 30
  see also education
Securities and Investments Board (SIB) 135
security
  domestic 64-5
  job security 14-15
  precautions 12
self defence 65
self-employment 15
  see also tax, self-employed
servants 12
serviced flats 79, 189
sex 55
shopping, mail order 74-5, 193-94, 201-03
skills, maintaining 27
social life 17, 30, 47-48, 50, 61, 72-3, 75, 88
social security 11, 20, 29
spouse
  allowances 10
  breaking the news 1-2
  can be male 32
  and capital gains 115
  career implications ix, 2, 8, 10, 13, 15, 17, 189
  and contract renewal 186
  culture shock 3
  and inheritance tax 117-21, 165
  return to UK 189
  and social life 50, 72-3, 75
  tax status 95-7
  visits to UK 76-7

work permits 15, 17, 24, 33
see also families; partners
State Boarding School Information
    Service 83, 208
storage 36-7
stress 55-6
syphilis 55
tax 12
    advice *see* advisers
    aircrew 101n 106
    allowances 42, 96, 108, 140n, 142
    appeals 109
    armed forces 104-05
    capital gains (CGT) xii, 8, 26, 28,
        112-17, 142, 145, 187
    capital loss 26, 113-4, 187
    complaints 109-10
    concessions 100
    crown servants 104-05, 108, 122
    domicile in other countries 124n
    domicile in the UK 94, 117, 120
    double tax agreements 124-26, 142,
        236-36
    emergency return to UK 100
    EU employees 105
    foreign earnings deduction 100-03
    implications for voters 85-6
    incidental duties in UK 106-07
    income tax rates
        abroad 126
        UK 92
    inheritance tax 117-21
        exemptions 117-19
    liability overseas 7, 21, 124, 126-30,
        149
    'look-through' provisions 103
    and merchant seafarers 101n 105-06
    non-resident in UK 92, 94-103, 113,
        187
    offshore oil and gas rigs 105
    and offshore pension plans 181, 188
    PAYE 26, 98, 102, 111
    on property income 172
    remittance basis 99-100, 191
    resident in UK 92-4
    and return to UK 23, 27, 186-87
    self-assessment 110-11, 229
    self-employed 104
    tax years 93, 186
    and terminal leave 187
    UK system 90-111
    value added tax 42, 121-24
    see also inland revenue
tax-havens 133
taxis 30, 45-46
taxpayer's charter 110, 228-29
telephone
    directories xii, 48, 194
    international codes 193
    phoning home 75
television and video equipment 38
terminal bonus 11
tests, psychometric 3
trailing spouse *see* spouse
travel arrangements 30
trusts
    offshore 120, 164-65
    venture capital (VCTs) 188
UCAS Handbook 84, 209
unemployment benefit 180
Union Bank of Switzerland, *Prices and
    Earnings Around the Globe* 6, 194, 233-34
valuables 36
visas 24
visitors, from home 75-6
voting 84-9
wallets, spare, for muggers 63, 65
war/civil unrest 49, 177
weapons 65
wills
    and forced heirship 130, 164-65
    and inheritance tax 119-20
wives *see* spouse
Women's Corona Society 16, 31-2, 195
    see also Corona Worldwide
work permits 15, 17, 24, 32-3
World Health Organisation (WHO) 34,
    54, 196

*) 0(81- 349- 4453: Finchley central. (Accountants)
   Burgh Kaprow Lewis

   Fiona ~~Colurego~~ Kerin.

) Hourly basis.